How Terror Evolves

How Terror Evolves

*The Emergence and Spread
of Terrorist Techniques*

Yannick Veilleux-Lepage

ROWMAN &
LITTLEFIELD
INTERNATIONAL

London • New York

Published by Rowman & Littlefield International, Ltd.
6 Tinworth Street, London SE11 5AL, United Kingdom
www.rowmaninternational.com

Rowman & Littlefield International, Ltd. is an affiliate of
Rowman & Littlefield
4501 Forbes Boulevard, Suite 200, Lanham, Maryland 20706, USA
With additional offices in Boulder, New York, Toronto (Canada), and London (UK)
www.rowman.com

British Library Cataloguing in Publication Information
A catalogue record for this book is available from the British Library

ISBN: HB 978-1-78660-878-9

Library of Congress Cataloging-in-Publication Data

Library of Congress Control Number: 2020933932

ISBN 978-1-78660-878-9 (cloth)
ISBN 978-1-5381-4981-2 (pbk)
ISBN 978-1-78660-879-6 (electronic)

This book is dedicated to my mentors
Jan and Marc

Contents

Acknowledgements

This book has been in development for several years; as such the list of people to thank is long. I will start with my family: my wife Ellie Ashton; my parents Dominique Veilleux and David Lepage; and my sister Chloé Veilleux-Lepage. None of this would have been possible without support and unconditional love they have provided me over the years. Thanks also go to my in-laws for welcoming me into their family and making me feel at home in the United Kingdom.

My interest in political violence was kindled as an undergraduate student at Carleton University. I owe a special debt of gratitude to my dear friends, the late Dr. Jan Fedorowicz, and Dr. Marc Tyrell with whom I spent countless hours – sometimes over a pint of Guinness – discussing these topics. Jan and Marc's unwavering support and friendship for the past 15 years not only shaped my career as an academic but the person I am today. I would also like to thank the friends from this time of my life: Michael McGoldrick, Denis Giroux, Jonathan Perron-Clow, Owen Hewitt, and Jake Graham.

At the University of St Andrews, I was extremely fortunate to fall into an intellectual community that provided the perfect mixture of rigor, humor, debate, and friendship. To me the beating heart of this community was embodied by the late Professor Nick Rengger. My heartfelt thanks will always be with my doctoral supervisors Professor Richard English and Dr. Bernhard Blumenau for their continuous support of my research, their patience and advice. I also owe incalculable debts to Dr. Tim Wilson, Dr. Gilbert Ramsay, Dr. Mark Currie, Dr. Nick Brooke, Gillian Brunton, and Julie Middleton. Each of them provided guidance, support, and friendship; I am deeply appreciative of their individual and collective efforts and I feel privileged have been a part of this esteemed institution. In addition, I would like to thank my cohort and officemates, particularly Emil Archambault and Jeff Fiorito. I would also like to thank Beth and Keith Shotton, and Lee Mahoney. These friendships are some of my most precious takeaways from my time at St Andrews.

I would also like to show my appreciation to the staff and students at the Transcultural Conflict and Violence Initiative at Georgia State University. In particular, I am deeply indebted to Ayse Lokmanoglu, Carissa Goodwin, Chelsea Daymon, and Dr. Wojciech Kaczkowski for their support during a challenging time.

This project was completed at Leiden University where I have been extremely lucky to find yet another group of supportive colleagues in the Institute of Security and Global Affairs. A particular thank you goes to my colleagues in the terrorism and political violence research group: Dr. Bart Schuurman, Dr. Tahir Abbas, Jeanine de Roy van Zuijdewijn, Dr. Jelle van Buuren, and Jennifer Dowling for creating such a collegial and exciting place to work. Thanks also go to Alisa Kerschbaum and Katharina Krusselmann for meticulously going over the proofs.

I would also like to thank Dr. Sarah Marsden and Dr. Akil Awan for providing early feedback, along with all those who have reviewed it. Thanks go to Professor Andrew Silke for not only serving as my external examiner and for endorsing this book, and to Dr. James Rogers for his kind endorsement as well. I would also like to thank the editing team at Rowman & Littlefield, particularly my editor Dhara Snowden, for her endless patience.

Preface

The nineteenth-century observation that terrorism constituted 'propaganda of the deed' has proven to be an enduring sound bite. And yet very often propaganda seems to have attracted far more analytical attention than deeds. Grubby details of actual violence are still frequently neglected in analysis. Overall, the general shape of terroristic violence – its shifting long-term dynamics, forms, and developments – remains strikingly understudied.

By contrast, this extraordinary study uses evolutionary theory as the inspiration for a close interrogation of terrorism through its acts. Dr Veilleux-Lepage's specific choice of focus – hijackings – is a rather inspired one. At the height of the hijacking carnival of the early 1970s, Ghassan Kannafani of the Popular Front for the Liberation of Palestine remarked that he had 'always said we don't hijack planes because we love Boeing 707s'. But his own actions rather suggested otherwise: such airplanes offered publicity opportunities that were quite simply unrivalled. Aircraft hijackings, indeed, are among the most idiosyncratic (but also darkly mesmerising) of all modern terroristic atrocities. Hijacking concentrates the threat of the most impersonal killing within the most intimate of theatres: its 'flying prisons' become instant global stages.

Here Dr Veilleux-Lepage proves impressively keen to get his hands dirty with sparkling detail. His sheer diligence in mining that detail speaks for itself, and its monument is a database of hijacking incidents that is approximately four times that of the renowned *Global Terrorism Database*. But his intellectual achievement in *How Terror Evolves* extends far further than the generation of a gigantic heap of fresh information. In essence, this is a study that offers us an explanation of how this peculiar form of political 'claim-making' has emerged, developed, and come to dominate the experience of air travel. And this proves to be a far more twisting and contingent tale than is often realised.

How Terror Evolves thus represents an accomplished academic debut from a rising star of the terrorism studies field: a disturbing illumination of how micro-developments can gradually accumulate to generate quite fresh horrors and an extended meditation on both the structure and agency behind terroristic spectaculars. A storehouse of insights, this is a book to visit regularly. Dr Yannick Veilleux-Lepage's groundbreaking new study deserves the widest readership.

Dr Tim Wilson
Handa Centre for the Study of Terrorism and Political Violence
University of St Andrews
11 December 2019

Chapter One

Introduction

The unexpected appearance of several armed men is met with brief silence before the ambient hum of the plane's engines is drowned in the ensuing confusion. Demands are articulated. Snippets of operational instructions are overheard, and individuals on board guess at the hijackers' motives, searching their understanding for the political meaning of the attack. Footsteps, with a tenor and cadence that feels out of place, vibrate along the aisle and up the interior of the fuselage. An argument ensues in the cockpit as the pilot explains, with increasing agitation, why the plane cannot go there, why he cannot be expected to do that. A change in direction is felt and the air grows tenser still. Exchanged glances among crew members are the silent markers of the choice with which all captives are suddenly confronted: to comply or to attempt a risky and potentially ill-fated attempt at intervention.

Such a narrative is perhaps most readily associated with the events of 11 September 2001. A reader of the aforementioned anecdote may even be prompted to consider whether it aligns most closely with accounts of American Airlines Flight 11, United Airlines Flight 175, American Airlines Flight 77, or United Airlines Flight 93. If most individuals were asked to look back further into the annals of hijacking history for the source of such a story, they would likely cite the events of El Al Flight 426 on 23 July 1968, which is most frequently considered to be the genesis of modern-day hijackings. While these events are integral to the history of modern terrorism – and are simultaneously important in relation to resultant political consequences and alterations to state response and air security – the story of hijacking as a technique of contention is one that is both broader and more long-standing than is commonly acknowledged.

Indeed, the first instances of hijacking as a technique of political contention can be traced to 1930s' Peru. On 26 August 1930, the second day of an uprising of Luis Miguel Sánchez Cerro against then-president Augusto B. Leguía, Cerro's men hijacked a Pan American-Grace Airways (PANAGRA) F7 Ford Trimotor mail aircraft, forcing the pilot to change course and drop anti-propaganda leaflets over Arequipa before transporting a group of rebels to a remote garrison to rally support. Both effective and novel, this event is one of many during the period that previously constituted a significant oversight in the understanding of the evolution of hijacking as a technique of contention. While fictitious, the narrative with which I opened this book could apply to this instance as well as to that of the flights hijacked on 11 September 2001. Through the widening of our purview, then, and through an evolutionary framework, it is the purpose of this book to put diverse iterations of hijacking into productive tension and conversation with one another to draw out new and significant observations about the ways in which hijacking – and, by extension, other techniques of political contention – move across nations, ideologies, and time.

This book provides a framework derived from evolutionary theory to facilitate the examination of terroristic innovation. This evolutionary approach is employed to provide three types of explanations for terroristic innovation: (1) proximate explanations, (2) developmental explanations, and (3) functional explanations. Proximate explanations are those that answer the question: 'what are the characteristics of a given terror technique and what is its purpose?' Developmental explanations address how techniques come about and are sustained. Further, as is the case in the methodology employed throughout this book, they can be used to evaluate how a given technique evolved over the course of its history. Finally, and most importantly, functional explanations address the question: 'how and why did a given terror technique spread, endure, and sometimes, disappear altogether?' Functional explanations, therefore, describe how evolutionary processes shape whether a given technique is adopted or rejected by various individuals and groups of claim-makers.

In their barest form, terror techniques can be understood as the product of a set of instructions on how to contest or change the existing political status quo in the face of an adversary: the state and its institutions. Focusing on acts of political violence and on the terror techniques employed, rather than on the actors and their motivations, I use this evolutionary framework to trace the processes through which the use of aircraft as weapons of destruction developed from the first instances of aircraft hijacking in 1930s' Peru, through Palestinian terrorism in the 1960s and 1970s, up to its adoption by al-Qaeda in the 1990s, leading to the 9/11 attacks. I argue that overwhelming evidence indicates that these attacks should be understood as mutation along an evolutionary path that began in the jungles of Peru nearly ninety years ago. A failure to situate the 9/11 attacks within the wider context of the long history of hijacking tells only a partial story and reinforces both the inaccurate perception of the exceptionality of the 9/11 attacks and the rather dubious notion of 'new terrorism'.

Importantly, while I draw on interdisciplinary influences, I situate this book within the field of terrorism studies and address a prevalent issue within that field. While scholarship on terrorism has seen exponential growth and important contributions since the events of 9/11, it has faced criticism on the basis, as Jackson (2007) articulates, of its 'tendency to treat contemporary terrorism as a new phenomenon' and for its 'persistent lack of historicity' (pp. 244–45). My aim here, therefore, is to develop a framework based on evolutionary theory, through which new historical insights can be identified and evidenced.

Importantly, this book also aims to correct both empirical and qualitative lacunae in the field of terrorism studies through this evolutionary approach. First, I have compiled the first comprehensive database of hijacking incidents, which provides a salient, extensive, and quantitative base of functional knowledge on the development of hijacking from its inception. While I do not address all incidents in detail within this book, developing such a catalogue formed a significant aspect of my methodology. Further, focusing on the action and modus operandi – rather than the actors or their ideologies – through an evolutionary lens has enabled me to produce a much more wide-ranging but focused trajectory of the history of hijacking as a technique of political contention (and, tangentially but significantly, to also consider the impact of criminal hijacking innovations that fall outside the scope of politically motivated action). This constitutes a significant narrative in which I draw out previously overlooked connections between seemingly disparate actions and innovations and craft a qualitative narrative of the story, as well as the historicity, of hijacking. One of the benefits of such an approach is that it enables me to produce novel and well-evidenced claims concerning the variation, transmission, and selection of the phenomenon of hijacking. One such claim is a new argument – based on both exhaustive data on hijackings and the overall trajectory of their evolution – that the 9/11 attacks were based on a long and iterative process of trial and error.

In chapter 2, I provide a discussion of the evolutionary theoretical framework for the present study, its potential applications to the field of terrorism studies, and an understanding of hijacking as a technique of contention specifically. After presenting a brief overview of Darwinian biology, including the key notions of natural selection and transmission, I address the applicability of the theory to social sciences, including an overview of the successes and failures of previous attempts at such a methodology. I then consider terroristic techniques as a unit of inheritance and, more importantly, outline my decision to consider techniques of contention – rather than the narrower concept of terrorism – as the salient unit of inheritance for the purposes of this study. I move, then, to a consideration of Charles Tilly's theory concerning repertoires of contention, which is this study's nearest relative in the sense that it includes the implicit understanding that techniques of political contention change over time. As well as delineating the ways in which I extend and correct Tilly's theory in terms of its failure to differentiate between changes resulting from structural shifts in given countries and techniques transported across societies, I also outline the key notions of propositional knowledge and modulation. Further, I consider evolutionary principles of variation, transmission, and selection in relation to their potential for addressing hijacking as a technique of contention. Finally, I detail various modes by which techniques of contention can be assessed on the basis of feasibility, legitimacy, and efficacy.

Building on chapter 2, chapters 3 to 7 apply the proposed framework to aeroplane hijacking, surveying a wide range of instances in which this technique was employed over history. This provides an empirically rich account of the development of hijacking as a technique of contention over time and space, demonstrating the merit of applying evolutionary theory to such phenomena, and sheds light on the mechanisms involved in the creation and diffusion of new terroristic techniques. In these chapters, I analyse different strains of aeroplane hijacking from 1931 to 2001 to identify the adaptations the technique has undergone, along with the changes in social, cultural, economic, technological, political, or religious context prompting these adaptations and innovations. The five strains identified are:

- the emergence of aeroplane hijacking in Peru and Cuba;
- hijacking for transportation;
- the use of hijacking by Palestinian claim-makers;
- criminal innovation; and
- the use of aeroplanes as weapons of destruction.

In chapter 3, I address two key and, generally overlooked, periods that are significant to the early development of hijacking: that which took place in the Andes, specifically Peru, in the 1930s, and that which took place during the Cuban Revolution. First, I consider the potentiality of airspace as a symbolic site with a great deal of illocutionary potential, which led claim-makers to use hijacking not only as an instrumental means to achieve an end (transportation or violence) but also as the act of contention in and of itself. Similarly, the Cuban Revolution saw the targeting of Cubana airline aircraft as a means of symbolically highlighting the government's vulnerability. I also explain the significance of, and evolutionary implications attendant on, a conspicuous lack of direct transmission of hijacking as a technique of contention across these two periods of time.

In chapter 4, I examine the use of hijacking as a means of transportation, primarily to the United States, by detailing how hijacking was used to escape the Soviet Union after World War II and by those seeking political asylum after the Cuban Revolution. Significantly – and one of the reasons why these hijackings do not appear in more narrowly defined studies (those that focus only on violent terroristic innovations as opposed to techniques of contention or those that address actors and motivations rather than techniques) – is that these iterations of hijacking were, for the most part, sanctioned by other states. In the case of flights from Soviet states, the United States encouraged this by way of propaganda to undermine communism. Further, both these trends toward hijacking as a means of transportation directly contributed to the diffusion of hijacking to the repertoire of contention of the black nationalist movement in the United States later during the 1960s and early in the 1970s.

In chapter 5, I consider the ways in which Palestinian hijacking – while it has been accorded more scholarly attention than the material addressed in the previous chapters – can be considered in new ways in light of an evolutionary perspective on techniques of contention. I address several significant hijackings perpetrated by factions of the Palestinian liberation movement(s) and contend that mass mediatization of such attacks had a direct impact on their transmission and subsequent inclusion in other groups' repertoires of contention. Further, I use this novel trajectory and analysis of Palestinian hijacking to advance an argument concerning the ways in which claim-makers reject, as well as adopt, techniques of contention.

A departure from the previous chapters' exclusive focus on hijacking as a claim-making technique, chapter 6 includes a discussion of criminal innovations to hijacking. I address the period between 1968 and 1973 in relation to the emergence of hijacking for extortion, using parachutes as a means of escape, and the novel threat of employing aircraft as a means of destruction. Importantly, these innovations affected the propositional knowledge base of diverse political claim-makers as well as air security authorities. I argue that both the reactive actions undertaken by authorities and the innovations enacted by criminal hijackers during this period were important to creating the environment within which 9/11 could occur.

Building on this understanding and the evolutionary trajectory addressed throughout the previous chapters, I argue that 9/11 was not a novel technique. Instead, it needs to be viewed in the context of numerous other incidents, such as a hijacking perpetrated by three fugitives who threatened to crash a hijacked DC-9 into a nuclear power plant unless their demands were met in November 1972 and other similar incidents using aircraft as a means of destruction and, indeed, by all innovations on hijacking as a technique of contention since 1930s' Peru. I claim that the 9/11 attacks were deliberately designed to exploit flaws in aviation security. After highlighting the long-standing understanding of aircraft's potential as weapons of destruction, which predates even aviation, I address instances of actual or threatened attacks involving the use of aircraft to destroy buildings and the targeting of key sites of national significance. Most significantly, I examine the hijacking on Christmas Eve in 1994 in which Abu Nidal operatives planned to crash an aeroplane into the Eiffel tower or explode it over Paris, arguing that this marks a direct precursor to 9/11 in the sense that it included hijacking with the intention of using an aircraft as a weapon and of targeting a national symbol to advance political aims. Similarly, I consider the details of the Bojinka plot, the most salient detail of which was the intent to hijack a plane and fly it into the headquarters of the Central Intelligence Agency at Langley. In sum, I advance an argument that the 9/11 attacks were the result of a long and extensive process of trial and error, an understanding of which can be advanced by considering hijacking as a technique of contention within an evolutionary framework.

Finally, in the conclusion, I provide policy recommendations and set out possible avenues for further research using an evolutionary framework, whether by counter-terrorism practitioners or scholars, to further investigate the mechanisms surrounding terroristic innovation and its diffusion and impact.

Chapter Two

An Evolutionary Approach to Terrorist Innovation

2.1 A BRIEF OVERVIEW OF EVOLUTIONARY THEORY

The evolutionary framework of the biological sciences is the legacy of Charles Darwin, whose book, *On the Origin of Species by Means of Natural Selection*, became the springboard for the development of almost all evolutionary theory thereafter. Indeed, Eldredge (1995) rightfully proclaims Darwin 'the founding father of evolutionary discourse, and all sides of the basic evolutionary disputes legitimately find their patrimony in his work' (p. 1). Similarly, the distinguished biologist Ernst Mayr (1988) lauds Darwin's theory of natural selection as the most revolutionary theory in history on the basis of the ideas it refuted as well as those it advanced. Darwin's theory of natural selection discredited the idea of creation – the belief that diversity of life on Earth was a result of divine intervention – thus, defeating Lord Kelvin's argument that life on Earth was new by estimating life on Earth to be at least several thousand million years old, and overcoming anthropocentrism by showing that humans are not a separate creation but rather the product of a common evolutionary process (Mayr 1988, 193).

What made Darwin's ideas unique was not his proposition that the environment encouraged organisms to adapt but, rather, his delineation of precisely how the environment encouraged, forced, or prompted organisms to adapt (Sterling-Folker 2001, 71). Downplaying the 'inheritance of acquired characteristics' described by his predecessor Jean-Baptiste Lamarck, Darwin concluded that all living organisms were not 'immutable' but, in fact, the 'lineal descendants of some other and generally extinct species' and identified 'Natural Selection [as] the main but not exclusive means of modification' (Darwin 1964 [1859], 6). Across his entire corpus, Darwin advanced

7

roughly five distinguishable ideas that constitute his theory of biological evolution: evolution, common descent, gradualism, multiplication of species, and natural selection.

Evolution is the premise that the world is 'neither constant nor perpetually cycling, but rather steadily and perhaps directionally changing, and that organisms are being transformed' (Mayr 1988, 198). While this notion is now understood as a scientific fact, the common belief at the time of Darwin's publication of *Origin of Species* was that the world was both unchanging and new and that each species transferred to the next generation characteristics that did not change. Darwin's scholarship brought about an important paradigm shift, which Mayr (1988) calls the 'First Darwinian Revolution', not only because it replaced the notion that Earth's natural life was unchanging, but also because it deprived 'man of his unique position in the universe' and placed 'him into the stream of animal evolution' (p. 215).

Common descent is the notion that every group of organisms descends from a common ancestral species. During Darwin's famous excursion in the Galapagos archipelago, his observation of many species of finches led him to conclude that they had descended from a common ancestor and consequently to postulate that tracing an animal's ancestry into the higher taxa could lead to the determination of a common ancestor of all species.

Proposing the notion of gradualism, Darwin advanced that evolution proceeds relatively slowly and gradually rather than by leaps and jumps. This represented a drastic departure from previous scholarship, which argued that new species could only be created by sudden and dramatic changes from one generation to the next. While most evolutionary theorists now accept gradualism,[1] the argument that evolution is gradual was one of Darwin's most controversial ideas at the time of its publication (Thayer 2004, 24).

Multiplication of species is the recognition of the great diversity of life existing at present and in the past. In this sense, Darwin understood that the extant species were only a portion of the life that must have existed on Earth through history and, thus, provided a scientific explanation for the origins of many species as well as the widely scattered dinosaur fossils, which were often attributed to the biblical Great Flood.

Arguably Darwin's most significant contribution, natural selection, is the mechanism of evolutionary change that focuses on heritable modifications that assist an organism's ability to survive and reproduce and that are passed on to subsequent generations. Darwin recognized that all organisms struggle for life in a dangerous and competitive zero-sum environment, where natural resources, including food supplies, are finite:

> Owing to this struggle for life, any variation, however slight, and from whatever cause proceeding, if it be in any degree profitable to an individual of any species, in its infinitely complex relations to other organic beings and to its

physical conditions of life, will tend to the preservation of that individual, and will generally be inherited by its offspring. The offspring, also, will thus have a better chance of surviving, for, of the many individuals of any species which are periodically born, but a small number can survive. I have called this principle, by which each slight variation, if useful, is preserved, by the term of Natural Selection. (Darwin 1964 [1859], 51)

The theory of natural selection provided an entirely new way of explaining the natural world: that heritable modifications, which help individual species (or as I will argue in the subsequent sections, ideas and behaviours) reproduce and survive, are passed to subsequent generations. More specifically, since natural resources are finite, populations cannot survive and breed with infinite success. Instead, all organisms within a given environment are in competition with each other: both indirectly, by consumption of scarce resources, and directly, as predators and prey.

According to Darwin, the organisms that become these predators and their prey have individual and entirely accidental characteristics or variations. Faced with constant competition between and within species, these variations can improve a particular individual organism's chances of survival. In breeding, the successful organism's favourable variation is then transmitted to a portion of offspring, who, in turn, benefit from an increased chance of surviving and breeding. With every surviving generation, the tendency for reproduction of this characteristic increases because both direct and indirect competition generates the 'preservation of favourable variations and the rejection of injurious variations' (Darwin 2017 [1859], 69), and these characteristics eventually become dominant.[2] Bowler (1984) invoked the giraffe's long neck as evidence of his theory, and it remains a frequently cited example:

In the original population of grass-feeders, some individuals would by chance have longer than average neck, others shorter. When the grass began to disappear, those with longer necks would be able to reach leaves on trees more easily; because they could exploit the alternative source of food more effectively, they would be healthier and able to breed more readily; their offspring would be more numerous and inherit the extra length of neck. Conversely, those animals with shorter necks would get less food and not breed so easily; in extreme cases they would die of starvation, although a difference in rate of reproduction is all the mechanism required. It then follows that, in the next generation, more individuals will come from long-necked parents than from short. (p. 157)

Not only would the inherited characteristic eventually cause a major change in the species, but the selection mechanism would also lead to species differentiation and hence diversity because variation in characteristics would also allow different populations to exploit different resources.

In 1865, six years after Darwin published *Origin of Species*, Gregor Jo-
hann Mendel published a paper on the reproduction of pea plants in which he
identified a previously unsuspected mode of heredity, which we now call
genes.[3] Modern evolutionary theory amalgamated Darwin's basic ideas and
Mendelian genetics to produce the evolutionary synthesis theory. As Thayer
(2004) suggests, evolutionary synthesis introduces several new means
through which evolution can occur: (i) *migration*, which occurs as breeding
migrants move into and out of a population, affecting the rate at which genes
move into and out of a population; (ii) *mutation*, which facilitates spontaneous novelty in DNA as a result of a natural process or event, copying error, or
structural chromosomal changes; and (iii) *genetic drift*, 'a change in the
frequency of a gene variant in a population due to chance' (pp. 27–29). As
such, according to evolutionary synthesis, evolution occurs as a result of both
natural processes and chance. In addition, two other forces of evolution have
also been identified by evolutionary scientists: (iv) artificial selection, long
practiced in agricultural and animal breeding, and (v) sexual selection, the
process by which some individuals gain reproductive advantage by being
more attractive to the opposite sex (Thayer 2004, 28–29).

The essence of the evolutionary argument is that most of the behavioural
and physical characteristics of a species evolve because '[t]hose whose genes
promote characteristics that are advantageous in the struggle to survive and
reproduce are rewarded through the transmission of their genes to the next
generation' (Kitcher 1985, 42). This process has three main components: (i)
variation, that members of a relevant population vary with respect to at least
one characteristic with selective significance; (ii) *transmission* (sometimes
called *heredity*), that there exist copying mechanisms to ensure continuity
over time in the form and behaviour of entities in the population; and (iii)
selection, that the characteristics of some entities are better adapted to prevailing evolutionary pressures and, consequently, these entities increase in
numerical significance relative to less well-adapted entities. In other words,
the evolution of an entity within a system involves three key principles:
variation, transmission, and selection.

To understand why particular variations are retained or eliminated, it is
important to examine potential forces of selection. In biology, some entities
are better adapted to their environment than others, therefore surviving longer and more successfully producing offspring (Aldrich et al. 2008). This
mechanism of selection, commonly known as "fitness", implicit in the phrase
'survival of the fittest', refers to 'the relative ability of a complex organism to
perform the functions demanded by the environment for survival' (Spruyt
2001, 113). The greater the ability to meet such demand, the greater the
success at reproduction. This Darwinian view promotes an understanding of
evolution as directional and progressive; however, contrary to the popular
interpretation of Darwinist theory, evolution is undirected, lacking a general

pattern of development, and unpredictable, because random mutations and selection by exogenous events drive the process (Spruyt 2001, 113–14). Therefore, as Gould (1980; 1989) stresses, there is no reason to believe that later stages in evolutionary phases yield more complex, or more intricate, solutions to environmental challenges.[4] While this is a very brief overview of evolutionary theory (and its application and evidence base within biological science), for the purposes of the present study, it is important to note that it is also possible to evidence these notions with salient examples from the field of social sciences.

2.2 APPLYING EVOLUTIONARY THEORY TO SOCIAL SCIENCE

While it is a cornerstone of current biological understanding, there is nothing inherently biological in Darwin's evolutionary theory. In its broadest sense, it is a logical conclusion from a set of specific assumptions and not a concrete description of a specific biological process (Dennett 1996). Darwin's theory describes the logic of evolution, rather than the process of biological evolution. In fact, it was only several years after the first publication of *Origin of Species* that the biological mechanisms of evolution, first discovered by Mendel, were made known to the scientific community. Importantly, then, Darwin's theory has significant implications for wider fields of inquiry, rather than being limited to biology:

> That evolution is a core concept in biology does not mean that it is an inherent-ly biological concept. Evolution can happen in other domains providing that conditions for an evolutionary process are in place. Thus, as economists apply-ing evolutionary ideas to economic phenomena, we can learn from the debates on evolutionary biology in order to understand better the logical status of concepts such as fitness, adaptation and units of selection, without in any sense needing to absorb the associated biological context. (Metcalfe 1998, 22)

Taken out of its biological context, Darwin's logic can be stated as consisting of three assumptions: (i) 'a population of agents have variation in fixed traits, behavioural patterns, or tendencies'; (ii) these traits, patterns, or tendencies can be 'transferred to other agents either through reproduction or emula-tions'; and (iii) the 'relative rate of this [transmission] is partially determined by these traits' usefulness in adapting the agent to its [ever-changing] envi-ronment' (Montgomery 2011, 12). Considering that the application of evolu-tionary analogies to social sciences has enormous promise and, given the tendency in political science to borrow insights and theoretical approaches from the natural sciences, the relative lack of cross-fertilization from biology into such disciplines is surprising (Montgomery 2011, 10). However, apply-ing evolutionary insights to social science can prove problematic, and scholars who have attempted such methodology have faced criticism on the basis of tautological reasoning.

Based on a rudimentary understanding of fitness, some scholars have implied that this characteristic should be investigated by empirically assessing actual survival. Low (2000) suggests that – when seen in such superficial and oversimplified terms – natural selection can indeed appear tautological: 'What works, works, so if you see it, it must be working' (p. 34). Popper (1972) offers a more sophisticated version of this argument, claiming that any condition where species exist is well-matched with Darwinian explanation because if those species were not adapted, they would not exist. In other words, Popper notes, adaptation is defined as the minimum requirement for life to exist in a specific environment; unfortunately, since nothing is ruled out, the theory lacks explanatory power. Arguing along similar lines, Gould and Lewontin use the term 'Panglossian paradigm', a reference to Dr. Pangloss in Voltaire's *Candide*, who argues that any calamity – earthquake, flood, or disease – happened for the best, to describe what they believe to be the excesses of adaptationism. This argument refutes that of biologists who atomize organisms into parts and explain each as direct, near-optimal paths of adaptation to their respective environments (Thayer 2004).

Despite these criticisms of tautology and Panglossian reasoning, properly understood, natural selection is in fact far from exhibiting either of these traits. With regard to the accusation of tautology, Sober (1984) demonstrates that the notion of 'survival of the fittest' is not tautological since the proposition is both empirically based and testable in its effect. In fact, Sober argues that fitness, as a 'disproportional property, can be assimilated as a cause of selection and therefore under certain conditions is not a tautology' (Durand 2006, 105).

> The fact that an organism has a certain level of fitness is not an *event*. An organism's fitness is more like a sugar lump's solubility than its sudden immersion in water. However, the fact that fitness is a dispositional property does not show that it lacks causal efficacy. Nor is the definitional connection of the fitness concept with (probably) survival and reproductive success a reason for holding that it is causally inert. (Sober 1984, 84)

As such, in opposition to Popper's criticism that Darwinian theory is not explanatory because nothing is ruled out, Darwinian theory does in fact rule out many possibilities. Indeed, the theory precludes the existence of an inefficient organism when a more efficient one exists. It eliminates mutations or changes that are theoretically impossible according to the laws of ontogeny, molecular biology, and genetics to achieve incremental steps. Lastly, it prohibits the establishment of new species without ancestors. Therefore, the phrase 'survival of the fittest' is not merely defined in terms of what endures but, rather, provides a causal explanation for why certain species survive. In other words, adaptation is a functional notion (in that it explains phenomena that lead to outcomes), and not, as Popper argues, a logical or semantic a priori definition. The nature of fitness is probabilistic and not deterministic.

An additional counterpoint to Gould and Lewontin's charges – that what exists is immutable and close to perfection – is that no modern evolutionary theorist suggests that evolution leads to the 'best' outcome. Instead, Mayr (1988) suggests that 'evolution is opportunistic, and natural selection makes use of what variation it encounters' and that natural selection is an 'optimization process, but one of a very special kind' (pp. 153, 105). In other words, selection functions optimally in a given environment but is subject to many constraints in environmental conditions, and the environment is almost always changing. As such, organisms, such as humans, must also continually change, evolving to suit their environment.

These major criticisms advanced against evolutionary theory and, indirectly, its application to social science, are useful to consider in that they help illuminate the dangers for natural or social scientists and challenge them to be aware of these concerns. However, as demonstrated, although these criticisms of tautological or Panglossian reasoning are useful for illuminating potential pitfalls, they should not impede the use of evolutionary theory to explain human behaviour. Indeed, these criticisms and the examples used to counter them, more than anything, serve to highlight the importance of paying sufficient attention to the properties of an adaptation as opposed to its reaction to its given environment, the importance of attention to ancestral permutations, and the value of selecting an appropriate unit of inheritance (or 'unit of analysis').

2.3 UNITS OF ANALYSIS

According to Durham (1991), an evolutionary explanation begins with the need to clearly identify an appropriate unit of inheritance. The identification of such a unit – whether it is genes, ideas, techniques, values, words, or even entire languages – depends on the nature and logic of the theory of selection itself and represents the cornerstone of such an application of evolutionary insight. Dietl (2008) notes that 'every field must struggle with understanding its most basic units' (p. 89). In fact, identifying an adequate unit of inheritance has generated a considerable amount of confusion in biology (Hull 1998; Ghiselin 1997; Gould 2002) as a result of conceptual problems on the meaning of causality (Dietl 2008).[5]

It is therefore not surprising to find similar problems in applications of evolutionary insights to social sciences.[6] Moreover, the identification of an adequate and appropriate unit of inheritance has been fraught with conceptual problems for both biological and social scientists. However, despite these previously encountered difficulties, flexibility in terms of units of analysis is generally acknowledged as one of the methodological advantages of an evolutionary approach (Rapkin 2001; Thompson 2001a). Consequently, various scholars have suggested appropriate units of selection – including individual human beings, cities, states, nations, nongovernmental organizations, firms, policies, behaviours, genes, ideas, norms, institutions, and societies of states – on the basis that they might be 'examined fruitfully from an evolutionary standpoint' (Rapkin 2001, 53).

While the selection of appropriate units of inheritance remains a subject of debate, evolutionary biologists have generally come to appreciate the importance of carefully selecting such units to avoid ontological confusion about causal agency in natural selection. Having recognized the importance of selecting an appropriate unit of inheritance subject to the evolutionary approach, Gould (2002) proposes two useful sets of criteria to evaluate the appropriateness of a unit of inheritance. First, the unit must have a discrete and definable beginning, an equally discrete and definite ending, and sufficient stability to merit continuous recognition as the same "thing". Secondly, the unit must manifest the essential properties that permit them to function as an evolutionary entity with the capability to act as a causal agent in the process of Darwinian selection. Ultimately, the principle of inheritance must prevail, and successive variations must in some sense be retained and then passed on (Hull et al. 2001). This does not imply, however, that units of inheritance must necessarily pass 'carbon copies' of themselves to the next generation: rather that they only increase the relative presence of their heritable attributes within their environment in a manner that causes replication to be different in some measurable way. This allows for the formulation of testable causal scenarios about which certain heritable characteristics yield increased reproductive success while others do not.

Definitional Problems

The difficulties in selecting an appropriate unit of inheritance to survey the emergence, transformation, and diffusion of techniques of political violence are further complicated by the fundamental disagreements within the field of terrorism studies about what constitutes terrorism and the field's profound and detrimental reliance on case studies that often lack generalizable characteristics or attributes.

As noted by Weinberg et al. (2004) 'few terms or concepts in contemporary political discourse have proved as hard to define as terrorism' (p. 777). Consequently, nearly all scholarly inquiry within the field of terrorism studies is bound to include a discussion of the 'problem of definition'. This problem is characterized by a lack of agreement on any one definition and the existence of contradicting definitions that can best be termed as a 'surplus of definitions'. This state of affairs has even led researchers, including Walter Laqueur (1977, 5), the 'founding father of Terrorism Studies', to cast doubts as to whether a settled agreed-upon definition is possible or even necessary, arguing that terrorism has appeared in so many different forms and under so many different circumstances that a comprehensive definition is impossible. Almost twenty years later, Laqueur (1999) reiterated his observation that any attempt to define terrorism 'is bound to fail' (p. 46), and despite the publication of thousands of books and articles on terrorism, the definitional challenge has shown few, if any, signs of abating.

Contemplating the definitional debate, Weinberg et al. (2004) argue that journalists, policy makers, and scholars have subjected the term 'terrorism' to three 'sins to which complex concepts are heir' (p. 778). First, they claim that terrorism has become an 'essentially contested concept': one whose meaning lends itself to endless debate but no satisfactory resolution. Indeed, like any social science concept, terrorism can be defined as whatever the disputants say it is, and therefore, it comes down to who has the power to define and who can argue their case long and hard enough for their definition to emerge triumphant. The implication here is that scholars of terrorism have widely acknowledged the fruitlessness of definitional debates and endeavours and have instead reverted to an intuitive understanding of the phenomena.

The second charge brought forward by Weinberg and his associates (2004) is that terrorism as a concept, especially as framed within media discourse, suffers from 'border' and 'membership' problems, where a violent act may be considered terrorism on some occasions but not on others, usually 'based upon the assumed motivations of the perpetrators' (p. 779). In fact, media coverage of terrorism has frequently been characterized by disputes over definitions, with critiques of the conceptualization of terrorism in the media highlighting inconsistencies in the use of the term and particularly taking exception to perceived double standards and subjectivity in the applications of the term to certain actors. These discussions have been particularly dominant in light of the recent mass shooting incidents in the United States. For example, following the killing of nine African American churchgoers in Charleston, South Carolina, in 2015 by Dylann Roof, authors writing for publications such as the *New Yorker, Salon.com, Foreign Policy*, and *The Atlantic* argued the attack deserved to be called 'terrorism' under both governmental and academic definitions (see Illing 2015; Groll 2015; Friedersdorf 2015). For example, the *Salon.com* article titled 'We Must Call Him a Terrorist' (Illing 2015) highlighted the significant contestation over the conceptualization of 'terrorism' within the media, arguing that debates over definitions of terrorism arise 'only when white people are the perpetrators'. Furthermore, noting the 'urgency' contained in the designation of an act as 'terrorism', the article suggests that the underlying assumption is that 'terrorism is about the colour of the criminal, not the intent of the crime', and that, as such, only violent crimes committed by 'brown men with bombs' constitute urgent security threats.

These criticisms are far from new. In fact, journalists and academics have long criticized the imbalance in media coverage, where politically motived murders committed in recent years by non-Muslims are less likely to be labelled as acts of terrorism by the media. In addition, violent incidents committed by non-Muslims receive less media coverage, are less likely to make the national news, and more commonly remain local news stories (Kearns et al. 2019). These patterns shape public consciousness regarding terrorism and the national policy discourse about counter-terrorism policy, keeping both focused on the threat of so-called jihadi terrorism. Anthony Richards (2015) echoes this assertion and argues that there appears to be a wholesale disregard for any serious endeavour to treat terrorism as an analytical concept' in public and political discourse; instead, the term 'has been shaped to serve the interests of the definers to the point that any common political will or purpose to address the problem of achieving a universally agreed definition has been overridden in favour of perspectives that seek to preserve and enhance those interests' (p. 2).

The third sin committed by the current conceptualizations of the phenomenon, identified by Weinberg et al. (2004) is the 'stretching' of the term. The term *terrorism* suffers from being stretched to the point of ambiguity and imprecision to cover a wider range of acts, such as 'narco-terrorism' and 'cyber-terrorism', the latter seldom involving any reference to violence or the threat of violence. Contemplating the issue of conceptual stretching, Gearty (1991) pronounces that the term terrorist 'resonates with moral opprobrium and as such, as far as the authorities and others are concerned, [it is] far too useful an insult to be pinned down and controlled' (p. 6), while English (2009) argues that the subjectivity of the term meant that 'one can end up merely with antiphonally chanted, mutually echoing abuse, and as a result with little clarity or analytical illumination' (p. 19). Likewise, Richards (2015) aptly highlights that the word 'terrorism' has also been employed to refer to a multitude of events. These range from protesters in Thailand, Tunisia, and Libya, to the 2010 Israeli raid on the so called 'Gaza Freedom Flotilla' (which was attempting to break the Israeli blockade of Gaza). It has also been used when denouncing the US invasion of Iraq, the US drone strikes in Pakistan, the 2011 North Atlantic Treaty Organization (NATO) intervention in Libya, Syrian rebels challenging the Assad regime, and even in connection with Julian Assange – founder of WikiLeaks – who was described by US Senator Mitch McConnell as a 'high-tech terrorist'. This demonstrates 'how the label is too often used without any rigor as to what terrorism is and what its parameters are' (Richards 2015, 2–3).

Pondering the conceptual stretching within governmental and law enforcement context, Hoffman (2006) illustrates how the social construction of the term *terrorism* within governmental context is deeply political, and the defining factor for the labelling of a group as such is, in part, linked to the organization's specific agenda. Richards (2014) laments this, arguing that the 'failure to craft an agreed-on definition of terrorism has left a vacuum' for state agencies 'to define terrorism in ways that serve their own perceived political and strategic interests' (p. 214). Echoing Richards' sentiments, Golder and Williams (2004) stress the need to 'describe the concept with as much precision as possible' fearing that otherwise, 'the power of the States may extend very far indeed' (p. 272), while Townshend (2011) argues that the need for a clear definition of terrorism for policy makers was sharply highlighted by 'the indefinite reach of President Bush's "war against terror"' (p. 2). In addition to lending itself to opportunistic appropriation, Gourevitch (2003) adds that this conceptual confusion and imprecise terminology usage have rendered the term meaningless, laying governments open to charges that they are undermining their own counter-terrorism efforts and attempts to generate international cooperation.

The aforementioned issues with the current conceptualizations of terrorism pose some unusual challenges that must be addressed by scholars. Most importantly, scholars of political violence must be aware and pragmatic about their conceptual choices. As Collier (1998) suggests: 'When such [conceptual] confusion arises, it is essential for scholars to engage in a self-conscious, critical evaluation that systematically appraises existing usage of concepts and seeks to channel it in more productive directions' (p. 5). Moreover, while definitions cannot be viewed in a binary fashion as either true or false, Tilly (2004) stresses that 'in social science useful definitions should point to detectable phenomena that exhibit some degree of causal coherence – in principle all instances should display common properties that embody or result from similar cause-effect relations' (p. 8).

Techniques as a Unit of Inheritance

Therefore, to avoid stretching the definition of terrorism beyond measure, I have chosen to consider a variety of forms of political contention, which I call 'techniques of contention', as the unit of inheritance (and analysis). Thus, rather than prolonging the protracted definitional debates, in this book, I will focus my inquiries on the techniques of contention employed by claim-makers to contest or change the existing political status quo in the face of their adversary – the state and its institutions (Tilly 1995).

'Reduced to its greatest simplicity', contentious politics involves the conflict between 'those who are more or less satisfied with the existing social order that want to conserve it and those for whom the existing order does not suit and so desires or want to change it' (Oberschall 1973, 33). According to Tilly (1995), contentious politics represents 'sustained challenges to power holders in the name of a disadvantaged population living under the jurisdiction or influence of those powerholders' (p. 369) motivated by real or perceived grievances. These 'powerholders' are deemed to have wronged or harmed individuals or groups to such a degree that these groups (or their representatives) are inspired to voice a dissident opinion and engage in claim-making actions whose purpose is to improve the conditions of said group. Unlike previous theorizations of collective actions, claim-makers are seen as rational actors assessing the environment in which they exist and, based on those assessments, selecting the manner – or rather the claim-making technique – they will employ to contest or change the existing political status quo in the face of an adversary such as a state and its institutions (Tilly 1995).

These claim-making techniques, along with all other techniques available to humankind, represent an epistemological entity and are, in their barest form, sets of instructions to manipulate environments (Mokyr 1998, 122) or alter human-made systems. All claim-making techniques available to a given society or held by a given group at a given time, when combined, represent a repertoire of contention (Tilly 1995). Tilly (1995) contends that people making claims against powerful adversaries almost always select their techniques, which he calls "tactics", from the determined "repertoire" that already exists – and that they are aware of – to make their claims. These repertoires represent only small subsets of all possible techniques feasibly available in the world. I consider the techniques contained in claim-makers' repertoires of contention, which include the deployment of threats and violence, in a manner that falls outside the societally accepted norms of claim making, to be 'terroristic'.

This focus on the technique itself separates the actions from the actors. Much as Simmel (1950) advocated the study of a pure form of "sociation" analytically separated from both agency and social structure, I argue the study of terrorism should focus on the nature of the technique rather than on the characteristics of the agents or organizations responsible for it. Crenshaw and Robinson (2010) identify several distinct advantages to such an approach. First, 'even a cursory examination of terrorism in the twentieth and twenty-first centuries demonstrates that today's terrorist organisations often become tomorrow's politics parties', such as the Irish Republican Army, Hamas, and the Irgun (p. 236). Secondly, most terrorist organizations can just as easily be characterized as 'social movement organisations that happen to employ terrorism as a strategic choice' (p. 236). Lastly, while the size and strength of an organization may shape its choice of claim-making techniques, such factors are more properly considered causes of said groups' choice(s) of different forms of claim-making techniques, rather than actual elements of those techniques. Thus, the attributes of techniques of contention should not be conflated with the attributes of (groups of) actors.

Seeing terrorism as part of a wider social movements provides several distinct advantages. First, it allows one to avoid the ahistoricity and lack of contextual rigour of which terrorism research has often been accused (Silke 2004; Ranstorp 2006; Della Porta 1995). Moreover, this approach does not solely focus on claim-makers but also on state practices (as part of the environment) and their subsequent effect on these groups and their choices, thus addressing the critique that terrorism research too often ignores the role of the state in contributing to the development of a 'terrorist' response (Alexander 1991; Della Porta 1995; Araj 2008).

2.4 TECHNIQUES OF CONTENTIONS AND TERRORISM

While extant work has not yet considered the application of evolutionary theory to terrorism studies, the notion that techniques of political contention undergo changes is not a completely novel idea. Indeed, the concept of repertoires of contention, first proposed by Tilly (1978), entails an understanding of how such techniques change over time.[7] Most importantly, this chapter demonstrates how evolutionary concepts are present within Tilly's conceptualization of contentious politics, although the author does not explicitly use evolutionary language. Repertoires of contention can be understood as a collection of claim-making strategies and techniques that a given group knows how to use and may choose to deploy to make a claim. These techniques might include strikes, lobbying, petitions, mass protests, hunger strikes, public demonstrations, and other forms of claim-making that are visible to an adversary, that is, usually a state and its institutions (Tilly 1995). Further, Tilly (1995) notes that repertoires of contention represent only small subsets of all techniques feasibly available in the world:

> The word repertoire identifies a limited set of routines that are learned, shared, and acted out through a relatively deliberate process of choice. Repertoires [of contention] are learned cultural creations, but they do not descend from abstract philosophy or take shape as a result of political propaganda; they emerge from struggle. People learn to break windows in protest, attack pilloried prisoners, tear down dishonored houses, stage public marches, petition, hold formal meetings, organize special-interest associations. At any particular point in history, however, they learn only a rather small number of alternative ways to act collectively. (p. 26)

This definition of repertoires of contention encompasses three noteworthy elements. First, in relation to the concept of evolutionary theory, repertoires are temporal and spatial; therefore, they are associated with specific histori-

cal periods within specific societies which change over time, but only gla-
cially (Mokyr 1998; 2000; 2005; 2006). Secondly, Tilly suggests that both
the makeup of the repertoires, and therefore, choices of techniques are constrained, meaning groups or individuals will routinely return to tried-and-
tested techniques. Lastly, the aforementioned concept of repertoires emphasizes practical constitution; in other words, repertoires of contention do not
emerge out of abstract thinking but, rather, out of struggle, activities of
everyday life and, perhaps most importantly, out of interaction with an 'adversary'.

In this section, I will outline a key tenet of my theoretical framework by
expanding and further developing Tilly's three definitional elements to advance the understanding of how and when techniques associated with terrorism enter various repertoires of contention. First while Tilly's characterisa-
tion of techniques of contention as evolving in specific times and places is
relevant to this study's evolutionary framework, it has some weaknesses. In
particular, it fails to adequately and explicitly differentiate between techniques emerging from within a society as a result of major structural changes
in state and those techniques that are transported between societies and consequently adopted. I also address Joel Mokyr's (1998; 2000; 2005; 2006)
distinctive theory on the role of useful knowledge in industrial innovation.
This theory explains how propositional knowledge (which encompasses a
society's understanding of nature) constrains the emergence of physical technologies or techniques to harness nature for the benefit of humans. This
notion is the foundation on which my theoretical framework is built by
introducing the notion of social technologies and contending that the same
logic can and should be applied to the emergence of social techniques, including techniques of contention. Finally, I explore the role of struggles
between claim-makers and the authorities and the impact of such interactions, arguing that claim-makers and authorities engage in a reciprocal relationship and respond tactically to the other's choice of techniques.

In sum, this section introduces notions of modularity and the groundwork
of evolutionary theory as they relate to repertoires of contention and, thereby,
lays out some basic foundations for the following section, which will explore
how techniques evolve and are diffused and why certain techniques – but not
others – become modular and are transported to other repertoires. Most importantly, I demonstrate how evolutionary concepts are present within Tilly's
conceptualization of contention, although Tilly does not explicitly use evolutionary language.

Modularity

Tilly views changes to repertoires as glacial, only resulting from major structural changes like significant state fluctuations in interests, opportunities, and

organizations (Tarrow 1998, 31). In *Contentious Performances* (2008), Tilly revisits the narrative of contention he proposed in *Popular Contention in Great Britain, 1758–1834* (1995) and argues that the prevalent forms of contention in Great Britain evolved from the eighteenth to the nineteenth century.[8] The eighteenth-century repertoire included various techniques of claim-making, including food riots, blocking, touring, threatening, parading, forced illuminations, attacks on public figures, breaking windows, and taking advantage of authorized public ceremonies to voice preferences (Tilly 2008, 79, 133). On the other hand, the nineteenth-century repertoire evolved to include public meetings, petitions, and demonstrations (Tilly 2008, 42). Similarly, Tilly's *The Contentious French* (1986) identifies two distinctive repertoires that developed between the eighteenth and nineteenth centuries in France. Tilly's treatment of the various repertoires of contention in France and Great Britain supports his claim that particular repertoires of contention are indeed specific to given historical periods and to specific societies; despite some similarities, methods of contention used by the eighteenth-century French were markedly different from those used by both the eighteenth-century British and the nineteenth-century French.

Tilly's work thus demonstrates that repertoires of contention develop and adapt over long periods of time in relation to specific historical settings. However, because of Tilly's almost-exclusive reliance on rich historical narratives to illustrate the changes to various repertoires of contention, he fails to articulate a precise mechanism to explain *why* certain techniques of contention arise, spread, ensue, disappear, or simply fail to emerge in given repertoires. While Tilly's work includes implicit evolutionary components, then, it is necessary to address specific elements of modularity, as they relate to both the concept of repertoires of contention and that of evolutionary theory. Rather than simply focusing on large structural changes in the state, as Tilly does, the following sections of this chapter address the source of variation in relation to changes in propositional knowledge held within a given society.

Although specific techniques of contention are products of specific contentious relationships and time periods, it does not necessarily follow that such techniques are contained within only one society at a given time. Instead, they are employed across a multitude of diversified contexts. For example, strikes and demonstrations were initially invented by a minority of pioneers in Europe. However, striking and demonstrating methods spread across borders; these techniques are now part of numerous repertoires of political contention and are generally understood by a majority of citizens, and not only in Europe but also in most modern states worldwide (Meyer and Tarrow 1998). Wada (2012) identifies techniques that have spread beyond the specific societal context in which they emerged as 'modular' techniques.

The notion of modularity, which draws on the field of diffusion studies (Soule 2004; Strang and Soule 1998; Givan et al. 2010), provides a lens by which to explain how techniques spread and can be exported by claim-makers (McAdam and Rucht 1993; Tarrow 1993). This represents a particularly important line of inquiry because it enables analysis of both the techniques of contention themselves and the mechanisms that led to their transportation across diffuse repertoires. Determining whether a particular technique has been subjected to an evolutionary process (and, therefore, represents an adaptation of an existing technique), constitutes a new technique altogether or already exists within another society's repertoire of contention is crucial to understanding whether or not a given technique represents a watershed moment in the evolution of political violence.

While Tilly's work does provide a useful basis for the integration of the notion of modularity into the concept of repertoires of contention, it does not provide us with a specific model that explicitly includes modularity. For example, Tilly (1978) argues that contentious groups often employ flexible repertoires of contention where their observation of other groups' tactics lead to the subsequent modification of their own techniques of contention. By imitating forms of collective actions used by other claim-making groups, claim-makers may increase their own effectiveness. The underlying assumption is that when one claim-making group uses a particular technique of contention successfully, others are more likely to follow suit (Oberschall 1989; Tilly 1995). In that sense, social movements 'do not have to reinvent the wheel at each place and in each conflict'; instead, 'they often find inspiration elsewhere in the ideas and tactics espoused and practiced by other activists' (McAdam and Rucht 1993, 58).

Whereas Tilly's work does not explicitly focus on the transmission of techniques, recent literature on contentious politics has begun to devote more attention to how claim-makers influence not only their adversaries, but also other claim-makers across movements and countries. For example, Sean Chabot (2010) analyses how the 'Gandhian repertoire' of nonviolent direct action was integral to the Indian nationalist struggle for independence from colonial rules and was employed by leaders and participants in the US civil rights movements in the 1950s and 1960s. Soule (1997; 1999) contends that connections among activists and organizations, as well as links through social and cultural identities, have contributed to the rapid spread of 'the shantytown' protest technique: that is, the construction of shacks from scraps of wood, tar paper, and plastics on US campuses between 1985 and 1990. Conversely, Wood (2007) identifies how police repression of new tactics such as black bloc (the wearing of black concealing and protective items of clothing to hide their identities and protect themselves from pepper spray) used in Seattle during the World Trade Organization protest in 1999 limited the diffusion of these techniques to other demonstrations in New York and Toronto.

Since repertoires of contention represent the sum of all claim-making techniques available to a given society at a given time (Tilly 1995), they are temporal and spatial entities. Diversity in techniques – as Tilly addressed when comparing eighteenth- and nineteenth-century British and French methods of contention – is directly linked to a core characteristic of cultural evolution. Cultures evolve in partial isolation – either geographical, historical, or social – from one another and, therefore, tend to diverge from one another as small differences accumulate, generation by generation. The influence of geography on the emergence of cultural differences, by either expanding or limiting the body of ideas and innovations available to different people, is both a longstanding and central component of evolutionary thought. According to this line of thinking, human cultural diversity is produced primarily by historical and geographical happenstance (Newson et al. 2010, 458). The purest examples of this phenomenon are related to symbolic aspects of cultural repertoires, such as language (Bettinger et al. 1996; Labov 2006; Nettle 1999; Thompson 2001a). When populations live in different habitats, adaptive processes of cultural change lead to diversification because the variants best suited to these respective habitats are most likely to be adopted.

That being said, convergence of cultural practices can also occur when populations live in environments that are discrete but similar (Johnson and Earle 2006). For example, groups that live in deserts will likely develop some similar practices, whether the desert is located in Australia or Tunisia. However, adaptive processes are affected by numerous historical factors that produce variations between populations, even if their survival pressures are similar. For example, the problem of carrying and storing water can be solved in a number of ways, and a culture that has already developed the skill of weaving waterproof baskets may never acquire the technology for producing pottery, and vice versa. Similarly, geographical, historical, and social separation permits small differences to accumulate between cultural pools. This may cause incipient techniques of contention to diverge. Modern history provides ample evidence to support Patrick's (2001, 146) claim that, without some form of isolation, diversity could not persist, as all local techniques would be swamped by globalizing culture. Therefore, the notion of modularity is significant in considering the transmission and evolution of techniques of contention. Further, it is necessary to consider the key role of propositional knowledge, which forms one of this book's underpinning principles of how and why techniques of contention are either adopted or rejected by various groups of claim-makers.

Propositional Knowledge and Techniques of Contention

Tilly also suggests that repertoires constrain behaviour by limiting the choices of techniques available for claim-making and influencing future choices. While Tilly (1992) makes numerous references to improvisation within repertoires and recognises that individuals will experiment with new techniques in the search for tactical advantage, he contends that claim-makers do this in small ways, staying at the edge of well-established techniques. As such, Tilly suggests that the 'prior history of contention . . . constrains the choices of action currently available, in partial independence of the identities and interests that participants bring to the action' (Tilly 1995, 29). Moreover, Tilly (1978) proposes that 'any given populations tend to have a fairly limited and well-established set of means for actions on shared interests' (p. 39). Therefore, whilst repertoires provide an array of possible techniques, they also limit individuals' choice of techniques: "people generally turn to familiar routines" even when, in principle, some other "unfamiliar form of action would serve their interest much better" (1986, 4).

For example, in the United States, the use of demonstrations and sit-ins are now widely recognised techniques of contention, and as a result, tend to be employed over other methods, especially due to their use by highly visible movements such as the Civil Rights, anti-war, feminist, and environmental movements of the past century (Traugott 2010, 19). University students who wish to protest institutional policy are therefore more likely to use these or similar tactics in order to voice their dissatisfaction and seek change, even if a novel approach might improve their likelihood of success.

However, whilst Tilly's concept of repertoires of contention implies that individuals selecting a technique of contention are restricted to techniques they are familiar with, 'know-how' or 'acquired competence' may further restrict the options available (Tilly and Tilly 1981). Knowledge of the existence of a technique is not sufficient; claim-makers must also have the abilities required to carry it out. Nonetheless, Tilly's work falls short of explicitly demonstrating why and how individuals lack knowledge, or how they come to attain it. In order to remedy this shortcoming in Tilly's work and to fully understand how 'know-how', familiarity, and 'acquired competence' limit the choice of which techniques individuals will use, I employ a theory proposed by economic historian Joel Mokyr.

Mokyr (1998; 2000; 2005; 2006) argues that the growth of physical technologies to harness nature for the benefit of mankind in recent centuries was driven by the accumulation of 'useful' knowledge and the declining costs of accessing it. Building on Kuznets' (1955) work, Mokyr understands knowledge as an economic resource necessary for societal improvement and economic growth. According to Mokyr (2005), useful knowledge 'deals with natural phenomena that potentially lend themselves to manipulation, such as artefacts, materials, energy and living beings' (p. 3). Therefore, useful knowledge is knowledge about any regularity or pattern of nature that may be harnessed for the purpose of generating economic value or otherwise benefitting human beings. In this sense, useful knowledge does not refer to the veracity of said knowledge or to any epistemological feature of its origin. This is not to suggest that all types of knowledge or epistemologies are equivalent, rather, that the economic and social usefulness of knowledge as an object has more relevance than its epistemology.

By focusing on the practical application of knowledge, Mokyr's theory of knowledge builds on Polanyi's (1962) notion of "tacit knowing". In doing so, Mokyr partitions useful knowledge into two distinct subsets. One is propositional knowledge, which describes and catalogues natural phenomena and the relationships among them. This roughly translates to explanations of 'what things are' and 'how they work'. The other subcategory is prescriptive knowledge, which contains instructions that can be executed to manipulate nature.

Propositional knowledge is defined as the union of 'observation, classification, measurement and cataloguing of natural phenomena', and the 'establishment of regularities, principles, and "natural laws" that govern these phenomena and allow us to make sense of it' (Mokyr 2000, 256). It includes formalized knowledge; practical informal knowledge; artisanal and agricultural knowledge; folk wisdoms; and any other natural phenomena (Mokyr 2002).

On the other hand, prescriptive knowledge, or repertoires of techniques, consist of the 'blueprints, whether codified or tacit, of techniques that society could carry out if it wanted', to manipulate nature for human purposes (Mokyr 2001, 5). In their simplest form, these techniques are a set of instructions or 'recipes' with which to manipulate environments and alter man-made systems. Indeed, the analogy of a cookbook is fitting in the sense that techniques, like recipes, can either be codified, as they are in cookbooks, or be implicit and tacit. Instructions on how to administer medicines or instructions for building a bridge are both clear examples of prescriptive knowledge.

Polanyi (1962) contends that the difference between these two subsets of knowledge boils down to observing that propositional knowledge can be 'right or wrong', whereas prescriptive knowledge, or techniques, 'can only be successful or unsuccessful' (p. 175). For example, while the knowledge of gravity necessary for bridge building is propositional, different techniques of bridge building are prescriptive knowledge and may therefore be successful or unsuccessful to varying degrees. Polanyi further argues that the same distinction is exemplified in patent law, which grants patents for inventions that are additions to the body of prescriptive knowledge, but not to discoveries, which are additions to propositional knowledge. In sum, prescriptive knowledge defines what a society is capable of doing and differs from propositional knowledge in that it defines a society's power over, and not just knowledge of, nature. Applying this to techniques of contention allows us to understand that a society is limited in its ability to create new techniques by its knowledge of the relationship between the state and opponents, a topic that will be subsequently explored.

Prescriptive knowledge and propositional knowledge are profoundly intertwined: All techniques (prescriptive knowledge) require propositional knowledge that, to some degree, 'explains' the phenomenon that is being manipulated by the technique. This set of propositional knowledge is the epistemic base of the technique. Mokyr's (2001) core contention, which he supports through the use of historical evidence, is that the emergence and evolution of techniques contained within a society's repertoire depends on the quality of its epistemic base. If the epistemic base of a technique is narrow, little is understood about how and why a certain technique works, and its evolution is thereby limited. Conversely, once the epistemic base is broadened as a result of a greater understanding of the technique's 'inner workings', resultant techniques can evolve much further.[9] While techniques (prescriptive knowledge) must necessarily be bound to propositional knowledge, there is no requirement for this epistemic base of any technique to be 'true'; rather, it needs only to conform to the accepted propositional knowledge of the time period. In fact, numerous techniques, from bloodletting and crop rotations to modern slim-down diets, have been used with some success despite the fact that they are based on propositional knowledge that is no longer accepted. In that sense, the epistemic base is bounded from below by a generated support: the very least a society must know about a technique is that 'it works'. However, as the epistemic base widens, and society learns more about the underlying natural processes at work, this in turn has an important impact on the further refinement of existing techniques or the emergence of new ones. In this sense, the composition of a repertoire is limited by the body of propositional knowledge existing within a society.

However, Mokyr's distinction between propositional knowledge and prescriptive knowledge does not explain why a particular technique exists within a specific repertoire. Rather, it provides two partial insights into why certain techniques *fail to emerge* within a given repertoire at a given time. Firstly, a given technique cannot emerge within a society that lacks the required body of propositional knowledge. For example, a society that lacks the body of propositional knowledge surrounding advanced physics is constrained from developing nuclear technologies (Mokyr 2002). In the same vein, it is unsurprising that sending parcel bombs did not enter the European repertoire of contention as a claim-making technique until after the invention of nitro-glycerine, which allowed for the relatively safe transport of explosives to their destination via mail (Laqueur 2001). Prior to this, claim-makers were limited by propositional constraints – a lack of knowledge of thermodynamics and chemistry – which prohibited their society from developing, manufacturing, and using such technology. Secondly, while 'the existence of a minimum epistemic base is a necessary condition for a technique to emerge and evolve, it does not describe anything like a sufficient condition for that technique to emerge' (Mokyr 2006, 317). Just because society has the propositional knowledge necessary to feasibly develop a parcel bomb, this will not necessarily lead to this technique's invention. In relation to scientific inventions, as well as to techniques of political contention, it stands to reason that many did not emerge previously simply because they did not occur to anyone, rather than because of a lack of propositional knowledge. Indeed, the possibility of deliberately crashing an aeroplane into a building existed long before anyone actually did it in practice.

Similarly, a shortcoming of Tilly's work is his failure to consider and adequately explore how knowledge constrains both individuals' choices of techniques and the overall make up of a society's repertoire of contention. In fact, Tilly's assertion that repertoires are more or less a fixed set of actions claim-makers follow during an episode of contention, results from the use of objectivist and culturally neutral language that treats actors as passive receptors and appliers of such mechanisms. It demonstrates little consideration of the claim-makers' understanding of their own societies and the historical periods in which they live (Brachet de Márquez 2014). While Tilly recognizes that claim-makers can make choices between a variety of techniques existing within the repertoires, he does not explicitly incorporate into his theory the notion that individuals are bound by different societal limitations. Therefore, these claim-makers may have an entirely different conception of what these techniques mean and different expectations of what they may lead to or accomplish. In this sense, we might explain the non-existence of sit-ins in eighteenth-century France based on the fact that repertoires of contention are at once structural, cultural, and social concepts. This encompasses not only what people do know how to do when they are involved in conflict with others, 'but also how they understand and attribute meaning to their actions at a given time' (Tarrow 1998, 30).

To properly elaborate how structural and societal norms influence and further constrain repertoires of contention, it will be useful to return to and expand on Mokyr's notion of propositional knowledge. In its original formulation, Mokyr limits propositional knowledge exclusively to knowledge about nature, rather than applying this concept to knowledge about society as a whole: that is, knowledge about social phenomena and the social systems that coordinate human behaviour and create structures of human interaction (Eggertsson 2009, 720; North 1994, 359–60). The impact of the concept of propositional knowledge on the understanding of the emergence of new social techniques, especially when compared to the work devoted to propositional knowledge about nature, has been limited (Nelson 2003, 15). As such, rather than an explicitly postulated and clear definition of knowledge about society, this line of thinking has produced a variety of vague definitions that consider knowledge about society as individuals' implicit understanding of the 'working rules' (Commons 1936), 'rules of the game' (North 1990), 'how the game is played' (Schotter 1981), 'governing structures' (Williamson 1985), and other related conceptions proposed by economists and social scientists. Faced with this lack of a clear and authoritative definition, it is useful to apply the concept of propositional knowledge to knowledge about society and, specifically, techniques of contention in the same way as the concept has already been applied to knowledge about nature.

Significantly, individuals rely on normative social theories or models (ethics, religious beliefs), explicit theories of social regularities, and the measurement and classification of social phenomena (Maddison 1982) to understand their social environments. These normative and positive theories and expectations – which may be reinforced by particular sets of rules, enforcement mechanisms, and behavioural regularities – represent how individuals perceive their social environment and its inner workings. Moreover, a large amount of this knowledge about society is non-codified, tacit knowledge that can only be expressed through actions. All societies contain a great deal of knowledge about the perceived inner working of the society in question, such as lessons learned, practical skills, and experience, which is stored in the form of behavioural and social norms. Like propositional knowledge about nature, propositional knowledge about society does not need to be 'true' in the sense of having been empirically tested or falsified. Rather, it simply needs to be more or less accepted as 'true' by the society for it to lead to the emergence of social techniques.

Returning to the question of techniques of contention, and expanding Mokyr's definition of propositional knowledge to include knowledge about how societies function, provides additional mechanisms to explain the constraints on repertoires. As will be discussed in greater detail in the subsequent section of this chapter, the core of politics of contention is interaction between claim-makers and those who seek to impose or maintain the status quo. As such, techniques of contention are directly linked to claim-makers' understanding of the societal system in which they operate and, incidentally, their understanding of how the population and the authorities will react to various techniques of contention. As the body of propositional knowledge about society expands, and new beliefs and notions emerge, the epistemic base of repertoires of contention widens. As previously described, this widening of the epistemic base allows for the emergence of new techniques, partly through the invention of new technologies or the adaptation of existing technologies and partly as a response to changing beliefs about society. Therefore, when faced with a new technique of contention, it is necessary to question whether this technique emerged as a result of technological changes or as the result of a new understanding of society's inner workings. This focus represents a significant departure from Tilly's analysis, which positions changes to repertoires as the glacial result of major structural changes in states. Instead, I posit that changes to repertoires occur not just as a result of actual changes in the state itself but also from changes in people's understanding of society's inner workings: namely, individuals' understanding of their relationship with the state.

Techniques of Contention: The Product of Struggle

Tilly's conceptualization of repertoires of contention stresses that they emerge out of struggle, activities of everyday life, and, perhaps most importantly, interaction with the 'adversary'. Tilly (2006, 27) uses the analogy of improvisational jazz music, or spontaneous skits by a troupe of actors to describe this form of interaction: composers provide the initial 'head' for a jam session, but 'the improvisations depend on a group of actors over whom they have little control' and who 'interact with one another, with opponents, and with those they are trying to attract' (Tarrow 2013, 16). As in a musical riff, the process implies a 'paradoxical combination of ritual and flexibility' (Tilly 1978, 22), in which neither element is allowed to completely dominate the other, lest the performance lose its effectiveness. Similarly, people learn a limited set of collective action techniques and they tailor them to 'the immediate situation and to the responses of other parties, e.g. antagonists, authorities, allies, observers, objects of their action, and other people somehow involved in the struggle' (Tilly 1993, 265). Furthermore, Tilly (1995) contends that various techniques of contention influence societal relationships such as 'police practices, laws of assembly, rules of association, routines for informal gatherings, ways of displaying symbols of affiliation, opposition or protest, means of reporting news, and so on' (pp. 26–27), thus, emphasising that the repertoire is one of interaction between actors.

Access to repertoires of any subset of techniques is not limited to individuals seeking to make a claim against powerful adversaries. The adversaries themselves also have access to a repertoire containing the various techniques to respond to collective action and dissent. These techniques can range from enacting legislative changes (such as instituting laws governing assembly and associations and those that criminalize speech) to military repression of dissent or even summary imprisonment or assassination of activists and dissenters. As such, claim-makers' repertoires of contention should be understood as being mirrored and directly influenced by the existing authority's own repertoire of techniques for enforcing the status quo. Therefore, any claim-making is directly influenced by the interplay between the techniques used by both the claim-makers themselves and their adversaries. This insight appears to be congruous with Tilly's (2005) argument that contentious political actors do not simply employ a single technique from within a repertoire of contention, but rather tend to engage in a series of contentious 'interactions' with the authorities. Ultimately, 'repertoires of contention are the established ways in which pairs of actors make and receive claims bearing on each other's interests' (Tilly 1993, 265). In other words, a repertoire of contention facilitates a dialogue, and not a monologue, in which claim-makers learn a limited set of techniques of contention and tailor them to both their immediate situations and to the responses of other parties. When choosing to employ a particular technique contained within a society's repertoire of contention, claim-makers do so by anticipating the authorities' reactions based on previous experience and on their particular understanding of their adversary.

To understand a claim-maker's strategic decision-making process (when made in relation to their adversaries), it is useful to distinguish between factors influencing the costs and benefits of the particular technique and the factors related to the goals of such action (Kriesi 2004, 78). Regarding both, claim-makers may anticipate positive, negative, mixed, or non-existent reactions. In relation to goals, authorities may be expected to respond either: (i) favourably, by changing their policies in the direction of the movement's goal, as was the case in the 1905 revolution in Russia, where an absolutist regime lacked the repressive capability to enforce its refusal of claim-makers' demands; or (ii) unfavourably, by maintaining the existing status quo or even changing its policies in the opposite direction to that which is desired by the group, as was the outcome in the Chinese student rebellion of 1989 (Tarrow 1998, 149).

While authorities may exhibit either positive or negative responses based on their appreciation (or lack of appreciation) for a given claim's validity, they may also respond negatively or positively to the technique used, irrespective of the claim's validity. For instance, positive reactions to claim-making techniques may include providing resources or moral support, or by recognizing the legitimacy of the technique itself. A good example of this is Western governments' recognition of petitions as a legitimate and encouraged claim-making technique through government funded websites. Alternatively, authorities faced with a technique of contention they deem illegitimate or unacceptable may decide to react in such a way as to apply sanctions that increase the cost of, and punish the use of, such a technique. Claim-makers will, therefore, make strategic choices on the basis of their appreciation of the specific chances of reform and/or failure and the risk of repression they face as a result of their efforts. As Gamson and Meyer (1996) suggest, the existing literature has focused extensively on this decision-making process, while largely ignoring the question of 'relative opportunity' that results from the ability to choose between various techniques (p. 283). Gamson and Meyer (1996) further argue that the opportunity for the use of a particular technique may shift based on an ever-changing configuration of actors and their structural context. Once a claim-making process between claim-makers and the authorities is set in motion, it will contribute to the modification of the larger political context.

As claim-makers and the authorities interact with each other – either by attempting to change or preserve the status quo – their adversaries obtain additional information on their opponents. This information can include which techniques exist in their adversaries' repertoires and under which condition(s) their opponents will employ a particular technique. This additional information represents an increase in propositional knowledge about society and, thus, forms the epistemic base for the emergence of new techniques. In this sense, existing repertoires of contention are both subject to and influenced by the societal relationships between those making a claim and their adversaries and, more specifically, on the acquisition of new propositional knowledge about society from their interactions.

For example, in 1976, when female strikers in South Korea were awaiting attack by riot police, a worker whispered 'men cannot touch undressed women, even if they are police' so hundreds of strikers stripped to their underwear, held each other tightly and sang union songs in a desperate attempt to thwart the assault (Koo 2001, 80). This example aptly illustrates how individuals making a claim can adapt their techniques based on their propositional knowledge about society: (i) 'the police will attempt to break up this protest by force' but (ii) 'male police officer will not touch undressed women'. Unfortunately for the strikers, while the police were momentarily dumbfounded by the emergence of a new and unfamiliar technique of contention aimed at resisting their efforts to regain control over the situation, they 'moved in and began to break up the protesters, hitting the women with bats, pulling screaming women by their hair, throwing them onto the ground, and dumping them into police vans' (Koo 2001, 81). In the aftermath of the police onslaught, the propositional knowledge about society changed, and based on this specific interaction with the police, the notion that 'police would not touch undressed women' was excised from the body of propositional knowledge about South Korean society in 1976.

The mechanism that explains why techniques of contention arise, spread, ensue, and disappear will be addressed in greater detail in the following section of this chapter. As demonstrated throughout this section, new techniques of contention are not only the product of individual struggles or 'moments of madness' – to borrow Zolberg's (1972) famous description – but rather are the by-products of numerous compounded historical interactions between claim-makers and the authorities. Given the nature of interactions between the claim-makers and their adversaries, it is clear that the emergence and development of various forms of authority must also be considered. Indeed, any change in the form of authority or the techniques by which this authority seeks to enforce the status quo necessarily affects the subsequent evolution of techniques of contention.

2.5 THE EVOLUTION OF CONTENTION

Applying the Darwinian principles of variation, transmission, and selection to techniques of contention requires an understanding of three properties: (i) a source of variation, or the continual appearance of new variants on which selection can act; (ii) mechanisms of transmission, or means by which the units are reproduced; and (iii) processes of selection, which explain the retention and rejection of alternative variants over time. I contend that, with regard to techniques of contention, the source of variation is change in social, cultural, economic, technological, political, or religious environments. These shifts represent changes in the propositional knowledge held within a society.

With regard to the transmission mechanism of techniques of contention, it is necessary to employ standard diffusion theory. The diffusion of techniques of contention occurs through: (i) direct communication between actors through their interpersonal networks, or (ii) non-relational ties (e.g., mass media that often appears to perform this function). Focusing on the mechanism of transmission provides important insights as to how new techniques of contention spread within a society and how they can be transported to other societies.

Lastly, I suggest that there are three potential sources of selection with regard to techniques of contention: (i) feasibility, which includes structural preconditions, the costs of a technique, and resource limitations; (ii) legitimacy: namely whether a technique is deemed just and right from the perspective of those who perform it and their constituents; and (iii) effectiveness, the probability that the technique will be successful and lead to the desired outcome.

Variation

First, it is necessary to address the ways in which the source of variation relates to the evolution of techniques of contention. Variation among replicating units supplies the raw material for selection in all evolving systems. In biology, the process by which this occurs is traditionally understood to be largely the result of random or 'blind' mutation.[10] However, according to the prevalent understanding of modern evolutionary synthesis, there are in fact two sources of genetic variation: mutation and recombination. Both sources of genetic variation are considered unpredictable phenomena in terms of the time at which they occur, the genes they affect, and the individual organisms concerned (Dobzhansky 1937; Simpson 1984). In particular, a central tenet of modern synthesis theory is the claim that genetic mutations occur at 'random' or by 'chance'. In contrast, variations within cultural systems are generally understood to be strategically and deliberately generated.[11] For example, Witt (2006) asserts that 'cultural, institutions, technology, and economic activities evolved according to their own regularities' (p. 8). This statement highlights the notion that, in contrast to biological evolution, human intentionality and purposefulness play an important role in human-made or cultural systems.

As Witt argues, cultural variations are consciously developed because humans possess foresight and creativity, learn from experience, modify existing practices, synthesise old habits, and invent novel solutions to current or anticipated necessity. This postulation is fitting when applied to techniques of contention. Importantly, Witt makes a distinction in the relationship between subjects and their environment in the context of cultural and biological evolution. Whereas, in 'classic Darwinian models, environmental impacts alter subjects in an involuntary fashion . . . humans can influence their environment as opposed to being mere passive reactors to the changes that affect it' (Thompson 2001, 4–5). In the biological world, environmental impacts refer to changes that make it difficult for an organism to survive in its current form within its current setting. These may include the introduction of a new predator, a shortage of food or shelter, or changes in climate. When applying this notion to the evolution of techniques of contention, environmental change refers to changes in the body of propositional knowledge within a society. Consequently, these changes affect the likelihood of certain techniques of contention (the unit of inheritance) being employed.

As described in the previous section, throughout history, propositional knowledge limited societies' access to feasible techniques because they lacked the required epistemic base. On the other hand, the existence of some part of propositional knowledge that could serve as an epistemic base for a new technique does not necessarily guarantee that such a technique will emerge. In other words, the existence of an epistemic base creates the opportunity for the emergence of new techniques rather than guaranteeing that it will be taken advantage of. This can be compared to evolutionary biology in that environmental change provides the opportunity for adaptation but does not make adaptation inevitable.

When faced with the emergence of a new variant of an existing technique, two questions are necessary in explaining the source of the variation: 'what propositional knowledge represents the epistemic base which supports this new variation?' and 'when/how did this propositional knowledge emerge?' It is crucial to understand the changes that alter a society's body of propositional knowledge because it sheds light on why new variations of techniques that were previously unthinkable or impossible emerge. These changes in propositional knowledge can include changes in social, cultural, economic, political, or religious contexts, as well as changes in the nature of the relationships between claim-makers and their adversaries (and, thus, the status quo).

The impact of changes in propositional knowledge—namely those related to changes in the nature of the relationship between claim-makers and their adversaries—on the emergence of new techniques of contention is consistent with the insights derived from work within the domain of political economy. Enders and Sandler (1993), Enders et al. (1990), and Im et al. (1987) report that claim-makers respond strategically to counter-terrorism measures when deciding which technique of contention to employ, thereby generating 'substitution effects'. This argument suggests that, when claim-makers observe an increase in a particular government counter-terrorism program, they will switch techniques and pursue attacks less likely to be affected by the government's efforts. For instance, Enders and Sandler (1993) demonstrate that, when the United States installed metal detectors in airports in the 1970s, aeroplane hijackings decreased but other forms of terrorism increased, a phenomenon that will be examined in more detail in the case studies in the following chapters. This insight can be applied to the evolutionary model at hand: the introduction of counter-terrorism measures alters claim-makers' understanding of their adversaries and of their strategic choices (choices of techniques and targets). In turn, this new propositional knowledge (e.g., a change in the environment) may create an incentive for claim-makers to innovate and develop new techniques of contention.

Transmission

Building on an understanding of the modes of variation that constitute and alter techniques of contention, it is necessary to consider how these techniques are then transmitted and diffused. In relation to evolutionary biology, genetic transmission is a slow, intergenerational process of inheritance, in which the transfer of heritable traits occurs through gametogenesis and fertilization (Patrick 2001, 144). Cultural transmission, by contrast, is a rapid, flexible, and continuous process, involving imitation and exploitation of the ever-proliferating avenues of human communication. Unlike genetic transmission, cultural transmission is not limited to parents and offspring, but instead involves various 'teachers' and 'learners'. Indeed, in principle, this process may involve the transmission of information between any one individual to any other individual(s). In other words, cultural transmission can include various transmission ratios: many-to-one, one-to-few, or one-to-many (Cavalli-Sforza and Feldman 1981).

As previously mentioned, repertoires of contention are inherently flexible and evolve as a result of changing propositional knowledge. Claim-makers, therefore, can observe other groups' techniques of contention and may choose to imitate said techniques to gain a tactical advantage over their adversary. When one group of claim-makers uses a particular technique successfully, others are then more likely to adopt this technique (Oberschall 1989; Tilly 1993, 1995). In other words, 'innovation is communicated through certain channels over time among members of a social system' (Rogers 1983, 14). According to traditional theories of diffusion, there are two main channels along which information, leading to the borrowing or imitation of (techniques of contention), can be transmitted: (i) relational ties (or direct transmission) and (ii) nonrelational ties (or indirect transmission) (Soule 1997). Transmission can occur either within the same society from one group of claim-makers to another or between two geographically distant repertoires of contention. With regard to the latter, it is important to note that, while particular techniques of contention can be invented more than once by different people in different societies, the rate of adoption far exceeds the rate of variation (Biggs 2013). As such, in most cases where claim-makers use a new variation of an existing technique for the first time, they are likely adopting it from others who have previously used it rather than inventing a novel solution themselves.

Relational models of diffusion maintain that information flows between actors through their direct interpersonal networks (Strang and Meyer 1993). Therefore, the rate at which information diffuses varies with the level of interaction between actors and with the density of interpersonal networks. As Soule (1997) suggests, social science has benefitted greatly from research on relational models of diffusion. In particular, researchers have attempted to map ties and communications between individuals to track diffusion of techniques of contention. For example, Singer (1970) interviewed five hundred African American individuals about their sources of information during the 1967 12th Street riot in Detroit. The results indicated that the chief source of information was in-person communication.

However, because it is not always possible to obtain precise data on who spoke to or is connected to whom, scholars frequently employ inferences to establish that direct contact has occurred. For example, Bohstedt and William (1988) suggest that the dense community networks formed in market transactions facilitated the spread of food riots across communities in Devonshire late in the eighteenth century. Similarly, Hedstrom et al. (2000) show that the diffusion of support for the Swedish Social Democratic Party in 1894 and 1911 occurred along the travel routes used by political agitators at the time. It is also possible to infer interpersonal communication via shared organizational membership. Givan et al. (2010) argue that 'people are sharing ideas, communicating, and facilitating the diffusion of social movements because they belong to the same movement organizations' (p. 10). Moreover, since individuals often belong to multiple organizations, they also serve as conduits of information between organizations. This idea is implicit in much of the research on the sit-ins of the 1960s. For example, Morris (1981) demonstrates that these sit-ins were not spontaneous and uncoordinated activities, but that pre-existing organizational ties facilitated the communication necessary for the spread of this technique of contention. Likewise, research on social movements in Latin America suggests that labour union members were important actors in the development of militant grassroots neighbourhood organizations in low-income urban communities (Stokes 1995). At the same time, Catholic Church activists inspired by liberation theology contributed to the spread of peasant associations in rural El Salvador, which eventually provided a social base for insurgent action (Wood 2003). Scholars have similarly been able to infer the occurrence of interpersonal communications by considering geographical proximity (Givan et al. 2010, 11). In this way, Petras and Zeitlin (1967) address how the Chilean mining industry exhibited high levels of Marxist ideology and activism, which eventually spread to nearby agricultural municipalities.

To address diffusion between geographically distinct groups, Rudé (1964) argues that the connections forged via emergent trade routes were necessary for the dissemination of information, including politics and social movements, among groups from disparate locations. Similarly, McAdam and Rucht (1993) identify individuals whose friendships and trans-Atlantic travels linked the American and West German student movements throughout the 1960s and early 1970s and led to the transmission of techniques such as the "teach-in". This demonstrates that the mobility of experienced individuals, or "teachers", has an important impact on the diffusion of techniques of contention across geographical areas; these teachers repeat familiar techniques in new locations, thus making local activists aware of them and that much more likely to adopt them.

Despite the varied and thorough research conducted on how innovations spread between directly connected actors, most scholars recognize that direct networks only account for part of the story and that the transmission of ideas or techniques among actors that are not directly connected must not be disregarded. In fact, Soule (2004, 295) considers why unconnected actors display high degrees of homogeneity in form, structure, ideology, and practice and how innovations might spread among such actors. One type of indirect tie identified in the diffusion study literature is the shared cultural understanding of claim-makers: what Strang and Meyer (1993) dub 'cultural linkages'. Essentially, claim-makers in different locales imitate techniques of similar, though disconnected, actors. For example, McAdam and Rucht (1993) argue that this process occurred in 1976 when activists in Seabrooks, New Hampshire, imitated a mass demonstration against a nuclear site that occurred in Germany two years previously.

In the absence of direct personal or organizational relations, mass media often performs the function of diffusing techniques of contention. For example, Spilerman (1976) reports that, during the urban riots of the late 1960s in the United States, rioting appeared to cluster in time. The riots, Spilerman claims, diffused throughout urban, black areas, through television coverage of civil rights activism. According to Spilerman, the media thus served as an indirect channel of diffusion by creating a cultural linkage among African Americans in different metropolitan areas and by familiarizing individuals all over the country with both the details of, and motivations for, the riots. Similarly, Singer's (1970) work on the 1967 riots in Detroit identifies the media, along with interpersonal communication, as a leading source of information on the riot within the city. Furthermore, Myers (2000) suggests riots that receive national media attention tend to prompt more riots nationwide, whereas smaller riots that only receive local media attention only increase riot propensities within the affected local area. Andrews and Biggs (2006) also highlight the importance of the media to spread the use of sit-ins in the civil rights movements. In a more contemporary context, an entire field of research is being devoted to understanding how the Internet facilitates the sharing of information and techniques of contention among groups that may otherwise have little contact with each other.

As addressed previously, repertoires of contention are temporal and spatial entities. Although they are therefore ever-changing, they are nonetheless specific to a given time and place. However, while new techniques of contention can emerge within a society as a result of changes to that society's propositional knowledge, they are more often adopted and transported from an existing repertoire elsewhere. In addition to asking 'what propositional knowledge represents the epistemic base which supports this new variation?' and 'when did this propositional knowledge emerge?' to understand emergent techniques of contention, we must also ask ourselves the following questions: "is this technique a product of (a) changing propositional knowledge within this society or (b) has this technique been used in other societies before?" If (a) is true and a new technique has emerged as a result of changing propositional knowledge within society, we must also ask: "has the technique been diffused to another society?" and, if so, "which one?" Conversely, if (b) is true and the technique of contention is observed in an environment in which it did not originate, one must ask: "where did this technique originate?"; "how did it come to be diffused to this environment?"; "was there already an epistemic base within this society to suppose this technique that could explain its emergence?"; "how has the appearance of this technique in this environment altered the existing propositional knowledge held within this society?"; and "does this technique differ in some way from the original iteration?"

As previously addressed, focusing on the mechanism of transmission provides important insights on how new techniques of contention spread within and between societies. Importantly, evolutionary processes are both incremental and path dependent. As Mokyr (2005) suggests, 'No species can change too much at one time, though neither biologist nor cultural evolution-ists will readily or easily agree on how much change is too much' (p. 319). With sufficient time, however, minute differences can become compounded and lead to quite different outcomes. Path dependence means that the forms of these final outcomes depend on the exact itinerary taken (David 1994). This implies that it is important to identify the historical process leading to a given outcome if we wish to fully understand said outcome because by examining the trajectory we gain insights about a technique's previous per-mutations and the contexts in which they arose, spread, ensued, disappeared, or simply failed to emerge in given repertoires.

Selection

To understand why particular techniques of contention are retained or elimi-nated, it is necessary to examine the potential forces of selection at play. In comparison to genetic information, there are many more ways for cultural information to be transmitted. Consequently, there are many more ways for cultural information to be differentially replicated (Patrick 2001, 144). Whereas cultural selection is the differential replication of cultural informa-tion, cultural fitness measures the relative transmission, or success, of vari-ants in techniques of contention. In genetic evolution, fitness depends on the consequences of the genetic variation for the organism. In cultural selection as it relates to contentious action, fitness depends on the consequences of the technique for the claim-makers. However, whereas organisms cannot choose their own genes, claim-makers can determine which technique of contention to employ to advance their claim.

The selection of techniques of contention, whether associated with terror-ism or not, entails rational choice (Hoffman and McCormick 2004; Pape 2003). As rational choice theorists point out, human beings may select or reject beliefs according to perceived likely consequences long before they select overt behaviour (Durham 1991). This process might be thought of, as Patrick (2001) argues, as 'rational "self-selection"' (p. 153). In the same way as biologists define a variation's 'fitness' as its usefulness for survival and reproduction, some ecological anthropologists contend that culture is adap-tive and subjected to a process by which fitness-enhancing traits are naturally selected for their current functions. In other words, humans consciously se-lect cultural elements such as ideas, norms, values, or techniques based on their perceived usefulness (Durham 1991). As Strang and Meyer (1993) ob-serve, cultural elements 'are adopted to the extent that they appear more effective or efficient than the alternative' (p. 488).

In fact, Tilly himself draws extensively on rational choice theory to intro-duce a set of assumptions that inform the totality of his work: namely, that claim-makers assess the costs and benefits associated with collective actions and claim-making, even though they have imperfect information regarding these costs and benefits (Krinsky and Mische 2013, 11). Tilly's insights are now deeply ingrained within political process theory. This now standard explanation of social movement mobilization emphasizes the role of political opportunities and mobilizing structures, along with repertoires of contention. Further, it refutes the formerly prevailing view that claim-makers, whether protesters or other social movement participants, were irrational mobs overwhelmed by collective mentality (Caren 2007). In other words, political process theorists argue that claim-making movements did not result from alienation or abnormal psychological dispositions but were instead a rational means to achieve political ends and resolve legitimate grievances.

Influenced by political process theory, in his study of the spread of self-immolation as a technique of contention, Biggs (2013) proposes three interrelated sources of selection to which techniques of contention are subjected: (i) *feasibility*, which refers to the structural preconditions and the costs of a technique and resource limitations; (ii) *legitimacy*, the sense whether a technique is 'just and right – from the perspective of those who are going to perform it' (p. 409); and (iii) *effectiveness*, the probability that the technique will be successful and lead to the outcome desired by the claim-makers. Biggs' explanation for why new claim-making techniques are adopted in new places emphasises the rational judgement of actors. If a technique is not considered feasible, legitimate, and effective, claim-makers will cease to employ it, thereby removing it from the repertoire of contention. For example, the Korean strikers who undressed in an unsuccessful attempt to thwart the riot police and then determined that the technique was ineffective removed it from their repertoire of contention. Alternatively, if a technique is not considered to be feasible, legitimate, and effective, it may simply never enter that specific repertoire of contention. This is the case of the conspicuous absence of the use of suicide bombing by organizations, including the Irish Republican Army, the ETA in Spain, the Red Brigades in Italy, the Baader-Meinhof gang in Germany, and the Shining Path in Peru, a question that will be addressed subsequently.

Feasibility can refer to structural preconditions (e.g., the unemployed cannot strike), resource limitations, or prohibitive costs of a given technique. Resource limitation has two evident components. First, a particular technique might be inaccessible because a society lacks the required propositional knowledge to enact it. For example, if a society does not have knowledge of advanced physics, it cannot develop nuclear technologies. Similarly, it would be inherently difficult for claim-makers to envisage mail bombs before the invention of dynamite, which allowed for the relatively safe transport of explosives.

Secondly, resource limitation includes situations in which a particular technique is inaccessible not because of a lack of propositional knowledge but, rather, because of limited access to the resource(s) required to enact such a technique. In fact, limiting claim-makers' access to resources remains one of the core strategies of authorities to maintain the status quo. This has ranged, for example, from limiting dissidents access to the press or Internet (as commonly employed by autocratic regimes), to raids and seizures of assets, and to the control of goods that can be used to employ a particular type of technique of contention deemed unacceptable by the authorities, such as banning large purchases of fertilizers to thwart the construction of ammonium nitrate and fuel oil bombs.

Legitimacy refers to 'the sense that the tactic is just and right – from the perspective of those who are going to perform it' (Biggs 2013, 409). Techniques of contention are selected for compatibility with the existing cultural environment. As Patrick (2001) argues, 'cultural selection is no mere "tinkerer", but "constraints of inherited form can bias cultural (like biological) evolution"' (p. 145). Just as technology can affect feasibility, a society's values, religion, norms, and so on, render some seemingly plausible techniques of contention socially inconceivable. In fact, Snow and his contributors (1986; 1988) have suggested that claim-makers' successes and failures depend, in large part, on groups' ability to frame the use of techniques of contention in a way that links claim-makers' grievances to mainstream beliefs and values. Taylor and Van Dyke (2007) argue that the Rastafarian movement demonstrates 'one of the clearest cases of a movement that met with success' because it employed techniques of contention that resonated with 'symbols, ideas and elements' held as important by 'both indigenous groups and national and international elites' (p. 282).[12]

Returning briefly to the question of suicide bombing, Kalyvas and Sánchez-Cuenca (2005) explain its conspicuous absence as a technique of contention in several protracted and violent conflicts, including the Northern Ireland Troubles, by invoking two important factors, *normative preferences* and *constituency costs*, both of which are directly tied with the perceived legitimacy of a given technique of contention. *Normative preferences* constrain claim-makers in that claim-makers tend to see themselves as acting in a just way (Gilbert 1995). Thus, the expression 'legitimate targets' – and, by extension, 'legitimate technique' – is not uncommon in the discourse of claim-makers who engage in acts of political violence. For example, the Provisional IRA (PIRA) has relied extensively on a wide range of exculpatory justification when civilians unconnected to the state apparatus have been killed: The killing was a mistake; the killing was accidental; the police or authorities did not take the warning seriously; collateral damage is a necessary component of any conflict; and so on (Kalyvas and Sánchez-Cuenca 2005). *Constituency costs* involve the preference and moral sentiments of claim-makers' supporters, on whom claim-makers depend. Claim-makers must recognize that a trade-off can exist between the intensity of any technique of contention employed and the maintenance of popular support. Supporters may share the same aims as claim-makers but disagree over the means by which to achieve these aims. These disagreements can be normative – that is, related to the legitimacy of the technique – or strategic, related to whether the technique used is the most efficient to accomplish said aims. With regard to normative considerations, it stands to reason that, unless suicide bombing is seen as a natural and proper action by the population, the use of this technique will only deepen the gap between claim-makers and the public at large. In the case of political conflict in Northern Ireland, it is plausible to surmise that, had suicide bombing been employed as a technique of contention by the PIRA, public support from Northern Irish republicans would have decreased as a result of perceived illegitimacy of this technique. Further, it is likely that support from the Irish community in the United States would also have dwindled. In fact, on several occasions, the PIRA, well aware of the adverse impact their particularly brutal attacks would have among supporters denied responsibility or attempted to attribute blame elsewhere for said attacks. [13]

The third selection pressure, *effectiveness*, refers to the probability that a technique will be successful, which depends on a myriad of factors, including novelty, militancy, and variety.

Novelty: although claim-makers typically choose from their fairly limited repertoires of contention when deciding on which technique to employ, empirical studies have demonstrated that innovative techniques are most successful in achieving policy changes. For example, McAdam (1983) suggests that the emergence of new techniques of contention employed by the US civil rights movement, such as sit-ins and freedom rides, were effective because they caught the authorities off guard. Similarly, McCammon et al. (2001) provides evidence that the British suffragette movement was successful in gaining women the right to vote partly as a result of their innovative use of the suffrage parade as a technique of contention. This technique puts hundreds of women on the streets to both publicize their claim for the right to vote and to 'resist the ideology of separate spheres that precluded women from participating in political life' (Taylor and Van Dyke 2007, 279).

Militancy: 'innovative techniques of contention are often successful because of the uncertainty and disruption they bring about' (Taylor and Van Dyke 2007, 280). Several early studies have concluded that claim-makers who employed disruptive techniques were more successful than those who opted for tamer means of claim-making (Tilly et al. 1975; Piven and Cloward 1979; Steedly and Foley 1979; Mirowsky and Ross 1981; McAdam 1983). For example, Gamson's (1990) pioneering work includes an examination of techniques of contention among fifty-three different groups of claim-makers in the US prior to the Second World War; Gamson argues that claim-makers who used violence were more likely to achieve both policy gains and access to political power. Similarly, McAdam and Su (2002), addressing the impact of anti-war protest on congressional support for US involvement during the Vietnam War, suggest that, for a movement to be effective, claim-makers must combine the use of disruptive techniques with a commitment to democratic politics of persuasion. However, more recent research, especially from within the field of terrorism studies, shows a much more complicated picture, with two opposing views on the issue. On one side, scholars argue that techniques of contention associated with terrorism are becoming increasingly popular because they are effective. Notably, Pape (2003; 2005) claims that terrorists achieved 'significant policy changes' in more than half the campaigns analysed. Furthermore, Pape (2003; 2005) contends that terrorism is particularly effective against democracies because of the electorate's high sensitivity to civilian causalities, which induces leaders to grant concessions to claim-makers who employ techniques commonly associated with terrorism. Conversely, other scholars suggest that there is little empirical evidence to demonstrate that violent techniques of contention are effective and, further, that these techniques are generally less effective than others.

Variety: the use of a variety of techniques of contention yields the best results in terms of policy change. Morris (1993) addresses the 1963 campaign against racial segregations in Birmingham, Alabama, to demonstrate how civil rights claim-makers simultaneously staged an economic boycott against the city's businesses, held sit-in demonstrations at local lunch counters, and staged large-scale demonstrations. This use of multiple techniques, Morris concludes, resulted in a community-wide crisis that authorities were unable to contain and explains the gains of the civil rights movements in Birmingham far more convincingly, in his opinion, than explanations offered up for the efficacy of either novelty or militancy. Scholars of the feminist movement, such as Rupp and Taylor (1987), Staggenborg (1991), and Gelb and Hart (1999) also provid evidence that, when the women's movement employed a vast array of techniques of contention simultaneously, it was more likely to achieve policy changes.

While scholars have advanced compelling arguments demonstrating the impacts of these three factors, *novelty*, *militancy*, and *variety*, on a given technique's efficiency, evaluating a technique remains inherently difficult for both claim-makers and sociologists (Soule 1999) because it can only be tested by putting a technique into practice (Biggs 2013, 409).

As Tilly (1995) points out, in modern societies, protest achieves its effects indirectly, through long and complicated chains of causality. Moreover, any episode of sustained contention invariably involves multiple techniques of contention; it can thus be difficult to measure the effectiveness of any particular one. To make matters more complicated still, since the cultural environment changes at a much quicker pace than the biological one, a novel technique that is found to be more effective relative to other techniques is likely to be repeated on subsequent occasions and may lose its efficacy over time. This may be because claim-makers' opponents, namely the authorities, may have either a positive or negative response to the claim based on their appreciation of or disbelief in a given claim's validity. Similarly, they may also respond negatively or positively – irrespective of their perceived validity of the claim – to the technique used to articulate it, thus changing the society's body of propositional knowledge. For example, during the Egyptian Revolution of 2011, demonstrators improvised techniques of contention by fraternizing with armoured units; by chanting their appreciation for the army, in contrast to their behaviour towards the hated police, protesters arguably made repression difficult (Ketchley 2014). In response to these techniques of fraternization, which required proximity on the part of the protesters, the army subsequently deployed military police to keep protesters at bay (Biggs 2013, 410).

In addition to feasibility, legitimacy, and effectiveness, it is necessary to recognize that the adoption of new techniques of contention may also depend on the various determinants of claim-making in general – grievances, opportunities, resources, networks, and so on. However, if a technique seems more feasible, more legitimate, or more effective than other existing techniques within a given repertoire of contention, then claim-makers within that society will be more likely to use the technique again on subsequent occasions. As such, when trying to understand why a certain technique may be adopted into or excised from a given repertoire of a contention, it is crucial to look at the technique's feasibility, legitimacy, and effectiveness in comparison with the feasibility, legitimacy, and effectiveness of other techniques within the repertoire against which it might be competing. The same is true when seeking to provide plausible causal explanations as to why a certain technique never entered a particular repertoire, despite the presence of the necessary transmission mechanism. Because claim-makers, as rational actors, adopt a competing choice-based approach when selecting one technique over another, we must ask ourselves the following question with regard to the role of feasibility: 'what are the structural and resource requirements of each of the competing techniques?' Once identified, we must investigate whether changes have occurred within the society, thereby either modifying the structural or resource requirements of the technique or impacting how feasible it is for claim-makers to employ said technique. To establish this, it is necessary to question whether new technological or structural developments linked to the technique have emerged; whether access to the required resources to enact a certain technique have widened or narrowed; and, crucially how these changes have affected the feasibility of one technique compared to other techniques available within claim-makers' repertoire. The same basic approach should be used to evaluate and understand how claim-makers (and their supporters, in the case of legitimacy) perceive the legitimacy and effectiveness of various techniques of contention when deciding whether to employ such techniques.

2.6 CASE STUDY STRUCTURE

To answer the questions laid out in this chapter and demonstrate how evolutionary biology can provide important insights on this study's chosen technique of contention, the evolution of aeroplane hijacking as a technique of political violence is charted in the following chapters. Each case study chapter (chapters 3–7) focuses on one of five strains of hijackings and is divided into three sections. Each section applies a different Darwinian principle: (i) the *variation* sections identify the adaptations the technique underwent in the period and places in question and the factors that led to the emergence and mutation of these adaptations; (ii) the *transmission* sections concern themselves with identifying the mechanisms that led to the transportation of adaptations across different repertoires; (iii) the *selection* sections explore the contexts in which various techniques of variants of techniques are adopted or rejected by a multitude of claim-makers, looking at how techniques of contention are frequently assessed by those who use them (or indeed choose not to) on the basis of feasibility, legitimacy, and efficacy.

As argued by Eldredge and Novacek (1985), the success of evolutionary analysis rests largely on the strength of the data employed. Therefore, to improve the robustness and accuracy of the data for this study, three sources of data were used: existing databases, newspapers, and references to hijacking incidents in the existing literature on the subject.

The resulting database comprised of 1,084 incidents of hijackings, successful or thwarted, ranging from 1930 until 11 September 2001 was created. The database I constructed for this project contained roughly four times more hijacking incidents than those listed in the *Global Terrorism Database*, the largest and most complete data set available to examine incidents of terrorism over time. Each incident within my data set is coded as a unique event, with all pertinent information available collected, including: the date, location, air carrier, the organization, or social movement responsible for the hijacking if applicable, the number of occupants on board the flight, the number of hijackers, and whether any fatalities or injuries resulted from the hijacking or attempted hijacking. In addition, each incident, where possible, includes a short note providing information about the motivation of the perpetrators and the results in terms of the outcome of the incident.

NOTES

1. Darwin's theory of gradualism remains the source of some debate among evolutionary theorists. This debate revolves around the definition and meaning of 'gradual'. Eldredge and Gould (1972) advance an argument for 'punctuated equilibria', the notion that the development of species is a slow process characterised by long periods of stability with little or no change interrupted by brief periods of rapid change. While their work has received considerable attention, many evolutionary theorists such as Dawkins (1996), Dennett (1996), and Pinker (1999) argue that it does not, in fact, represent a new argument. For an excellent survey of this discussion, see Somit and Peterson (1992).

2. It is worth noting that, contrary to the original Darwinian theory of natural selection – where individuals with particular characteristics best-suited to particular environmental demands have an advantage in reproduction – another biological perspective downplays the importance of adaptation for reproduction (Spruyt 2001). That view postulates that varieties of species that are not well adapted to a particular environment may survive, even displace others, purely because of differential fertility and fecundity (Grant 1985, 92–94).

3. In his original formulation, Mendel did not use the term 'gene'; in fact, the term was not used until 1909. Instead he referred to the 'particulate' transmission of hereditary factors (Avise 1998, 8).

4. It is important to note that biologists disagree among themselves about the importance of speciation events. Within evolutionary theory, some adhere to a gradualist view of evolution, whereas others see far more rapid change. Punctuated equilibrium suggested that critical changes in the environment will lead to dramatic and fast transformation, followed by long periods of slower, incremental change and relative stasis thereafter (Gould and Eldredge, 1972). On the other hand, gradualists suggest that 'incomplete taxonomies and lack of evidentiary proof of gradual change does not demonstrate that evolution does not work by long-term selection over sometimes minute differences' (Spruyt 2001, 115). See the discussion in Simpson (1984) and Somit and Peterson (1992).

5. Evolutionary biologists have also proposed a large variety of units of inheritance – some more appropriate than others – ranging from lengths of RNA, genes, chromosomes, antibodies, cells, organisms, groups of organisms, species, clades, communities, and even ecosystems (Dietl 2008).

6. For example, in the original formulation of Richard Dawkins' (1976; 1982) work on cultural evolution, the unit of inheritance was the meme; that is to say an idea, behaviour, or style that spreads from person to person within a culture. According to Dawkins, memes are replicated and transmitted among carriers. These memes structure minds, inform worldviews, behaviour, customs, artefacts, and institutions. Unfortunately, an insufficient body of empirical research has addressed Dawkins' conceptualization of memes. In fact, the literature on the subject has remained almost entirely devoted to theoretical antagonisms, internecine battles, and scholastic elucidations of prior writings on memes (Aunger 2006, 178). Much like the poorly chosen use of artefacts hindered much of George Basalla's otherwise pioneering attempts to provide a coherent evolutionary approach to technology, the pitfalls in isolating the appropriate unit of knowledge or culture has undermined much of Dawkins' proposition of 'memes' as an analogy of genes (Mokyr 2006, 315). The term *meme* has become increasingly popular to refer to nongenetic units of transmission. Susan Blackmore's *The Meme Machine* (2000) provides a useful introduction to memetics. Additionally, for an excellent critical evaluation of meme literature, see the collection of essays for and against meme theory edited by Aunger (2000).

7. For later development of the repertoires of contention technique, see both Tilly's later work (1986; 1995; 2006; 2008) and expansions of the concept proposed by other scholars (Traugott 2010; Beissinger 1998; Mueller 1999; Steinberg 1999).

8. Wada (2012) adeptly notes that Tilly's time period labels 'indicate relative tendencies rather than critical breaks in the form of contention' and therefore '"eighteenth-century" or "nineteenth-century" only offers a rough approximation of a complex time table' (p. 548). As such, a single episode of contention in the nineteenth century could combine techniques present

in both the eighteenth-century and nineteenth-century repertoires or could include only the nineteenth-century repertoire.

9. For example, early steam engines were invented despite a limited understanding of thermodynamics and, therefore, steam engines developed slowly because of a reliance on propositional knowledge that was gradually accumulated by engineers. However, the work of scientists, such as Sadi Carnot, furthered the underlying propositional knowledge of thermodynamics, and thus allowed for rapid improvement of the efficiency of steam machines for transportation and industrial uses. The invention of the internal combustion engine occurred more than a century later, when scientists made the necessary theoretical breakthroughs in thermodynamics (Cardwell 1994).

10. This core tenet in Darwin's original conception, which saw variation as 'spontaneous', 'accidental', or 'chance' – and continues to represent an important part of modern synthesis's consensus view – has recently faced important challenges. In the last thirty years, experimental research in molecular genetics, in particular on micro-organisms, has shown that certain molecular mechanisms – so-called 'mutator mechanisms' – can regulate mutation rates (increasing or decreasing them) in response to certain selective forces. Because of this causal connection between mutation rates and selective substrates, Jablonka and Lamb (1995; Jablonka et al. 2006), along with other biologists, historians, and philosophers of biology (Shapiro 1999; 2005; Sternberg 2006; Keller 2002), have questioned modern synthesis's claim that all genetic mutations occur by 'chance' or at 'random'.

11. It would be unwise to affirm that all variations within human-made systems are the product of strategic and deliberate processes, transcription, random, or copy errors, individual idiosyncrasies, linguistic mistranslation, textual mistranscription, or faulty memory are in many way analogues to blind mutation and drift in genetic transmission (Eerkens and Lipo, 2005; Patrick 2001, 143). For example, linguists have documented a good deal of individual variation in speech, some of which are probably random individual variants (Labov 2006). Similarly, small human populations might well lose rare skills or knowledge by chance, for example, due to the premature deaths of the only individuals who possessed them (Diamond 1978).

12. Buffonge's (2001) analysis of the Rastafarian movement shows how it was able to mobilize support and alter mainstream political discourse about the poverty of rural and urban Jamaicans by incorporating elements of Jamaican myth, story, and religion to reggae music as a means of articulating claims.

13. Examples include the Abercorn Restaurant bombing, when, on 4 March 1972, a bomb exploded with no warning in Belfast, killing two young Catholic women and injuring more than 130 people (English 2012, 156); the Claudy bombings, when, on 31 July 1972, three car bombs exploded mid-morning on the Main Street of Claudy in County Londonderry without warning, killing nine civilians (Clarke and Johnson 2001, 78; English 2012, 159); the Birmingham pub bombings, when, on 21 November 1974, two bombs exploded in two public houses in central Birmingham, England, killing 21 and injuring 182 others (English 2012, 169–70); the assassination of Joanne Mathers, a 29-year-old who was gunned down while collecting census forms in Derry on 8 April 1981 (Clarke and Johnston 2001, 126; English 2012, 208); the Harrods bombing, when a car bomb exploded outside Harrods department store in central London amid crowds of Christmas shoppers on 17 December 1983, killing six and injuring 90 others (Clarke and Johnston 2001, 143; English 2012, 247); or the Remembrance Day bombing, when a bomb exploded near the town of Enniskillen's war memorial during a Remembrance Sunday ceremony, killing 11 people, many of them old-age pensioners, and injuring 63 others (Maloney 2002, 341; English 2012, 255–56).

Chapter Three

The Emergence of Aeroplane Hijacking

The origins of aeroplane hijacking can be traced to two troubled periods of accelerated nationalism: the first in Peru during the early 1930s and the second thirty years later during the Cuban Revolution. While these two periods have generally been omitted from contemporary narratives on hijackings, the use of aircraft by Peruvian and Cuban revolutionaries foreshadowed future generations of hijacking. Both periods are useful to consider in relation to the evolutionary framework established in the previous chapter. Particularly noteworthy is the conspicuous absence of transmission between the Peruvian and Cuban cases, which suggests that, as a technique of contention, hijacking was invented at least twice, by two different sets of isolated claim-makers who had no contact with each other.

In the *variation* section, these two case studies will be looked at in greater detail; both are instances in which civil aviation became a site of contention through the hijacking and use of aeroplanes against state actors. In both cases, the emergence of hijacking as a technique of contention was directly linked to the influential notion that aerial control could be equated with the legitimacy and sovereignty of the existing regime, which represented a new and important form of propositional knowledge. This clear association between state legitimacy and the display of state power through aviation prompted challengers to seize aeroplanes not only when they were an instrumental part of an act of contention (e.g., cases in which planes were used for bombing, transport, etc.), but also when the capture *was* the act of contention itself. Control of aeroplanes served as a symbolic challenge to state control. In Peru, hijacking entered the repertoire of contention following Peruvian rebels' successful capture of a plane flown by government agents seeking to drop loyalist propaganda on a rebel-held city. Learning from the government's success, the rebels mimicked the state's technique and engaged in aerial propaganda drops of their own, leading to more hijackings of government planes. In this case, not only was the hijacking instrumental in that it allowed the rebels to access a technique that would otherwise be unfeasible for them, but it was also highly symbolic; it allowed them to access a technique that was seen as belonging solely to government's repertoire and thus challenge the government's monopoly of the skies. The Cuban Revolution is an unusually salient example of this phenomenon, as the 26th of July Movement purposefully targeted the national airline, Cubana, and made a public relations art form out of embarrassing the government with a number of highly visible and symbolic attacks; these acts were not sporadic incidents but, rather, a conscious campaign that finally forced the national airline to suspend flying, proving the technique highly effective.

In the *transmission* section of this chapter, I argue that despite their similarities – both in the ways the technique was realized and in the contexts in which they emerged – there is no evidence showing that Cuban revolutionaries were influenced or inspired by (or even knew of) the use of hijackings by Peruvian revolutionaries nearly three decades previously; this technique was not adopted by Cuban revolutionaries but reinvented by them. Finally, in the *selection* section, I demonstrate that the reinvention of the same technique in two geographical disparate contexts can be attributed to the similarities in the propositional knowledge held by these societies, namely the states' relationship with airpower. Moreover, the repeated use of hijackings in both cases can also be attributed to the fact that aircrews displayed an immediate initial willingness to comply with hijackers' demands, showing both revolutionaries and counter-revolutionaries that hijacking was a feasible technique of contention. In fact, once both revolutions were successful, counter-revolutionaries in turn adopted hijacking either in an attempt to reverse the revolution or as a means of leaving the country. In both cases, the pattern of adoption and replication of hijacking as a technique of contention predicted the subsequent pattern of the technique's selection: When successful, hijacking is replicated while failed hijackings tend to curb future imitation of the technique. This perhaps explains why the technique had to be reinvented; in Cuba, hijacking was replicated successfully by counter-revolutionaries and then continued to be replicated worldwide. In contrast, in the Peruvian case counter-revolutionaries failed to successfully replicate the technique, and it was abandoned and subsequently largely disappeared from the Peruvian repertoire of contention. This pattern of selection would later prove crucial to understand the fate of hijacking in the late 1960s and 1970s, which is discussed in chapter 6. Success breeds replication; failure leads to extinction.

3.1 VARIATION: THE SYMBOLIC APPEAL OF AVIATION

Airspace in the Andes

In 1929, Pan American-Grace Airways (better known as Panagra) entered the South American market with the establishment of a route structure of 14,000 miles (Gunston 2001, 278). Flying in such regions, Panagra was confronted with local corruption, domestic political violence, and most importantly, military coups and leftist revolts spurred by the Great Depression (Hiatt 2016).[1]

Within this context, Panagra, which was contractually bound to serve its hosts 'in time of war or great national crisis', saw its aircraft regularly commandeered by South American government forces conducting military operations against their enemies (Newton 1978, 324). For example, during the Chilean naval mutiny of 1931, the Chilean government commandeered two Panagra planes and their crews to send troops and supplies to quell the revolt. This mode of operations persisted despite censure from Panagra officials in New York, who argued that such involvement in a domestic power struggle would violate the terms of their insurance (Newton 1978).

The relationship between the state and Panagra was central to the emergence of hijacking during the Peruvian revolts of the early 1930s. The emergence of hijacking as a technique of contention in Peru can be directly linked to the longstanding notion that control of airspace equates state sovereignty and legitimacy. Indeed, the importance of aircraft as a political tool was already well ingrained within the Andes by the 1930s (Hiatt 2016, 131). Far from a neutral technology, aeroplanes participated in constructing an oligarchic vision for Peru, with successive governments employing aircraft, at times commandeered from Panagra, to defeat rebels, reinforcing the capital's centripetal pull, and demonstrating the reach and ability of the state.

In 1931, when word reached Lima that Luis Miguel Sánchez Cerro, then a lieutenant-colonel, was threatening an uprising in Arequipa, President Augusto B. Leguía dispatched two commandeered Panagra planes to Arequipa, each carrying pro-Leguía leaflets, copies of a Lima-based, pro-Leguía newspaper, *La Prensa*, and a twenty-five-pound bomb. This symbolic use of airpower represented an effort to demonstrate the reach of the Leguía regime and thus quell any unrest (Hiatt 2016, 133). However, the planes – one of which was piloted by Harold B. Grow, an American who had arrived in Peru in 1924 as a military attaché before being appointed to the command of the Peruvian Navy Air Service – were surrounded by pro-Cerro rebels during a refuelling stop, and both pilots were arrested (Hiatt 2016, 133). Grow was put on trial for the intended aerial bombardment of a city. Cerro denounced Grow as a 'mercenary and a vulgar agent of the dictator' and accused him of 'violating the rules of public right' by his intention 'to fly over Arequipa and bomb the city, without caring about the tremendous consequences of his action' (*New York Times* 1931e). At his court-martial, Grow professed his undying love for Peru and claimed that he was not on a mission to attack the city but, rather, was ordered to drop leaflets (*New York Times* 1931f). Either way, the rebels' ability to halt Grow's mission clearly demonstrated that the state did not have full control of the airspace, thus symbolically stripping it of some of its power.

In another incident, on 26 August 1930, Sánchez Cerro's men seized another Panagra F7 Ford Trimotor mail aircraft on its routine duties. This time, rather than simply detaining the pilot, Cerro's men forced him to pilot the plane and drop anti-government propaganda leaflets over the city of Arequipa, using the state's technique against it. The pilot was then forced to transport a group of armed rebels to Tacna, Peru, which enabled them to rally a remote garrison against the Leguía regime. An account of the upheaval in Peru published in the *New York Times* illustrates the centrality of captured aeroplanes to this event:

> [The] prefect of Tacna was killed when he refused to line up with the Southern military junta which began the Peruvian revolt in Arequipa last week. He was shot by Commander Beytia, a Tacna officer, who flew yesterday to Arequipa and placed himself under orders to Colonel Sánchez Cerro, Chieftain of the revolt. Commander Beytia returned today in the same plane, accompanied by Lieutenant Maldonado, a delegate of the Arequipa junta. They were met at the Tacna airfield by Colonel Lune, the prefect, and his aid Lieutenant Vizcarra. Commander Beytia presented credentials from Colonel Sánchez Cerro and demanded delivery of the prefecture. (*New York Times* 1930)

The seizure of Panagra planes and pilots on the ground provided rebels with the ability to rally support from hard-to-reach garrisons quickly and to engage in propaganda drops – a technique they had ostensibly copied from the Leguía government. However, while tactically useful, these acts were perhaps even more important because of their symbolism: The rebels could now rival the state in its control of airspace.

Interestingly, if slightly ironically, the tables were once again turned in February 1931 after the successful overthrow of Leguía by Cerro and his supporters. Cerro's Arequipa-based supporters, disillusioned by his apparent failure to fulfil his promises, sought his removal, and the restoration of the deposed President Leguía (*New York Times* 1931c, 1931b). As fighting broke out in the streets of the capital (*New York Times* 1931a), pro-Leguía men, undoubtedly mindful of the successful deployment of this technique the previous year, seized a Pan Am Airways aircraft leased to Panagra and chartered by the US government to deliver registered mail in Peru, along with its US pilot, Byron Richards. Seeking to replicate the success achieved by Cerro's men six months previously, Leguía's supporters demanded that the five hundred pounds of mail in the plane be removed and that the plane be flown over

Lima and Central Peru to 'distribute leaflets written by [pro-Leguía] rebels at Arequipa' (*New York Times* 1931d). However, while under armed guard, Richards and his co-pilot persuaded the pro-Leguía rebels to allow another Pan Am airmail plane to collect the mail. Once the other plane had departed with the mail safely on board, the pilots declared they had 'no desire or intention of being implicated in any way in their affairs and preferred to remain absolutely neutral' (Phillips 1973, 24) refusing to make the propaganda flight.

Undeterred by this failure, a pro-Leguía faction quickly attempted to seize another pilot, Elmer Faucett, after he conducted a propaganda drop over rebels in Arequipa on behalf of the government. However, after forcing him to fly to Talara to fill up with petrol and oil in preparation for a subsequent pro-Leguía propaganda drop, the plane was quickly seized by soldiers loyal to the president on landing (Phillips 1973). Attempts by pro-Leguía rebels to deprive the new government of aircrafts with which to conduct propaganda drops were thus met with routine failure, which explains why hijacking was winnowed out of the pro-Leguía rebels' repertoire of contention.

Applying the framework proposed throughout the previous chapter, it is easy to identify the propositional knowledge leading to the emergence of hijacking within the Peruvian context: Air power is both a coercive instrument wielded by the state and a symbol of that state's power and control. By the early 1930s, the notion that airpower could be equated with the legitimacy of an existing regime and sovereignty of a state was well established, not only in Peru but also throughout South America (Hiatt 2016). In fact, Willie Hiatt's (2016) extensive study of aviation in the Andes situates Peru's willingness to mobilize aeroplanes in warfare in the context of the aftermath of the country's defeat during the War of the Pacific (1879–1883).

In the decades following the War of the Pacific, the Peruvian government, with five borders still in dispute, increased its investment in aviation and received aeroplanes purchased by civilians and donated to the Peruvian military (Hiatt 2016). Political leadership also adopted the notion that aeroplanes would allow the country to lay tangible claim to disrupted territories. During the inauguration of a new aerodrome in Lima, for instance, President Leguía proclaimed the importance of aircraft to his modernization project saying, 'Let's populate our seas with submarines and our skies with aeroplanes, and this way we will not only establish our borders but also banish forever the tragic ghost of war' (Hiatt 2016, 132). The use of aerial power to quash revolts and mutinies elsewhere in the Andes[2] also served to further solidify the propositional knowledge linking aerial power with sovereignty and to display the superiority of a state vis-à-vis its challengers (Black 2016).[3]

In Peru, the rebels' capture of Grow and his plane, therefore, had a profound impact on both the propositional and prescriptive knowledge held by Cerro's men and society as a whole; aerial control was no longer to be seen as absolute or immune to challenges. As I have argued previously, the core of all techniques of contention is the claim-makers' understanding of the nature of the political environment created by the state, which forms their propositional knowledge about protest actions and society as a whole. Historically, the nature of state authority has meant that claim-makers must shape their own techniques of contention in response to the state and its actions. Claim-makers, therefore, often attempt to 'mimic' state techniques and create an opposing structure of societal organization paralleled with that of the state. In Peru, for example, claim-makers mimicked the government's technique of airborne propaganda drops. As such, the state's technique can be understood as the precursor to the emergence of a new claim-making technique.

Cerro's men also sought to mimic the state's legal apparatus with the imprisonment and trial of Grow, which was widely covered in US newspapers. This exercise served to reinforce the rebels' legitimacy. As Weber (1988) contends, this reinforcement of legitimacy is a crucial exercise in turning evasive power into a durable political position. Weber (1988, 470) further argues that a group's legitimacy depends on social actors considering a given political order obligatory or binding. By subjecting Grow to a court-martial, Cerro's men sought to establish their control over legal institutions, thereby highlighting the illegitimacy of Leguía and his agents. By seizing planes that would otherwise be contractually obligated to serve the state in its operations against the rebels, and by mimicking the state's use of these aeroplanes, Cerro's men augmented their claim to legitimacy and worked to negate Leguía's sovereignty. Thus, Cerro's men employed hijacking as a useful tool to out-manoeuvre the establishment and embarrass the state by capturing highly valued planes and using them to distribute rebel propaganda. Furthermore, the seizure of Grow and his plane generated new prescriptive knowledge: Planes and pilots could be seized during refuelling stops at remote airfields. Rather than prosecuting these pilots for their government links, Cerro's forces could instead coerce them into employing their skills and aircraft to advance the revolutionary cause. The Peruvian case, therefore, not only demonstrates the clear association between state legitimacy and the display of state power through aviation but also illustrates that seizing aeroplanes can function as a symbolic, as well as instrumental acts of contention. Rather than solely using hijacking of aeroplanes in a tactical way, this technique of contention also entails the visible symbolism of flying unhindered over a territory as a legitimizing act. In this way, airspace can be viewed as a site of contention because wresting control of aeroplanes directly challenges state power; this is perhaps even more clearly exemplified by the use of aeroplane hijacking in Cuba during the late 1950s.

The Cuban Revolution

Aircraft hijacking all but completely disappeared after the incidences in Peru in the 1930s but re-emerged as an overtly politically motivated act during the last five months of the Cuban Revolution within the context of armed clashes and extreme political changes during the final stages of Fidel Castro's revolution against Fulgencio Batista Zaldivar. Despite no indication that the Cuban rebels were inspired by the hijackings in Peru, the 26th of July Movement, like Cerro's men in Peru nearly three decades previously, specifically targeted the country's civil aviation company, Cubana de Aviación. By hijacking planes, Castro's men sought to both accomplish defined tactical objectives on the battlefield and to symbolically highlight the government's vulnerability.

On 22 October 1958, three members of the faction diverted a Cubana de Aviación S.A. (better known as Cubana) DC-3, which was flying from Cayo Mambi to Moa Bay, and forced it to land at a rebel-created airstrip in the Oriente Province (Phillips 1973, 42). Two weeks later, on 6 November, Cuban revolutionaries hijacked another Cubana DC-3 flying from an airport in seaside Manzanillo, near the rebel-held Sierra Maestra, to Holguin and diverted it to the same Oriente airstrip (*Times* 1959). In preparation for both hijackings, Raúl Castro, showing organizational prowess surprising to those who perceived him as overshadowed by his brother (Thomas 1970), built a temporary air base with his own public works corps, which he had equipped with tractors. On landing at Castro's Oriente airstrip, both planes were appropriated and deployed, in turn, to support the insurgency by dropping propaganda leaflets, conducting improved aerial bombing raids, strafing targets, and transporting troops and weapons. These two planes – along with two P-51 Mustangs, a Cessna-195, a T-28 Trojan, all purchased in the United States, and a captured Vought Sikorsky OS2U-3 Kingfisher – composed the entirety of Castro's air force during the later stages of the revolt (De La Pedraja Tomán 2006, 152–53).

Raúl Castro's adoption of hijacking 'deprived Cubana of nearly one-fourth of its planes, worth $1,160,000' (*Times* 1959). Moreover, as a 'radio broadcast warned Cubans not to fly on Cubana planes as they risked being shot down' or hijacked, Cubana ceased flying most domestic routes less than two months after the first hijacking of one of its planes (*Times* 1959). As such, the hijacking of these planes not only provided Castro with a rudimentary 'air transport force to service rebel columns marauding in Camaguey and Las Villas provinces', but it also 'helped sever the government's air link to beleaguered Santiago, already virtually cut off by land' (*Times* 1959), further weakening the already limited reach of the Batista regime. Cubana's decision to stop serving most domestic routes can therefore be seen to symbolize the government's vulnerability and foreshadow its imminent collapse. Thus, the decision to intentionally target the country's national airline, ostensibly because it 'transported President's Batista's troops' (Phillips 1973, 43), should be understood not as a series of sporadic and unconnected incidents but, rather, as a conscious campaign targeting the state and its legitimacy.

In addition to attacking the state in this symbolically meaningful way, hijacking was also used tactically by the rebels. To overcome logistical limitations, hijacking was employed on at least one occasion in 1958 to supply Castro's men with much-needed weaponry (Heres 2010, 97). Without a reliable arms-smuggling network traversing the Maestra Mountains, equipping a force large enough to attack Batista's well-trained and well-disciplined soldiers had presented a previously insurmountable challenge. In addition to smuggling weapons purchased in Miami and Venezuela on rented aircraft – a method that accounted for the transport up to 70 percent of all weaponry employed by Castro's men – weapons were also sent covertly to Havana and Varadero on board Cubana aircraft (Heres 2010, 97). On 1 November 1958, members of the 26th of July Movement opted to hijack a plane to transport more weaponry. Minutes before it landed, five passengers onboard Cubana flight CU-T603 drew firearms, announcing they were members of the 26th of July Movement and opened a hatch to retrieve uniforms and military gear stowed in a sub-floor compartment. After donning their uniforms and making their way into the cockpit, they ordered the crew to take the plane to Raúl Castro's small airstrip to deliver a shipment of smuggled arms, grenades, and military supplies ("Investigation of Cubana Crash and Other Matters" 1958; "Incoming Telegram" 1958b). However, the airstrip was unsuitable for a plane of this weight and speed, and after several aborted landing approaches, the flight was diverted to the airfield at Preston ("Incoming Telegram" 1958a). Upon approaching Preston, the plane ran out of fuel and crashed into the waters of Nipe Bay ("Investigation of Cubana Crash and Other Matters" 1958).

As US officials sought to make sense of the hijacking via telegrams between the State Department and the American Embassy in Havana, Ambassador Smith dispatched a vice-consul to Eastern Cuba to interview the three passengers who were thought to have survived ("Investigation of Cubana Crash and Other Matters" 1958; "Incoming Telegram" 1958a, 1958b). Although news accounts indicated that there had been seventeen fatalities, three of the hijackers, who were never found and presumed dead, were in fact rescued from the water by Castro's men. Two of them, it was later revealed, quickly ascended through the ranks of the Cuban regime. [4]

By targeting Cubana aeroplanes, Castro effectively pursued an obvious national symbol of the Batista regime. As in the case of Panagra in 1930s' Peru, Cubana functioned as a symbol of the nation, thereby demonstrating the legitimacy of the existing regime. Indeed, by 1955, Pan Am had begun selling its ownership shares of Cubana to the Batista regime (NACLA Newsletter 1971). As Raguraman (1997) argues, the history of commercial aviation is linked intrinsically to nationalism, with national governments originally using their airlines to connect colonies and overseas territories; since the First World War, airlines have functioned as culturally important symbols that closely connect airlines to their states. Raguraman (1997) describes this 'flag-carrier' effect as the 'collective sentiment of nationalism provided by an airline which proudly displays the name and flag of a nation' (p. 240). In fact, according to Bennett (2014), twentieth-century thinking grouped airlines, passengers, and nations together in the belief that 'a country's passengers effectively belong to its flag carrier' and, therefore, to their country. Thus, during the early years of commercial aviation, the focus was not on flying internationally but on serving national interests. Therefore, airlines such as Cubana became representatives of their respective nations.

As Raguraman (1997) states, flag carriers acted, and continue to act, as highly visible global ambassadors of the home country and as the government's 'chosen instruments' for promoting national identities on an international level (p. 241). The existence of this close association between flag-carriers' and nations not only explains why Peruvian and Cuban revolutionaries sought to target airlines closely linked to the political authority they sought to challenge but also represents the propositional knowledge on which claim-makers based their understanding of this technique of contention. The understanding that control of airspace (and of aircrafts) is intrinsically linked to the notion of a state's legitimacy and sovereignty was clearly appreciated by the hijackers in both contexts; by challenging the states control of airspace or access to aircraft, claim-makers directly undermined their adversary. By using this knowledge to wrest power from the state, and thereby legitimizing their own claims, the rebels in both countries were able to use hijacking as a technique to support their own aims and were highly successful. This same propositional knowledge also served to underpin the later adoption of hijacking by black nationalist groups in the late 1960s and early 1970s, along with the repetitive targeting of El Al operations by Palestinian claim-makers, which will be addressed in the following two chapters.

3.2 TRANSMISSION: A CONSPICUOUS LACK THEREOF

According to conventional evolutionary insight, rates of adoption far exceed rates of variation (Biggs 2013), or in the case of techniques of contention, adoption outstrips innovation by far. Therefore, when the same innovation emerges within two different contexts, it is crucial to ask questions relating to transmission: How does an innovation travel from one location (or, in the case of this study, one particular repertoire of contention) to another? To answer this question, it is important to recognize two factors. First, as the use of hijacking as a technique of contention had been winnowed out in Peru in the early 1930s largely because of repeated failures of hijackers, transmission to Cuba is improbable because of the time that had passed between these two waves of hijackings and their geographical distance: It seems unlikely that the techniques were diffused through relational ties. Moreover, there is no concrete evidence that Cuban revolutionaries were familiar with the use of hijacking during the Peruvian revolts of the 1930s; there is no indication that they read about the Peruvian hijackings in the media or were exposed to them through any other medium. Nonetheless, it is possible that the Cuban revolutionaries had heard about the previous hijackings, in which case, it would be important to consider the means of transmission. However, in the absence of any concrete evidence of this, the most plausible explanation that remains is that hijacking instead re-emerged in a Cuban context as a result of a similar propositional knowledge about the state, its behaviour, and most importantly, the state's use of aircraft to display its power, reach and legitimacy.

Importantly, while Peruvian hijacking events in the early 1930s garnered significant exposure in the international press in their immediate aftermath, they are nearly entirely omitted from historiographies of terrorism or discourse on aviation security. A survey of every article published in two of the most pre-eminent aviation legal periodicals in the United States, the *Air Law Review* and the *Journal of Air Law*, between 1930 until 1942 failed to produce a single mention of a crime, 'terrorism' or the need for law enforcement with regard to aeroplane hijacking (Karber 2005). This suggests that even those directly involved in aviation and aviation security were either unaware of or largely uninterested in the phenomenon. Instead, the most salient account of hijacking prior to the Second World War appears in a work of fiction, James Hilton's best-selling novel *Lost Horizon* (1933). In 1937, *Lost Horizon* was adapted into a US drama-fantasy film, directed by Frank Capra. Despite the fact that the book and film reached a wide audience and, arguably, spread prescriptive knowledge about the existence of hijacking, the technique remained very rare, with only one incident worldwide between 1933 and 1943, when on 21 October 1935, a lieutenant of the US Air Force hijacked a plane with the intention of flying it to Lithuania. Instead, the greatest threat to civilian aviation during the interwar period and the Second World War emerged from the periphery of the war zones, where at least twenty-three civilian aircraft were downed as a result of air-to-air shooting by industrial powers.[5] The decade following the Second World War saw the emergence of a different manifestation of hijacking to the cases of revolutionaries in Peru and Cuba. Whereas in the Peruvian and Cuban contexts, the use of hijacking represented a deliberate and systematic campaign to challenge the legitimacy and power of their adversary in a highly public and symbolic manner, this new strain was dubbed 'hijacking for transportation'. This phenomenon saw individuals seeking to leave the Soviet Bloc hijacking aircraft as a means of escape. This strain of hijacking, which began in 1947 and was geographically constrained to Europe until the end of the Cuban Revolution, will be discussed in much greater detail in the following section and in greater depth in the following chapter. The impact of this strain of hijacking for transportation, as will be discussed, were wide reaching, particularly with respect to hijacking committed by Cuban nationals seeking to leave post-revolutionary Cuba. However, the impact of this European strategy on the Cuban revolutionaries' decision to adopt hijacking as part of a deliberate and systematic campaign against the Batista regime remains unclear.

3.3 SELECTION: THE ADOPTION OF HIJACKING BY COUNTER-REVOLUTIONARIES

The final element to address in relation to these early instances of hijackings relates to the reason for the repeated use – or adoption by new groups of claim-makers for their own means – of the technique. In other words, in this section I will explore which circumstances and contexts lead to hijacking being retained or eliminated by Peruvian and Cuban revolutionaries or being used by those who later sought to reverse these revolutions. In all cases, effectiveness – the probability that the technique can be successfully deployed and lead to a desired outcome – appears to have been the defining factor that determined whether Peruvian and Cuban claim-makers continued to conduct hijacking after initial forays.

In Peru, the success of using US aircraft and pilots in support of the Peruvian revolution led to imitation by counter-revolutionaries loyal to Leguía. There are several accounts of attempted seizures of aircraft after he was overthrown. However, Cerro's regime, along with Panagra, having learned from the event of the revolution, quickly took extensive precautions to thwart the threat of counter-revolutionary elements seeking to commandeer planes to destabilize the new regime; for example, Panagra started issuing radio warnings to the aircrafts if destination or refuelling airports were under threat, allowing pilots to then make emergency landings at other island berths. Pilots also radioed approaching airports to ensure that they were still controlled by the government before landing to avoid planes being captured. Through these measures, hijacking became unfeasible for Peruvian claim-makers loyal to Leguía.

Conversely, following the Cuban Revolution, claim-makers in other South and Central American states appear to have emulated Castro's technique of hijacking planes to obtain a tactical advantage over their adversaries. Of the twenty-four hijackings that occurred in the Americas between the end of the Cuban Revolution and 1963, nineteen can be classified as 'hijacking for transport', mostly between Cuba and the United States. These instances will be discussed in length in the following chapter.

After transport, the next leading motivation appears to have been the overt support of revolutionary activities, particularly the dropping of propaganda leaflets. Prior to the Cuban Revolution, the use of the technique to distribute propaganda leaflets had not been employed by non-state actors since the Peruvian revolution. However, during and in the aftermath of Castro's revolution, this technique was quickly adopted by South and Central American revolutionaries, becoming well established within their repertoires of contention. More interestingly, apart from one instance in 1961, when a Transporter Aeros L1049 from Casablanca to Lisbon was hijacked by six heavily armed men and used to drop leaflets over Lisbon, this practice did not surface outside Latin America until 1992, when a hijacker forced a pilot to fly low over Ho Chi Minh City, Vietnam, to drop anti-communist leaflets. This suggests that Castro's successful seizures of planes for the purpose of dropping propaganda had only achieved recognition and replication within a relatively narrow geographically confined area.

Perhaps the most notable adoption of hijacking following the Cuban Revolution was that of Batista loyalists seeking to leave revolutionary Cuba. The period between the end of the Cuban Revolution in January 1959 and May 1961 saw a distinctive geographic cluster of hijackings, with flights originating from Cuba and headed to the United States accounting for fifteen out of nineteen total hijackings worldwide. This indicates a widespread adoption of the technique by those wishing to leave Cuba, thus emphasizing the importance of geographical proximity in the diffusion of techniques of contention. While these hijackings have traditionally been treated as apolitical, they nonetheless serve to highlight the hijackers' dissatisfaction with the state, which I will explore in more detail in the following chapter.

NOTES

1. As observed by Beth Day (1976), foreign 'mail pilots were endangered as revolutions swept the continent like prairie fires' (p. 29). Indeed, in the early 1930s, Panagra aircraft were fired on by irate farmers who claimed that low-flying planes crossing the high passes in the Andes were causing their herds to stampede (Day 1976, 30). Panagra pilots also engaged in armed standoffs with rival airlines, notably in 1931, when in what would later be referred to as the 'Battle of Lake Montenegro', a Pan Am pilot made an emergency landing at a rival airline's installation at Lake Montenegro (Josephson 1999, 74–75). Similarly, in 1931, a Panagra-owned plane leased to a local carrier was fired on by a ground-based machine gun and chased by an Argentine pursuit fighter after refusing to comply with demands for a bribe (Newton 1978, 324). Panagra employees were also subjected to violence on the ground; in 1930, a passenger threatened an employee with a firearm before being incapacitated by a flight mechanic, who struck the passenger in the head with a pyrene bottle (Grooch 1938, 91).

2. During the Chilean naval mutiny of 1931, the use of Panagra aircraft to attack mutineers combined with the government's uncompromising demand for complete surrender caused an immediate and marked decline in the mutineers' morale. Later in 1934, the city of São Paulo

was subjected to aerial bombing, demonstrating the strength and determination of governmental forces in the face of provincial opposition. Elsewhere on the continent, air attacks were also employed during federal forces' successful suppression of a large-scale constitutionalist revolt in Brazil (Black 2016, 85).

3. As early as immediately after the First World War, the early 'prophets of airpower' such as Douhet, Mitchell, and Trenchard highlighted the strategic importance of aerial power – particularly the potential offered by strategic aerial bombing. For a greater exploration of this topic, see Gray (2016). Moreover, for an in-depth on the use of aerial power to curb revolts and mutinies, see Black (2016).

4. Manual Fernandez Fálcon became Chief of the Counterintelligence Directorate at the Interior Ministry. Emundo Ponce de León, the presumed ringleader, was promoted to lieutenant and, two months later, was assigned to a police station as second in command. In the end, the United States did not pursue Ponce de León or the others involved in stashing weapons on the plane and commandeering it. Remarkably, in 1994, Ponce de León sought and was granted admission to the United States as a naturalized citizen, where he lived under a pseudonym in Miami until reports of his location began circulating among South Florida's Cuban community ("Relatives Claim Passenger in 1958 Plane Crash off Cuba Was a Hijacker" 2008; Tester 2012).

5. Most notably, the Empire of Japan followed a pattern of indiscriminately targeting civilian aircraft, and was thus responsible for all commercial air casualties in the Pacific and more than 40 percent of total worldwide incidents between 1938 and 1945 (Gidwitz 1980, 41; Karber 2005, 532–33).

Chapter Four

Hijacking for Transportation or 'Freedom Flights'

A strain of two geographically distinct but causally related waves of hijacking emerged as the Second World War drew to a close. These waves of hijacking occurred in response to the spread of global communism and were led to by those seeking to escape regimes they deemed oppressive; initially by individuals seeking to escape the Eastern Bloc and, later, in the aftermath of the Cuban Revolution, by those seeking to escape Fidel Castro's regime by claiming political asylum in the United States. Extensive media coverage of these so called 'freedom flights', paired with quasi-government support among Western states led to the adoption of hijacking by Americans fleeing US-style 'Jim Crow' racism or the Vietnam draft.

While the existing literature on terrorism and aviation security generally recognizes the existence of this strain of hijacking – in contrast to the previously discussed events in Peru and during the Cuban revolution that are usually ignored – such analyses tend to be superficial at best, with the events often dismissed as irrelevant or not categorized as politically motivated. In fact, Holden's (1986) definitive work on aeroplane hijacking categorizes these incidents as cases of 'hijacking for transportation', an entirely distinct category from the politically motivated hijackings of the late 1960s onwards. Aggarwala (1971), Arey (1972), and Loy (1970) make similar distinctions. More recently, examining attacks on commercial aviation between 1947 and 1996, Merari (1999) also categorized the 847 hijackings found during this period into two groups: those committed for personal interest, such as transportation to a non-scheduled destination, and those committed for political motives by terroristic groups, state agents, and criminal organizations. In the *variation* section of this chapter, I survey these two waves of hijacking and address the subsequent innovations made to the technique by Marielitos seeking to return to Cuba. I argue that treating so-called 'freedom flights' or 'hijacking for transportation' as separate from what other authors (Aggarwala 1971; Arey 1972; Merari 1999; Phillips 1973) call 'politically motivated hijacking' is highly problematic. First, it is impossible to divorce exit from a repressive regime from its political meaning. Secondly, such an approach fails to recognize the profound impact these events had on the existing propositional and prescriptive knowledge of the societies in which they took place and, thus, their direct influence on the subsequent evolution of hijacking, such as those made by Marielitos in the 1980s.

In the *transmission* section, this chapter goes on to demonstrate how Western states sought to further politicize – and in doing so publicized – dramatic escapes from the Soviet Union, including hijackings, to challenge the legitimacy of this regime. In so doing, they unintentionally spread prescriptive knowledge about these hijackings to an audience far exceeding Cuba and the Soviet Union. This spread of knowledge was also accentuated by the hasty reconfiguration of legal instruments in the West to facilitate future escapes from the East to the West. This process involved the establishment of a set of implicit norms, later known as the 'Havana Rules', whereby hijackers would receive only nominal sanctions if they conducted themselves in a manner aimed at minimizing risk to passengers, crews, and aircraft. These factors, I argue, had a profound influence on the propositional and prescriptive knowledge of claim-makers in the Western world.

Consequently, in the *selection* section of this chapter, I consider the influence of this new propositional and prescriptive knowledge on the wider civil rights movements of the 1960s. I contend that the tumultuous wave of hijackings in the United States during the late 1960s and early 1970s, perpetrated for various reasons, cannot be explained adequately without understanding the two preceding waves of Eastern Bloc and Cuban hijackings and the response of Western states. Efforts by Western states to further politicize and facilitate dramatic escapes from the Soviet Union and Cuba had profound and unintended consequences of spreading prescriptive knowledge about hijackings to an audience that far exceeded their geographical surroundings. In sum, I argue that Western perspectives and media efforts surrounding these waves of hijacking, which celebrated hijackings as courageous bids for freedom from communism's grasp, directly contributed to the diffusion of hijacking to the repertoire of contention of the black nationalist movement in the United States during the late 1960s and early 1970s and, indeed, all subsequent strains of hijacking. Indeed, only once claim-makers – and individuals motivated by financial gain (as discussed in chapter 6) – from within Western states began adopting hijacking in action against Western governments did these governments begin to engage in multilateral security efforts to curb hijacking. In addition to this shift in security efforts, it is important to consider the ways in which the period of development addressed in this chapter – namely, the use of hijacking by claim-makers seeking to advance the black nationalist cause or to protest the US involvement in Vietnam – relates to the developments of hijacking in the Middle East.

4.1 VARIATION: FREEDOM FLIGHTS AS A FORM OF CONTENTION

During the Second World War, the Soviet Union expanded its civilian aviation fleet, largely due to the occupation and destruction of western Union of Soviet Socialist Republics (USSR) and the overloading of the remaining rail lines for heavy military transportation needs. This expansion was facilitated by the large quantity of US lend-lease transport planes obtained over the course of the war (Davies 1983, 535). This rapid expansion, and an inherited array of former government and military vehicles, left dissidents with an opportunity to use the Soviet-run transportation systems to flee the country after the war (Davies 1983, 294–99). Within this context, Soviet authorities were faced with what Lissitzyn (1971) calls 'hijacking for travel purposes' (p. 83), or 'freedom flights', a subdivision of a much larger movement of displaced persons and political refugees seeking, often at the encouragement of Western states, to escape Soviet-occupied Eastern Europe and the harsh regimes installed there. This movement saw the use of various innovative techniques, including hijacking planes, trains, trucks, or tanks, and tunnelling to freedom.

As Mueller (1999) argues, escape, flight, and exodus are all actions that demonstrate 'varying levels of dissatisfaction with the conditions left behind and claims on some alternative life space' (p. 701) and, therefore, are clearly political actions. The most systematic examination of exit as a technique of contention is presented in Hirschman's (1970) treatise *Exit, Voice, and Loyalty*. Hirschman argues that 'exit' and 'voice' represent alternative modes of contention available to dissatisfied customers, employees, and citizens who are displeased with the quality of food and service they receive, the condition of their employment or, in this case, the nature or effects of government policies. In Hirschman's (1970) theory, an exit is basically free because the cost of non-participation is generally null. In opposition, voice requires creativity, effort, and organization. Therefore, in his original formulation, Hirschman (1970) suggests that an exit would always be the preferred means of expressing dissatisfaction, were it not for loyalty, which 'holds exit at bay and activates voice' (p. 78). However, in later work, Hirschman (1992) acknowledges that his original theory failed to account for cases 'where exit and voice are both in short supply, in spite of many reasons for discontent and unhappiness' (p. 81). Applying Hirschman's formulation to authoritarian systems, Mueller (1999) argues that exit actions such as escape, seeking asylum, or emigration – especially in contexts where freedom of movement is legally prohibited – should indeed be interpreted as inherently politically disruptive 'actions designed to further personal and group interest by seeking either to leave a state against resistance or to secure the right to leave' (p. 702). Therefore, all such exit actions are inherently politically contentious because they directly threaten the legitimacy of a state, particularly in the case of authoritarian regimes. Indeed, the flight of large numbers of people from a political system, particularly when it entails significant risk to those who exit, such as those fleeing the Iron Curtain, undermines a regime's hold on power, discredits it, and threatens its legitimacy as a functioning political system to the wider international audience and to those who stay.

Freedom Flights from the Soviet Union

According to the Secretary-General of International Civil Airport Association, the illegal seizure of a passenger aircraft as a means of escaping Soviet control or as a mode of transportation 'was not generally realized until 1947', when three Romanian army officers hijacked an internal civilian flight and diverted it to Turkey, where they requested political asylum (International Civil Airport Association 1971, 1). Very few details are available about this first incident, apart from a short description in Choi's (1994) overview of terrorism and aviation: 'Three Rumanian [sic] army officers hijacked a Rumanian civilian aircraft carrying ten people to Canakkale province in Turkey and requested political asylum . . . one of the crew members was shot dead for refusing to pilot the aircraft . . . the officers were taken into custody, and the seven civilians were freed' (p. 3). Scholarly analysis on the event is also lacking, despite the fact that the incident appears to represent the emergence of 'hijacking for transportation' in the Eastern hemisphere. In fact, between 1948 and 1958, of the thirty-three attempted or successful hijackings worldwide, twenty-three originated from within the Soviet sphere of influence, and all of these were motivated by an attempt to flee the Iron Curtain. The majority of these attempts included some form of violence, particularly towards crew members. Hijackers' use of weapons was made necessary by the fact that crew members, including pilots, were often armed in communist countries. In fact, as early as 1948, Soviet authorities attempting to curb aeroplane hijacking began employing 'air marshals' to defend aircraft from seizure (Phillips 1973, 266).

Freedom Flights from Cuba

In Cuba, Castro's seizure of Havana, and the subsequent capitulation of the Fulgencio Batista government on 1 January 1959, led to an exodus of former government officials and loyalists, resulting in approximately 10 percent of the Cuban population leaving the country (Pedraza 2001, 413–17).[1] The use of hijacked aeroplanes to leave Cuba began in the immediate aftermath of the revolution. On 1 January 1959, the day the Batista government surrendered, a Cubana flight out of Havana was diverted to New York by a group of Batista supporters (Karber 2005). Between 1 January 1959 and 8 August 1961, of the twenty-one hijackings worldwide, thirteen were committed by Cuban hijackers seeking asylum in the United States.[2] This trend continued until Cuba's adoption of *Cuba-United States Memorandum of Understanding on Hijacking of Aircraft and Vessels and Other Offense* in 1973, which will be discussed in this chapter and which prompted an extreme reduction in hijacking between the United States and Cuba between 1973 and 1980. However, the initial success of this accord was later undermined by Cuban exiles in the United States, known as Marielitos, further innovating on the technique and deploying it, between August 1980 and August 1983, to return to Cuba.

The Use of Flammable Liquid by Marielitos

In April 1980, capitalizing on the Jimmy Carter administration's rhetoric on refugee and human rights, Castro unexpectedly reversed his prohibition of emigration, announcing that whoever wished to leave for the United States could do so via the Cuban port of Mariel. Taking matters further, he extended the offer to Cuban prisoners and psychiatric patients, declaring that the United States could have Cuba's 'chicken thieves' (Smith 1987, 212–13). The crisis escalated when, on its own initiative, the Floridian Cuban-American community organized a boatlift in May 1980 to bring over estranged relatives: US immigration authorities were consequently overwhelmed by the arrival of 115,000 Cubans over the next two months (Smith 1987). However, in summer 1980, a number of Marielitos – individuals who emigrated from Cuba during the boatlift – decided, for a variety of reasons, to use a hijacked aircraft as a means of returning home to Cuba, sparking a new wave of hijacking for transportation.

Akin to black nationalists seeking refuge from racial inequality in the United States (which will be discussed in detail in the *selection* section of this chapter), a frequently cited reason for the departure of Marielitos is the lack of opportunities and the prejudice they faced in the United States. Although Cubans with professional skills in need of adaptation to the United States were heavily targeted by federal grants provided to local universities and community organizations to create intensive retraining programmes, the majority of Marielitos faced a harsh reception (Organista 2007). Not only did the Marielitos arrive in the United States during an economic recession, but 75 percent were also blue-collar workers. Moreover, while some were forced to leave Cuba, the majority had been allowed to leave, given their desire to escape the island's growing poverty. As such, they were initially denied the federal financial support granted to political refugees (Organista 2007). On arrival, the Marielitos were housed in temporary tent cities and sent to military detention centres for security screening. US apprehension over the Marielitos stemmed from Castro's well-publicized 'tainting' of the migration stream with hardened criminals, mental patients, homosexuals, and others deemed 'undesirable' to society at the time. Although fewer than 4 percent were actually felons or mental patients, the exaggerated media attention focused on these subgroups fuelled US fears (García 1996).[3] Angered at the crowded conditions in detention camps and prisons, many inmates rioted and clashed with National Guard troops.

Over the next three years, between August 1980 and August 1982, twenty-two American aircraft were seized and diverted to Cuba by Cubans wishing to return home. One noticeable innovation during this wave of hijacking was hijackers threatening to use gasoline and flammable liquids, such as rubbing alcohol, to set fire to crew members or the aircraft itself. Indeed, of the twenty-two aircraft diversions to Cuba, at least seventeen involved flammable liquid, indicating the rapid spread of this new prescriptive knowledge throughout the Cuban diaspora. The threat of igniting flammable liquids as a technique of coercive leverage exploited an existing weakness in the screening process. The walk-through metal detectors introduced in US airports in 1973 were obviously ineffective at detecting liquids or inflammable substances. Although X-ray machines could alert the operator to questionable containers in cabin baggage, they could not identify the contents. Preventing the technique of using flammable liquids in hijacking thus necessitated increased reliance on manual inspections by security personnel. In other words, would-be hijackers innovated on existing techniques in response to the resource limitations caused by the introduction of X-ray machines, which had made hijacking less feasible. The rapid increase in the use of flammable liquid demonstrates innovation in terms of weapon selection to ensure the successful commandeering of an airliner.

The spread and adoption of this innovation can also be attributed to its effectiveness. This effectiveness is related to an increase in the violence of this technique; aware of the catastrophic effect of a fire on board a plane, cabin crews generally opted to comply with the hijackers' demands when faced with such threats. This willingness to comply to hijackers' demands meant that hijackings became an increasingly effective avenue by which to voice contention. In fact, between August 1980 and March 1984, only one out of twenty-three hijacking attempts using threats related to flammable liquid was foiled. Exasperated by the spread of this technique, faced with great difficulty in curbing it, and cognizant of the danger it posed to passengers, crew, and aircraft, a frustrated Federal Aviation Administration (FAA) official commented that the use of flammable material as a means of diverting aircraft would not stop 'until we begin hanging hijackers at airports, an altogether implausible but not unsatisfying solution' (Livingstone 1983, 16–17).

The contagious frequency, combined with the danger, of this flammable liquid hijacking innovation forced the United States and Cuba to collaborate once again. As a result, on 16 September 1980, Cuba publicly announced that Marielitos had made a one-way trip and that returning hijackers would either be imprisoned or extradited. The following day, Cuba's resolve was tested when two Marielitos, who claimed to be 'tired of all the robbing and killing' in New York City, diverted a Delta flight from Atlanta to Cuba (*Arizona Republic* 1980, 5). The hijackers were immediately arrested by Cuban authorities and extradited to the United States the following day; both hijackers were indicted on charges of air piracy and sentenced to forty years in prison. As in 1973, the extradition of hijackers from Cuba to the United States had a profound impact on existing propositional knowledge and served to stop further adoption of hijacking by Marielitos seeking to return to Cuba. While the use of flammable liquid would remain a feasible way to hijack a plane, the renewed cooperation between the United States and Cuba had a serious impact on the effectiveness of the technique because hijackers faced arrest, extradition, and prosecution in the immediate aftermath; this profoundly altered the existing propositional knowledge as the end result of an otherwise successful hijacking was likely to be imprisonment rather than escape.

4.2 TRANSMISSION: SUPPORTING HIJACKING FOR PROPAGANDA PURPOSES

In the aftermath of the Second World War, the Harry S. Truman administration began to encourage flight escape to the West. In recognizing the beneficial symbol of freedom flights from behind the Iron Curtain and the intelligence value of escapees, the US government allied itself with, and sought to encourage, escapees, while simultaneously castigating the Soviet Union for its forcible movement East of millions of prisoners and purportedly unwilling repatriates.[4]

This contest was often described by its Western architects as a 'battle for men's minds'. Its origin can be attributed to the intensity of US media interest in prominent defectors such as Victor Andreevich Kravchenko, Igor Sergeyevich Gouzenko, and Oksana Stepanova Kasenkina, a fifty-two-year-old schoolteacher who hurled herself from a third-floor window of the Russian Consulate in New York's Upper East Side, insisting that she would rather die in America than be returned forcibly to the 'worker's fatherland' (as quoted in *Life* 1948). The story received a twenty-five-part serialization in the *New York Journal-American* (Carruthers 2005). According to the Policy Planning Staff, the principal strategic arm of the US Department of State, these stories, by creating 'a wide breach in the Iron Curtain', were more effective in 'arous[ing] the Western world to the realities of the nature of communist tyranny than anything else since the end of the war' ("PPS 54: Policy Relating to Defection and Defectors from Soviet Power" 1949). By breaching the Iron Curtain, defectors not only provided a glimpse inside the Soviet Union for those in the West, but, more importantly, their actions also served as an example for others in the East to navigate the same course.

The Policy Planning Staff imagined the ideal-typical defectors as 'important government and party officials, military officers, the intelligentsia, the managerial class and highly qualified technicians' ("PPS 22: Utilization of Refugees from the Soviet Union in U.S. National Interest" 1949). Incidentally, this profile corresponded rather well with those who employed hijacking as a means of escaping to the West. 'Convinced that the Stalinist system is evil', these individuals, US authorities assumed, would voluntarily place themselves under US jurisdiction ("PPS 22: Utilization of Refugees from the Soviet Union in U.S. National Interest" 1949). This was an attractive prospect to US authorities in a zero-sum climate, in which Washington's gains represented direct losses for the Kremlin. Responding to these incidents, Western authorities (i) sought to capitalize on compelling stories of escapees in which Americans, 'restless to take a personal part in the East-West struggle', could feel invested ("PSB Draft Program for Soviet Orbit Escapees" 1951) and (ii) reconfigured legal instruments hastily to facilitate future defection to the West. Both initiatives would have important repercussions for the future transmission of knowledge about hijacking as a technique of contention and, subsequently, for replication of the technique. In other words, US authorities sought both to make hijackings more feasible – by removing legal barriers – and more legitimate, as a welcome means of expressing political grievances.

According to Carruthers (2005), the Policy Planning Staff worried that Americans would not provide sufficient emotional support to escapees and, more importantly, would not support the government's attempts to facilitate their escape. Therefore, the Policy Planning Staff used its contact with news and entertainment organizations to 'bombard U.S. audience with particularly ingenious breaches of the curtain' (p. 931):

> Newsreels showcased the Ollarek family, who fled Czechoslovakia in a 'freedom duck' – an amphibious jeep stolen and steered across the Morava River into Austria 'under dramatic circumstances'. Ivan Pluhar, a Czech who tunnelled out of a prison camp near uranium mines, where he had been sentenced for anticommunist activity, was subsequently admitted into Yale Law School with much fanfare. . . . Almost all personal narratives ended with a ringing declamation that explicated the larger meaning of escape. Having lost a leg when a landmine exploded, impeding – but not preventing – her escape, Mrs. Kapus told her American rescuers: 'I shall be happier with one leg in America

than I would have been with two legs in Communist Hungary'. A Polish pilot who flew his MiG to Denmark was reported by *Life* as jubilantly announcing, 'Kommunizm Kaput!' And when a Czech 'freedom train' crashed into West Germany in September 1951, carrying an engineer and thirty-two passengers, its driver exclaimed, 'We are all here in the West – and the climate is wonderful!' (Carruthers 2005, 931–32)

Alongside this media attention, the vehicles employed by the escapees were often used in parades to raise funds for Radio Free Europe's mission to spread the word about successful escapes from behind the Iron Curtain. These publicity campaigns facilitated the spread of prescriptive knowledge about the actual techniques escapees employed (Carruthers 2005; Fried 1998; Caute 2008). For example, in 1954, under the sponsorship of the National Committee for a Free Europe, a 'Freedom Tank' toured the United States. Onlookers were entreated to place donations inside the armoured car in which eight Czechs had careened to 'freedom' (Fried 1998, 48). Americans were also exposed to the drama of these breakouts through escapee memoirs such as Peter Pirogov's *Why I Escaped* (1950), Vladimir Petrov's *My Retreat from Russia* (1950), and Louis Fischer's collection, *Thirteen Who Fled* (1949), all of which detailed the grim conditions behind the Iron Curtain and the hair-raising details of escapes. These exploits were also represented in cinema, in films such as *The Journey* (1959) and *Man on a Tightrope* (1953). These dramatic stories acted as an entry point for US citizens into what Fried (1998) termed Cold War 'pageantry'. Further, such portrayals arguably served to spread prescriptive knowledge about hijacking of commercial aircraft by Soviet escapees among the wider US public.

Indeed, because most hijackers were seen as seeking to flee 'evil communism' across the Iron Curtain, these actions were initially viewed as nonthreatening, a perception the US Department of State carefully cultivated. Indeed, the Cold War predisposition to look the other way when hijackings involved émigrés originating from despised regimes effectively sent the message that those committing this offence to escape communism would be given political exemption and would not be subject to extradition.

The United States took a similar attitude to exiles from Cuba, which also contributed to the spread of prescriptive knowledge about hijacking among Americans. The Dwight D. Eisenhower administration welcomed these Cuban exiles, recognizing their potential use as political weapons against Castro's regime. This prompted Castro to accuse the United States of playing politics with Cuban migrants by welcoming as 'heroes' those who were considered 'enemies and traitors' of the Cuban state (Masud-Piloto 2014, 139). Indeed, the US policy towards Cuban émigrés in the immediate aftermath of the Cuban Revolution was modelled on its attitude towards émigrés from the Soviet Union. The John F. Kennedy administration similarly determined that welcoming refugees from Cuba, especially trained professionals, would accelerate the revolution's demise, embarrass the regime at home and abroad, and create a crippling brain drain within Cuba. To support these efforts, the federal government publicly emphasized Cuban exiles' rapid adjustment to living in the United States, as well as their gratitude at being welcomed into a democratic society (Gero 1997, 18; Arey 1972, 317). Émigrés who arrived in the United States via hijacked planes or stolen boats were lauded by the US press as exemplifying the failures of Cuban revolutionary experiments and the extreme desire of Cubans to escape the yoke of communism.

Given the widespread publicity the technique received, it is unsurprising that it gained a place in Americans' repertoire of contention and that hijackers began diverting US flights to Cuba and elsewhere, and in May 1961, the first hijacking going from the United States to Cuba (excepting the 1958 hijacking of CU-T603 committed by Castro's men described in the previous chapter) was perpetrated by Antulio Ortiz, a US citizen. Ortiz would later be affectionately nicknamed 'Numero Uno' by the Cuban press (Gero 1997, 18; Arey 1972, 317). Ortiz, who harboured pro-Castro sentiments, stated that the hijacking was in retaliation for the multiple Cuban planes diverted to the United States and not returned to the Cuban government (*Miami News* 1961).

The efforts by successive US administrations to popularize hijackings as a means of destabilizing their foes had clearly backfired. This is perhaps most saliently evidenced by a particularly intensive wave of hijacking between 1968 and 1973, which seemed to have been sparked by three hijackings that occurred in quick succession and were extensively covered in the US media, therefore spreading new propositional knowledge about hijacking among the US public. The first of the three initial hijackings that garnered incredible media attention in the United States took place on 9 February 1968, when a marine private attempted a hijacking of a US military charter flight out of South Vietnam (Phillips 1973, 271). Eight days later, on 17 February 1968, a private plane from Miami was diverted to Cuba (Evans and Murphy 1978). Then on 21 February 1968, an alleged murderer hijacked a Delta DC-8 flight from Tampa to Palm Beach, diverting the flight to Havana to escape justice, the first successful hijacking of a US commercial jetliner. During the following period, between 1968 and 1973, at least eighty-eight commercial or private aircraft originating from the United States were hijacked and diverted to Cuba.

Analysing the demographics of perpetrators fleeing to Cuba between 1968 and 1972, Holden (1986) provides interesting insights into individuals' motivations. According to Holden, approximately 30 percent were either Cubans or Hispanics 'merely seeking transportation home' in the face of a travel ban to Cuba enforced by the State Department (p. 882). The second-largest group, representing another 20 percent, were 'Black Americans, who committed the hijackings during a period of militant civil rights activities', which involved claims for the creation of a black nation and anti-Vietnam war sentiment (pp. 882–83). The remaining 50 percent included an assortment of individuals and groups with a wide-ranging set of claims or motivations, including those protesting the Vietnam War, perceived colonialist and imperialist injustice, and those seeking to support Castro's communist revolution (Holden, 1986).

The Cuban Revolution had a profound influence on early ideologies of the black nationalist movement in the United States (Von Eschen 1997; Reitan 1999), which largely explains the transmission of the technique across the Gulf of Mexico. This included envisioning Cuba as a haven from US white supremacy and as an opportunity to forge political connections with African diasporic and global anticolonial movements. As such, black nationalists constituted a disproportionate number of Cuba-bound hijackers, arguably motivated in part by their perceptions of Cuba's racial project. Interestingly, this paralleled previous notions of Cuba by US Pan-Africanists, who understood the island nation as a vital part of the African diaspora, whose fate was bound up with that of black Americans (Latner 2015). As Guridy (2010) and Brock and Castañeda Fuertes (1998) argue, the movements of people of African descent between Cuba and the United States early and in the mid-twentieth century influenced black nationalism in the United States long before Cuba's revolution. Following the Cuban Revolution, Cuba's new government institutionalized structural changes that channelled the nation's material wealth and human capital into a socialist system and soon enshrined education, health care, and housing as universal human rights to which all Cubans, irrespective of race, were entitled. This move bolstered the nation's reputation as a racially egalitarian 'haven' from US-style Jim Crow racism. Cuba's official endorsement of black American tourism to a land 'free of racism' was supported by guests such as boxing legend Joe Louis. Furthermore, Castro's famed stay at Harlem's Hotel Theresa in 1960, where he met with Malcolm X – and the Cuban leader's strongly worded denunciation of racism in the United States – contributed to the island's appeal as a Caribbean sanctuary from de facto racial apartheid (Latner 2015, 31–32).[5]

Moreover, Cuba's image as a sanctuary for black nationalists was closely related to the revolutionary government's propensity to grant asylum to Americans.[6] In fact, so influential was Cuba's reputation as a sanctuary and a haven from extradition to the United States that rioting prisoners at the Attica Correctional Facility in New York in 1971 requested safe passage to Cuba or another 'non-imperialist' nation as one of their demands (Latner 2015, 23). This perception informed popular understandings of the Cuban Revolution among Americans well into the late 1960s and early 1970s and provided a framework for hijackers to articulate their actions within the context of the racial and social upheaval of the period. Despite this, a considerably small amount of critical attention has been devoted to the relationship between the black nationalist movement and Cuba after 1961. Moreover, although hijacking became a highly mediatized form of contention by black nationalists, only one published work devotes significant attention to this issue (see Latner 2015). Instead, much of the academic scholarship on hijackings to Cuba between 1968 and 1973 has been limited by an unwillingness to treat the hijackers as anything more than mentally ill idealists and common criminals.

4.3 SELECTION: LEGITIMIZING 'FREEDOM FLIGHTS'

To properly understand how and why hijacking entered into and spread within Soviet and Cuban escapees' repertoire of contention, and later that of black nationalists, it is crucial to more deeply examine the propositional knowledge created by Western states' response to the technique.

In addition to Western governments intentionally drawing public attention to so-called 'freedom flights' from the Soviet Union and Cuba, they also hastily reconfigured legal statutes and instruments to facilitate the escapees in a legislative sense. This required adjustments to both domestic and international law. Domestically, US immigration legislation was amended to allow the selective opening of its national borders to escapees (Loescher and Scanlan 1986). Internationally, the international refugee regime was solidified to 'duly privilege victims of political oppression over others who were pushed from, or elected to leave, their countries of citizenship' (Carruthers 2005, 912). However, in the absence of international law and agreement between the democratic West and the communist East on the issue, informal norms were developed, and individual countries' legal systems were left to ponder appropriate responses to hijacking.

Largely motivated by the enmity between Western states and the Soviet Union, the former tended to treat hijackers as victims of political persecution, much to the dismay of the Soviet Union, whose position was one of 'peremptory extradition', whereby the plane, passengers, and hijackers should be automatically returned to the state of origin (Sweet 2002). Moreover, since these hijackings typically resulted in neither loss of life nor financial gain, receiving countries generally sought to 'assert [their] sovereign right to grant asylum to political refugees' and were unwilling 'to prosecute the hijackers and refused to surrender fugitives to other states' (Joyner 1974, 4). A norm developed, therefore, in which Western aircrews, carriers and even governments would not seek to resist hijackers actively, provided that they did not endanger the survival of the aircraft or threaten harm to the passengers. This norm, which would later form the basis for the Havana Rules was further entrenched by a legal case pertaining to the 1951 hijacking of a Yugoslavian

National Airlines domestic flight by the pilot and co-pilot, who diverted the plane to Zurich. The Swiss High Court hearing the case ruled that:

> the important juridical principle is enunciated that the choice of means to effectuate a hijacking can indeed control this legitimacy of ends sought to be attained, to the point where impermissible means involving, for example, unnecessary or disproportionate use of force could operate to vitiate a claimed political objective altogether. (McWhinney 1975, 65–66)

This politicized inconsistency between the democratic West and the communist East, and the general acceptance of hijacking as a legitimate means of political activity within the Western world, would arguably later be used as a model of argumentation by others who emulated it against the West. Whether future hijackers were specifically aware of the intricacies of this ruling is arguably irrelevant; more important is that they saw the effects of it in the refusal of Western states to extradite their predecessors.

By publicizing the exploits of escapees, including those who employed hijacking – and by refusing to extradite them – an important body of propositional knowledge about the anticipated reaction of authorities within Western states was established and extensively transmitted throughout Western countries: namely, that hijacking would not trigger a violent response by the authorities under certain conditions and, provided that the crew, plane, and passengers were unharmed, hijackers could expect to be treated as asylum seekers. In this sense, early successes by defectors of the Soviet Union to the West, along with their treatment by the West (which rarely involved prosecutions or reprimand), clearly motivated emulations of the technique in the following decades.

This change in propositional knowledge – whereby Western states would praise rather than punish the non-violent, politically motivated theft of vehicles by escapees – was exacerbated further by the US response to the exodus of former government officials and Batista loyalists following the Cuban Revolution. According to McWhinney (1975, 65–66) Cuban hijackers escaping communist Cuba were treated in a similar fashion to their Eastern European counterparts, building on the implicit norms established as a result of the wave of hijackings in Eastern Europe during the 1950s by individuals seeking to leave the Iron Curtain, norms that were reinforced by the 1952 Swiss Federal Supreme Court ruling. They received only nominal sanctions, provided they followed the informal Havana Rules, which stipulated that: (i) The hijackers were fleeing a government they deemed oppressive, and (ii) no passengers or aircrew would be injured or otherwise mistreated. Indeed, flight crew members were often instructed not to resist armed hijackers – largely out of consideration for the safety of their passengers but also because of implicit support of escapees.

Following the introduction of security guards on board Cubana flights, and the subsequent violent altercations between hijackers and these security guards, the lack of prosecution indicates that US authorities deemed any injury to security forces or uncooperative flight crew exculpable if the seizure succeeded and the plane and passengers were neither endangered nor destroyed (McWhinney 1975, 69). In other words, propositional knowledge emerged that, as long as the United States held the departure state of any hijacked aeroplane in greater opprobrium than they did the act of hijacking itself, hijackers were likely to be granted asylum and to evade prosecution.

The rather permissive approach developed during the waves of immigration out of Eastern Europe and Cuba had a profound effect in terms of legitimizing hijacking. In relation to this study's theoretical framework, the effective deployment of a technique is only one of three variables, along with legitimacy and feasibility, necessary for its further emulation. By failing to prosecute hijackers rapidly and harshly – or at all in many cases – and instead hastily reconfiguring legal statutes and instruments to facilitate escapees, the authorities added to the existing bodies of propositional and prescriptive knowledge by delineating the criteria for a successful hijacker, making the technique more feasible. Further, and perhaps more importantly, this attitude constituted a de facto recognition by the West of this technique as a legitimate means of escaping a regime deemed oppressive. With this additional propositional knowledge about the perceived legitimacy of the technique, and keenly aware of the prescriptive knowledge necessary to deploy it, claim-makers within the United States quickly adopted hijacking for their own ends.

Among black nationalists, hijacking was executed or articulated in such a manner as to transform what might otherwise have been viewed as attempts at escaping criminal charges or acts of extortion, into acts of overt claim-making. In part, this occurred as a result of increased awareness of hijackings as an effective technique through which to gain concrete political demands. For example, later recounting his hijacking and diversion to Cuba of an Eastern Airline flight between Atlanta and Miami, Lorenzo Kombu Ervin, a member of the Black Panther Party, framed his actions as an act of political protest:

> Since the FBI was going all over the country looking for me, I had only two choices available: go underground in the U.S. or get out of the country. . . . Because there were so many plane hijackings going on at this time, I hit on the idea of commandeering an aircraft to fly me to Cuba for political asylum. . . . I wanted it to be known by the passengers that this hijacking was a political act, so I planned to pass out a statement explaining my actions. I had anti-war leaflets printed by an underground printing company, which I planned to take aboard the plane. I also drafted an application letter to formally request the Cuban government to grant me asylum on the grounds of political persecution

in the United States and racial oppression. . . . I went into the restroom shortly after takeoff, checked my gun to be sure it was loaded, and then went into the aisle where I stated to both passengers and crew in my most dramatic voice that the airplane was being hijacked: 'This aircraft is being commandeered by cadre of the Black Liberation Movement. I will not hurt any of you, do not panic. This is an armed protest action against the U.S. war in Vietnam and the domestic war against black America. We are going to Cuba, please do not interfere'. (Keynen and Rhodes 2012, 403–4)

Ervin's choice to frame his action as part of the larger black nationalist social movement is in no way unique. As aforementioned, black nationalists frequently saw Cuba as a symbol to further their revolutionary struggle, with Havana functioning as an imaginary transnational space in which African Americans and other revolutionaries could forge links with a radical global public as a result of the presence of representatives from Third World political movements. In addition to ideological alignment, black nationalists hoped that Cuba would provide them with a location in which to volunteer or receive guidance and practical instruction to further their cause back home. Indeed, William Lee Brent (2000), a member of the Black Panthers, successfully hijacked an Oakland to New York flight while on bail on 17 June 1969 and diverted it to Cuba. Brent later recounted: Black nationalists 'came with stars in their eyes, hoping the Cubans would train them in guerrilla warfare, arm them, and sneak them back to the States to engage in armed struggle' (p. 235).

However, the arrival of hijackers affiliated with black nationalism presented a delicate situation for the Cuban government. While Cuba remained committed to a position of support for black nationalist groups such as the Black Panther Party, and 'did of course use the incidents to embarrass the US government internationally' (Reitan 1999, 92), the Cuban government began to find the stream of hijackings economically costly and politically unhelpful in terms of normalizing their relations with Latin American countries. Most problematic of all though, was the potential security risk these incoming flights posed:

[The] risks were high since Cuban [officials] did not know if these planes were on a mission to attack the Island (à la Bay of Pigs) if they carried CIA or FBI spies posing as U.S. dissidents, or if they brought genuine fighters fleeing the United States for political reasons. (Reitan 1999, 92)

As such, although the Castro regime was routinely vilified in the US press for encouraging hijackings, and US imperialism was likewise pilloried in Havana's rhetoric, once their ideological excitement dissipated, black nationalists experienced 'some justifiable confusion and frustration' once they landed in Cuba (Reitan 1999, 92).

Upon arrival, hijackers 'received a surprisingly hostile welcome', which included 'interrogation by Cuban intelligence followed by temporary incarceration' until a determination could be made as to their identities and motives, followed by 'forcible evacuation to work camps' (Reitan 1999, 92, 107). This practice demonstrated the clear tension between Havana's public rhetoric of 'Cuba as a revolutionary haven for all oppressed black [revolutionaries] who could get there' and the regime's belief that 'air piracy' was 'a chronic security threat' because the black nationalist movement was 'so permeated with FBI and CIA agents that trusting unknown asylum-seekers could prove quite dangerous' (Reitan 1999, 92, 107). Citing a general 'climate of insecurity . . . in air and ocean navigation' caused by rampant hijacking, the Cuban government issued *Law No. 1226*, stipulating that hijackers could be held 'criminally liable under Cuban laws' and could be prosecuted in Cuba or extradited to the United States. This law, along with the *Cuba-United States Memorandum of Understanding on Hijacking of Aircraft and Vessels and Other Offenses*, signed on 25 February 1973 (which will be discussed in more detail in chapter 6), changed propositional knowledge about the fate of hijackers landing in Cuba and, therefore, led to a dramatic decline in hijackings originating in the United States in the mid-1970s.

Although Cuba had won the battle for African American public opinion since 1959, media coverage of Cuba-bound hijackings between 1968 and 1973 ultimately provided the US government with a rare triumph in its image war against Cuba in relation to the question of racial equality coverage of the hijackings in the United States: Cuba was no longer framed as a racially egalitarian utopia. In addition, black nationalist hijackers were portrayed in the media as psychopathic criminals running from justice, even when they articulated claims of political repression. In doing so, the media stripped the actions of black nationalist hijackers of political meaning and agency, which perhaps goes some way to explaining why so little scholarly attention has been devoted to these hijackings. Similarly, the lack of scholarly attention to the wider political meaning of 'freedom flights' committed by individuals wishing to escape the yolk of communism explains why these incidents, despite their crucial importance to the ever-shifting existing propositional and prescriptive knowledge surrounding hijacking and its transmission, have been largely ignored by the wider body of terrorism and aviation security literature. Incidents involving non-politically motivated hijackings committed by criminals (discussed in chapter 6) have also been largely ignored within this body of literature because of their lack of politicization, despite how influential these events have been on the evolution of the technique. Overall, what emerges as important in the evolution of hijacking as a technique of contention is not the motivation of the individual actor or group; rather, what emerges as most influential is what they contribute to the prescriptive knowledge – through their innovations – and the creation of new propositional knowledge of society by virtue of the responses their actions receive from the media and governments with which they interact.

NOTES

1. Approximately 125,000 Cubans reached the United States between January 1959 and March 1961, including 14,000 unaccompanied children, who arrived under the auspices of Operation Peter Pan (Pedraza 2001, 413).

2. On 16 April 1959, a flight from Havana to Isle of Pines, Cuba, was diverted to Miami by four gunmen. Nine days later, on 26 April 1959, four hijackers, including a general who had served under Batista, hijacked a domestic Cuban flight; they demanded to be taken to Miami, but settled for Key West due to a fuel shortage. On 2 October 1959, a Cubana flight from Havana to Santiago de Cuba was diverted to Miami. On 12 April 1960, three crew members and an accomplice hijacked a domestic Cubana flight and landed in Miami, where they set fire to the four engines. On 5 August 1960, a pilot and co-pilot diverted a Madrid-bound flight from Havana, Cuba, to Miami. Two weeks later, another pilot hijacked a Cubana flight from Havana to Varadero, landing in Fort Lauderdale. On 28 August 1960, the pilot of a domestic Cubana flight, along with two accomplices, rerouted a plane to the United States. On 29 October 1960, a security guard was shot and killed during the hijacking of a Cubana flight, which was diverted to Key West. On 8 December 1960, five individuals attempted to hijack a Domestic Cubana flight; however, after a gun battle, which resulted in one death, the plane crash-landed at Cienfuegos Airport. The hijackers were condemned to death by the Castro regime. Another Cubana flight was diverted to the United States on 14 April 1961. On 3 July 1961, eleven men and three women successfully hijacked a Cubana flight to Varadero and rerouted it to Miami, wounding the on-board security officer. Lastly, on 9 August 1961, five Batista loyalists hijacked an Aerovias flight from Havana to the Isles of Pines and diverted it to Miami, killing the pilot and two others and injuring six more.

3. According to Organista (2007), the extreme fear of Marielitos among Americans is best exemplified by Brian De Palma's 1983 remake of the classic James Cagney gangster film *Scarface*: 'The updated version begins with footage of the Mariel boatlift, followed by the detention centre interrogation of Tony Montana, a Marielito criminal played by Al Pacino. The rest of the film depicts Tony's violent rise as a cocaine drug lord who flaunts a buxom Anglo-American girlfriend, buries his face in a mountain of cocaine piled on his desk, and wields a bazooka-size gun while screaming, "You want to fuck with me?!" in a feeble Cuban accent' (p. 32). Organista (2007) argues that 'America's almost neurotic overreaction and restrictiveness' resulted in Marielitos protesting violently during the 1980s (p. 32).

4. Under the provision of the Yalta Conference of 1945, British and US authorities agreed to and assisted in delivering – at gunpoint where necessary – more than two million people into Soviet custody, including several thousand Russians who had never been Soviet citizens, along with many individuals who feared, and not without reason, that they would swiftly be dispatched to the gulags (Carruthers 2005, 915).

5. As argued by Reitan (1999), 'the Cubans saw an opportunity emerging in the United States to call international attention to the race riots and violence against Blacks, which was reaching boiling point. Beginning at that time and continuing for the next five years, talk of racial war and the impending Black-led revolution was commonplace in the Cuban media; it was here that the image was planted in the hearts and minds of Black militants that a racial paradise had been born in the Caribbean' (p. 24).

6. In 1961, the chapter president of the National Association for the Advancement of Colored People (NAACP) for Monroe, North Carolina, and a promoter of the 'armed self-defense' doctrine, along with his wife, had obtained asylum in Cuba after fleeing kidnapping charges (Tyson 2009). In the late 1960s, several other prominent black nationalists, such as Robert Williams, Huey P. Newton, Eldridge Cleaver and Stokely Carmichael, would also seek asylum in Cuba (Reitan 1999).

Chapter Five

The Global Impact of Palestinian Hijackings

Events in the Middle East in the late 1960s and throughout the 1970s forever transformed global aviation security and the way hijacking was understood because of how overtly politicized, mediatized, and at times violent, these events were. As Guelke (1995) notes, this led to a change in attitude toward hijacking – and hijackers – globally:

> Once Palestinian groups resorted to hijacking for the purpose of hostage-taking, attitudes towards hijacking for any purpose tended to harden, and in particular, the somewhat jocular view that had been taken of hijacking between America and Cuba in the early 1960s became a thing of the past. (p. 49)

As well as overlooking this shift from a cavalier view to a harsher perspective, scholarship on hijacking and in the field of terrorism studies more broadly has tended to exaggerate the initial adoption of hijacking by Palestinian claim-makers as an innovative breakthrough devoid of any historical antecedents. The ahistorical treatment of these events – and of other techniques of contention – has permeated terrorism studies and has been coupled with a predilection for a selective use of historical cases, often seemingly chosen specifically to reinforce preconceived ideas or to suit the predetermined needs of scholars. This has contributed to a failure to consider the wider contexts and the mechanisms that drive the spread and acceptance of new techniques of political violence. In fact, many scholars cite the adoption of hijacking by Palestinian groups as the origin of the modern era of transnational terrorism (Sandler 2005; Chaliand 1977; Hoffman 2013). This is due in part to the exploitation of 'the full impact of modern technology', which 'endowed . . . individuals or members of small groups' with 'capacities they never had before' (Rapoport 1989, xii), with disregard for previous iterations that also clearly fully exploited modern aeroplane technology. Similarly, Tucker (1997) also argues that the nature of hijacking changed drastically in the aftermath of El Al Flight 426. Indeed, while Tucker concedes that aeroplane hijackings were not uncommon prior to the El Al Flight 426 incident, he argues that 'these were not generally or consistently called terrorism; nor were those who committed them generally or consistently called terrorists', but instead that hijackers were called 'bandits, rebels, guerrillas, or later, urban guerrillas, revolutionaries, or insurgents' (p. 2). While this does indicate a shift in attitude towards hijackers, it does not provide convincing evidence that the technique itself underwent any significant change.

As demonstrated in previous chapters, claim-makers had a long history of hijacking aeroplanes to advance political agendas prior to 1968. Therefore, instead of positioning the El Al Flight 426 incident as the origin of modern hijacking, I will instead consider the adoption of hijacking by Palestinian groups as significant for two reasons. First, in the *variation* section of this chapter I argue that the adoption of hijacking by the Palestinian liberation movement, particularly the Popular Front for the Liberation of Palestine (PFLP) and its splinter groups, led to a period of rapid variation. This strain of hijacking represents a period of rapid variation in aeroplane hijackings, as claim-makers responded to countermeasures introduced by airlines and governments with increasingly innovative means to advance their claims. In the *transmission* section of this chapter, I address the question of diffusion and its influences in more detail, contending that the highly visible and publicized nature of these hijackings and attacks had the profound impact of rapidly diffusing hijacking. As a result, the technique was transmitted from the Palestinian liberation movement's repertoire of contention to that of other social movements worldwide. Finally, in the *selection* section of this chapter, I investigate why – despite the tremendous amount of publicity surrounding Palestinian hijackings and the rapid transmission of the hijacking to other social movements – the adoption of hijacking was far from universal, with some groups eschewing the technique as a result of perceived high constituency costs, ideological issues, or consecutive failures when attempting to replicate Palestinian approaches.

5.1 VARIATION: RAPID INNOVATIONS IN THE FACE OF A DETERMINED ADVERSARY

Following Israel's decisive victory during the Six-Day War against Egypt, Jordan, and Syria in 1967, Israel's occupation of the Gaza Strip, West Bank, Golan Heights, and Sinai caused despair and paralysis among Palestinians (Krause 2017, 147–48). As a consequence, the Palestinian resistance (including the Palestine Liberation Organization [PLO], in general, and Fatah in particular) gained a reputation as the only political actors able to redress the balance following the Arab military failure. Recognizing that their desire for liberation would not be achieved by the armies of Arab states, the PLO moved its operations within refugee camps and attempted to act as a legitimate authority.[1] Within this context, the armed struggle against 'Zionist colonisation' increasingly became a 'source of political legitimacy and national identity, the new substance of the "imagined community" of the Palestinians' (Sayigh 1999, 196). This allowed the PLO to gain popularity with large swathes of Palestinians who saw them, if not as ideal, then as perhaps their only means of emancipation from their perceived oppressors.

Faced with Israel's undeniable military superiority, the PLO opted for the Vietnamese and Cuban models of guerrilla warfare, seeking to turn the Middle East into a 'second Vietnam' (Chamberlin 2011, 21). 'By casting themselves as liberation fighters', writes historian Paul Chamberlin (2011), the PLO hoped to access 'networks of international support emanating from revolutionary centers like Beijing, Algiers, Hanoi, and Havana and [to] become a focus of international press' (pp. 21, 41). In addition to the PLO, the PFLP – which was formed by a merger between several organizations – also resorted to a guerrilla warfare strategy (Schweitzer 2011).

Addressing the PFLP leadership in 1967, Wadie Haddad, then leader of the group's military wing, explained the rationale behind adopting guerrilla operations:

> Trying to get men and weapons across Jordan into Israel is a waste of time and effort. Armed struggle of that type will never achieve the liberation of Palestine. . . . We have to hit the Israeli army in a qualitative way, not a quantitative way. This is a particular animal, the IDF; we cannot fight it plane for plane, tank for tank, soldier for soldier. We have to hit the Israelis at the weak joints. . . . What do I mean by the weak joints? I mean spectacular, one-off operations. These spectacular operations will focus the world's attention on the problem of Palestine. The world will ask, 'What the hell is the problem in Palestine? Who are these Palestinians? Why are they doing these things?' At the same time, such operations will be highly painful for the Israelis. High-profile, sensational operations, carried out by thoroughly trained people in secure underground structures – this is how we shall hit at the painful joints. In the end, the world will get fed up with its problem; it will decide it has to do something about Palestine. It will have to give us justice. (Mahnaimi and Abū Sharīf 1995, 59–60)

Elaborating on this shift in strategy, Haddad explained that the main idea was to employ a new technique: the hijacking of an El Al airliner and holding its passengers and crew hostage in exchange for prisoners held in Israel. According to Haddad, if such an operation failed to gain the attention of the international media, then the likelihood was that nothing would: 'It shouldn't be necessary to use actual violence. We don't even have to hit Israeli targets all the time. But we must be a constant irritation, a bug under the skin of the developed world. We must make them lose patience with Israel and Palestine that hard way' (Mahnaimi and Abū Sharīf 1995, 59–60). Although the deployment of a new technique within the context of the Palestinian liberation movement would not ultimately precipitate Israel's downfall, it would, as Haddad argued, draw sufficient international attention to the Palestinian plight to force a resolution (Schweitzer 2011).

The Inspiration for the Hijacking of El Al Flight 426

The hijackings committed by the PFLP (and its splinter groups) involved the synthesis of three pre-existing innovations: (i) the internationalization of the conflict, as mentioned previously, (ii) hijackings elsewhere, notably in North and Central America, and (iii) politically motivated kidnappings, such as the 1967 kidnapping of exiled former Congolese President Moise Tshombe by Francis-Joseph Bodenan.

According to Phillips (1973) the kidnapping of Tshombe was important in that it not only represented 'the first time a passenger was held captive as a result of a skyjack and used as a political bargaining counter', but it also gave the PFLP 'the idea of kidnap by skyjacking for political extortion' (p. 102). On 30 June 1967, a British-owned and operated HS 125, en route from Palma de Mallorca to Ibiza, Spain, was diverted at gunpoint to Algiers, Algeria, by Francis-Joseph Bodenan, the man who had chartered the aircraft (Phillips 1973, 103). On board was the exiled former Congolese President Moise Tshombe, who was then imprisoned by the Algerian government on landing, in an apparent effort to pre-empt and quell an incipient Katanga revolt (Gibbs 1991). The hijacking and subsequent kidnapping and detention of Tshombe provoked a major international dispute. Although the Congolese government demanded that Algeria extradite him to Congo, where he would be quickly executed on his return, the Algerians resisted the extradition demands and continued his imprisonment. After two years of continued imprisonment, Algerian authorities announced Tshombe's death from an apparent heart attack. As a result of Tshombe's pro-Western leanings and his alleged connection with the death of Patrice Lumumba, the first democratically elected prime minister of Congo, this kidnapping received extensive press coverage.

Phillips (1973) suggests that Haddad's decision to adopt aeroplane hijacking was in part attributable to this high-profile hijacking, which occurred only twenty days after the Arab-Israeli ceasefire. Interestingly, despite strong evidence of Algeria's involvement, Algeria received no diplomatic or legal punishment for their detention of Tshombe (Rousseau 1967; McWhinney 1975, 12). This lack of punitive action is significant, considering that the PFLP chose to land in Algeria during the hijacking of El Al Flight 426, seeing it as a safe haven, which will be discussed in more detail later in the chapter.

Akin to subsequent operations perpetrated by the PFLP and its splinter groups, the technique employed during the kidnapping of Tshombe offered many of the advantages of a barricade hostage situation, with several additional benefits. First, the hijackers were able to relocate from a site surrounded by hostile security forces to a friendly territory (Dolnik 2007). Second, during the late 1960s (as discussed in the previous chapter), the hijacking of an aeroplane was achievable with minimal force, as demonstrated by the fact that successful hijack weapons globally included items such as razor blades, coloured water, sharpened toothbrushes, rope, dining knives, and cigarette lighters. Lastly, the nature of a flight obviates concerns regarding hostage escaping or potential rescue missions (Dolnik 2007, 32).

The Hijacking of El Al Flight 426

At the outset of its armed campaign after the Six-Day War in 1967 there was a shift in the propositional knowledge, which, it is argued, formed the epistemic base for the adoption of hijacking by the PFLP. That the kidnapping of Tshombe so closely coincided with this shift in the PFLP's understanding of their adversary adds credence to the argument that Tshombe's kidnapping inspired the PFLP in their hijacking of El Al Flight 426.

The PFLP's cross-border attacks into Israel from neighbouring Jordan (the PFLP's primary base) at the outset of its armed campaign after the Six-Day War, were both fruitless and inordinately costly, leading to a change in how the PFLP understood their adversary. As Israel grew adept at intercepting fighters by establishing a robust anti-infiltration system, including infrared and sonic detection devices, fences, mines, and patrols via land and air, Palestinian claim-makers quickly acquired the propositional knowledge that they could not effectively fight within Israel, nor could they penetrate deeply enough from the outside to inflict any real damage on Israeli territory. Therefore, these cross-border attack techniques were deemed unfeasible. Moreover, these techniques involved high constituency costs because Israel's reprisals targeted the PFLP's host nations, namely Jordan and Lebanon.

These selection pressures in and of themselves would have been sufficient to winnow out cross-border raids in favour of other more feasible and less costly techniques. However, the selection pressures were further increased by the ineffectiveness of cross-border attacks, which did not garner sufficient international attention for the Palestinian predicament. These multiple selection pressures, combined with changes in their PFLP's propositional knowledge of their adversary made changes in technique inevitable, as summed up by Abu-Sharif and Mahnaimi (1995):

Given the Palestinians' inability to meaningfully strike within Israel, Haddad argued that the fight should not be confined to Israel but [should] rather span the global, targeting Israeli interests abroad. Not only would the PFLP seek to thereby exploit Israel's relative weakness abroad, but it also would draw worldwide attention to the Palestinians' plight and internationalize the conflict. (pp. 59–60)

In such an attempt to exploit Israel's relative weakness abroad and to draw international attention to the Palestinian predicament, the PFLP carried out the first hijacking of a commercial flight departing from or destined for the Middle East on 23 July 1968, when three PFLP hijackers seized an El Al Flight 426 travelling from Rome to Tel Aviv. Armed with pistols and hand grenades, the hijackers entered the cockpit, assaulted the co-pilot, and ordered Captain Oded Abardanell to divert the plane to Algiers (Taillon 2002, 17). In a new variation on the existing technique of hijacking, the PFLP demanded the release of Palestinian militants detained in Israel in exchange for the hostages on board, in the hope of forcing Israel to recognize and negotiate with Palestinian claim-makers (Hoffman 2006, 63).

While the El Al Flight 426 incident is certainly significant in that it is the first instance of a hijacking of a commercial flight in the Middle East, and as the first instance of hijacking as a means to initiate prisoner release, many scholars have overstated its distinction from previous examples of hijacking. For example, Hoffman (2006) argues that the hijacking of El Al Flight 426 was unique and significant because it represented the first time a plane was hijacked to make 'a bold political statement' instead of 'simply the diversion of a scheduled flight from one destination to another – as had been the case since [the] seemingly endless succession of homesick Cubans or sympathetic revolutionaries from other countries had commandeered domestic American passenger aircraft simply as a means to travel to Cuba' (Hoffman 2006, 63). However, as I have argued, hijackings originating from Cuba or bound to Cuba, or those that took place within the context of the Cold War, cannot be simply divorced from their wider political meaning and context. That said, Hoffman does make an undeniably valid point regarding the 'boldness' of the claim-makers' statement; their grievances and aim to exchange their hostages for Palestinians imprisoned in Israel was clearly and directly articulated. However, Hoffman (2006) positions the PFLP's conscious targeting of El Al, Israel's national airline, in opposition to previous hijackings in which 'the choice or nationality of the aircraft that was being seized did not matter' (p. 55). This statement suggests a slight lack of historical perspective. As evidenced throughout this book, claim-makers have long understood the link between commercial aviation and nationalism since the beginning of commercial aviation and, as a result, had frequently targeted national carriers long before this event. In fact, this represented a cornerstone of Fidel Castro's campaign against the Fulgencio Batista regime through the use of Cubana and, to some extent, the hijacking campaign of pro-Luis Miguel Sánchez Cerro rebels in 1930s' Peru using Panagra. Moreover, hostage taking was far from a novel technique and was not even a new iteration of aeroplane hijacking as mentioned in the previous section.

Rather than overstating its novelty, then, we might attribute the significance of El Al Flight 426 to a near-perfect convergence of a series of factors: the clear articulation of political statement, the purposeful targeting of a specified 'enemy state', the holding of hostages, and the execution of the hijacking itself. Further, it is significant on the basis of facilitating the transmission of prescriptive knowledge held by the PFLP to claim-makers worldwide. Due to the extensive media coverage of this event, its details were widely diffused and it became understood that: (i) a group could seize a large group of hostages by seizing a controlled environment like an aircraft; (ii) seizing an aircraft inflight meant no entry or exit was immediately possible and that the movement and behaviour of hostages could be closely monitored by a handful of people; (iii) the potential consequences of a government ignoring or rejecting the terrorists' demands could be obviously catastrophic; and, importantly, (iv) a group could essentially create a traveling 'theatre' that, due to the intense media coverage that attended such an event, could be used to attract and focus the world's attention on the plight of the passengers and, therefore, draw attention to the claim-makers' demands.

The PFLP's decision to target an El Al plane departing from Europe appears to have had three motivating factors. Firstly, based on existing propositional knowledge, Europe was seen as a 'soft entry point'. With tight operating margins, the profitability of this system was predicated on a 'flow through' model of tight connections at major international hubs, which – combined with increasingly large enplanement and crowded terminals – made the screening of passengers and detection of weapons difficult (Karber 2005, 831). Relatedly, there was a great deal of variability in the security measures of different European airports (Dierikx and Bouwens 1986). Secondly, Europe's geographical proximity to friendly Arab countries in North Africa or the Middle East was undoubtedly a factor, as previous hijackings in a North American context had shown that refuelling in hostile countries left hijacked planes vulnerable to intervention by security forces. Lastly, Western carriers had adopted the US non-confrontational 'Havana Rules' with El Al pilots instructed to meet hijackers' demands. Indeed, the pilot of Flight 426 later summarized this policy by stating, 'If an eighty-year-old woman had pointed a gun at me and demanded that I landed in her son-in-law's garden in Algeria, I would have complied' (Byman 2011, 42). However, in the aftermath of the 1968 hijacking, El Al quickly revisited this policy by hiring sky marshals on aeroplanes, introducing rigorous passenger searches and baggage screening, and training pilots in methods to disrupt a hijacking (Byman

2011, 42). In fact, one clear indicator of Israel's efficiency in quickly instituting measures to improve El Al security to deter future attacks is the fact that there were no other successful hijackings of El Al planes. This change in behaviour of the state forced the PFLP to further innovate, arguably contributing to the veritable cat-and-mouse game that ensued.

Ground Attacks and Destruction of Hijacked Aircrafts

Emboldened by their first success, and immediately responding to Israel's counter-hijacking measures, PFLP operatives further innovated on the existing prescriptive understanding of hijacking by deliberately operating outside the Havana Rules, both by endangering the lives of passengers and crews and by damaging aircraft. Two new innovations emerged: first, the deployment of ground attacks against El Al planes at European airports and later, the deliberate destruction of hijacked aircraft. These two innovations caught the attention of international community – still mostly operating under the propositional knowledge afforded by the Havana Rules – and showed them to be woefully unprepared.

On 26 December 1968, the Palestinian-Israeli conflict escalated from the previous form of hijacking, with its presumed 'civility' of negotiation, by attempting to deliberately damage a civilian plane without regard for the fact that it was full of passengers. Two Palestinians attacked an El Al Boeing 707 with grenades and submachine gun fire as it took off for New York from a layover in Athens, killing one mechanic and injuring two others. According to media reports, during the attack, the attackers 'fired about 25 bullets' and '[f]our incendiary hand grenades . . . against the engines', while 'one of [two men] scattered copies of a leaflet identifying them as members of "The Popular Front for the Liberation of Palestine"' (*Times* 1968a). In contrast to the hijacking of El Al Flight 426, the attackers were not concerned with a highly mediatized prisoner exchange but rather sought to garner international attention by targeting a symbol of Israel, an El Al flight.

Two days later, in response to the 26 December ground attack, Israeli commandos from the army's elite Sayeret Matkal forces launched 'Operation Gift', taking over Beirut International Airport (*Times* 1968b). The Israeli commandos then systematically destroyed all commercial aircraft belonging to Arab airlines at the airport by detonating explosive charges in the noses and undercarriage wheel wells of each aeroplane. The attack resulted in the destruction of thirteen planes, whose worth had been estimated by British insurers at $43.8 million (*Times* 1968c; Falk 1969, 417), sending a clear message to the supporters of the PFLP. This response established the pattern of action and reaction that would come to typify the relationship between the State of Israel and various Palestinian resistance organizations (and their supporters) for the next five decades.

By seemingly holding all Arab nations collectively responsible for PFLP actions, Israel significantly altered propositional knowledge for these states as well as Palestinian claimants: Arab states providing assistance to Palestinian hijackers would now incur significant retribution from Israel. In many ways, this contributed to Jordan's subsequent crack down on the PFLP and the PLO, which will be addressed in more detail in the next section.

Undeterred by this punitive treatment of their supporters, and perhaps inspired by it, the PFLP escalated their actions to the deliberate destruction of aircraft, along with the targeting of airports and airline offices. This technique entered the Palestinian repertoire of contention in full force during 1969 when on 18 February, El Al Flight 432, scheduled from Zurich to Tel Aviv, was attacked as it was taxiing. Four members of the PFLP, armed with assault rifles, incendiary grenades, and dynamite, mortally wounded the plane's co-pilot (Herf 2016, 116–18). On 8 September 1969, as part of a coordinated attack against Israeli embassies in Bonn, Brussels, and The Hague, the El Al office in Brussels was attacked with hand grenades (*Times* 1969). Another El Al office in Athens was attacked with hand grenades on 27 November 1969, resulting in one casualty and fifteen injuries, and a bomb was found in the El Al office in Berlin on 12 December 1969 (Herf 2016, 116–18). Similar attacks took place the following year: on 10 February 1970, the El Al counter at Munich-Riem Airport was attacked with hand grenades and other explosives; the El Al offices in Istanbul and in Tehran were both damaged by explosions on 25 April and 9 June, respectively; and explosives were mailed to the El Al office in London on 6 October (Herf 2016, 116–18).

Indeed, in addition to the aforementioned attacks, the PFLP bombed several European and Israeli targets throughout 1969, including Israeli-related businesses and a Marks and Spencer outlet in London (Herf 2016, 116–18). These attacks, with each target personally selected by Haddad, expanded the groups' plan to attract Western attention and built on its declared agenda of international revolution, focusing less exclusively on Israeli targets by broadening the movement's activities worldwide to take aim at the wider 'U.S.-led imperialistic world' (Schweitzer 2011).[2]

Expanding beyond El Al Flights

Innovating further, and as part of this wider campaign against the 'U.S.-led imperialistic world', the PFLP combined hijacking with the subsequent destruction of aircraft when two PFLP members seized a US TWA Flight 840 from Rome to Athens to Tel Aviv,[3] diverting the plane to Damascus, Syria, on 29 August 1969. Upon landing, the attackers forced the passengers to deplane and destroyed the cockpit using explosives provided by an accomplice on the ground. While the United States demanded that Syria arrange the release of all hostages, the Syrian regime refused – seeing an opportunity to use the PFLP's action for their own benefit – and instead permitted only a dozen crew members and ninety-three non-Israeli passengers to leave; an additional four Israeli passengers were released the following day, while the remaining two Israeli passengers were detained until December when they were released in return for seventy-one Syrian and Egyptian soldiers held by Israel (Schweitzer 2011; Naftali 2005, 35–36).

This incident marked a shift from exclusively targeting El Al flights, which the PFLP had justified as legitimate by insisting that the airline was not really a civilian target but rather, as George Habash, Secretary-General of the PFLP, often argued, 'a military objective because it transports military personnel and material' (Cooley 2015, 146). Instead, as the changing security environment made the hijacking of El Al planes increasingly unfeasible, the PFLP chose to target other Western aircrafts. The PFLP rationalized this broadening of targets to include other airlines by pointing out their role in both supporting Israeli 'imperialist' interests and in connecting Israel with the rest of the world (Sayigh 1999, 214).

The Dawson's Field Hijacking

By 1970, the PFLP had nearly tripled in size and significantly upgraded its capabilities and was therefore able to successfully conduct operations which would previously have been unfeasible for the group. This organizational growth was put on full display when the PFLP once again targeted Western airlines as part of their so-called 'Airplane Operation', its most specular undertaking to date (Schweitzer 2011). The Airplane Operation, typically referred to as the Dawson's Field hijackings (Dierikx and Bouwens 1986, 163), initially intended to hijack three aeroplanes all en route to New York – a destination arguably chosen to maximize the illocutionary effect and there-fore the effectiveness of the action – and to land all the planes at an isolated strip in Jordan.

This plan was built on the PFLP's previous hijacking successes, most recently the 22 July 1970 hijacking of an Olympic Airway Boeing 727 from Beirut to Athens. In that incident, the hijackers successfully negotiated the release of seven Palestinians held in Greek jails in exchange for the passen-gers after landing in Athens; this included the release of perpetrators of three prior attacks against Israeli aircraft and installations on Greek soil (for which the attackers had already been condemned under Greek law). The rapidity of the Greek government's response in striking a deal added to the PFLP's propositional knowledge. Indeed, international law scholars claim that this propositional knowledge on the effectiveness of hijacking in procuring con-cessions from states emboldened Palestinian groups in the run-up to the Airplane Operation (Rousseau 1970; McWhinney 1975).

The Airplane Operation was launched on 6 September 1970, when TWA Flight 742, departing from Frankfurt with 144 passengers and 11 crew members, and Swiss Air Flight 100, departing from Zurich with 143 passengers and 12 crew members, were successfully hijacked (Schweitzer 2011). However, the hijacking of the third plane, El Al Flight 219 from Amsterdam, did not go as planned. Haddad's plot called for four operatives to carry out the hijacking and, although Leila Khaled and Patrick Argüello – the latter a member of the Sandinista National Liberation Front – managed to board the plane, posing as a married couple, the two other operatives were denied boarding by El Al security. Khaled and Argüello were unable to successfully take control of El Al Flight 219 by themselves, as the Israeli pilot, who had been trained in counter-terrorism tactics as a direct result of the 1968 hijacking of Flight 426, entered into a steep nosedive after being alerted to the hijacking attempt, which threw the two operatives off balance (Schweitzer 2011; Mahnaimi and Abū Sharīf 1995, 81). In the ensuing commotion, both hijackers were subdued; an undercover security officer fatally wounded Argüello and passengers restrained Khaled. The plane then made an emergency landing at London Heathrow Airport, where Khaled was arrested and Argüello succumbed to his wounds on the way to a hospital (Naftali 2005).

The Airplane Operation went further astray when, having been denied boarding on El Al Flight 219, the other two operatives in Amsterdam opted to buy tickets on Pan American Flight 93 to New York. Although they successfully hijacked it with its 153 passengers and 17 crew members, the spontaneous diversion from the original plan proved problematic: Pan Am Flight 93 was unsuitable for Haddad's plan because the Boeing 747 was too large for the sandy landing strip at Dawson's Field. The hijackers instead diverted the flight to Beirut, refuelling and picking up several additional operatives and enough explosives to destroy the entire plane. The plane subsequently landed at Cairo International Airport, where, after all the hostages had been evacuated, the explosives were detonated, destroying the plane.

Despite these difficulties, Swiss Air Flight 100 and TWA Flight 742 both landed as planned at an abandoned British airfield in Jordan known as 'Dawson's Field', where PFLP operatives, including Haddad, were waiting on the ground to secure the plane and aid in the handling of the 306 hostages (Naftali 2005; *New York Times* 1970). The PFLP announced that they were not targeting US civilians themselves but rather US policies and demanded the release of prisoners held by countries with citizens among the hostages, most notably Switzerland, West Germany, Israel, and the United Kingdom. The UK government also was presented with a demand to promptly release the newly arrested Leila Khaled (Schweitzer 2011). As the United States held no such prisoners, Haddad announced that the US hostages would be released once all the other countries had complied with his demands ("Jordan, Vol. V, July 1/70-September 30/70" 1970).

At Israel's urging, the United States expended considerable political capital to convince the nations involved to create a unified front and agree to release prisoners only as long as all hostages – irrespective of nationality – would be released, too ("Hijacking. Operation Center, Situation Report [Sitrep] #4" 1970; Naftali 2005, 43). Three days into the crisis, a British Overseas Airways Corporation flight en route from Bombay to London was hijacked by a Palestinian PFLP sympathiser acting independently from the PFLP. The flight was also diverted to Dawson's Field. The unexpected arrival of Flight 775, with an additional 114 hostages, increased the number of UK citizens from two to thirty-eight, increasing pressure on the UK government to release Khaled (Naftali 2005).

On 12 September 1970, prior to the announced deadline and having removed hostages from the planes, the PFLP destroyed all three with explosives, with the media in attendance (*New York Times* 1970). The videos and photographs of this scene became some of the best-known visual symbols of the Palestinian international resistance movement in particular and of international terrorism in general (Schweitzer 2011). The following day, the BBC World Service broadcast a British government announcement in Arabic saying that the United Kingdom would release Khaled in exchange for the hostages, and the crisis formally ended on 30 September, with Western European nations exchanging Palestinian prisoners for their hostages (*Times* 1970a, 1970b). Despite its false start, the Dawson Field hijacking operation proved to be one of the most effective of the PFLP, not only effectively achieving the release of Palestinian prisoners but also gaining international attention.

The Emergence of Proxy-Bombs

In the aftermath of Dawson Field, and adapting to the changing security environment, notably the introduction of profiling of El Al passengers, the Popular Front for the Liberation of Palestine-General Command (PFLP-GC), a breakaway faction of the PFLP founded by a former Syrian army captain and demolition expert Ahmed Jibril (Hudson 1999, 154), also sought to innovate in their own right. Eschewing hijackings, the PFLP-GC instead resorted to employing unknowing mules to take explosives on board El Al flights. Dolnik (2007) suggests this innovation was 'inspired by the case of Jack Graham, who, in 1955, killed 38 passengers by planting an explosive in his mother's suitcase' in the United States (p. 83). Graham might have in turn been inspired by the actions of Joseph-Albert Guay, a Quebec man who, in 1951, planted a bomb in his wife's suitcase to bypass a divorce, obtain life insurance money, and elope with his mistress.

In each case, young PFLP-GC operatives would be sent to Europe to form relationships with women from inconspicuous countries. After a few weeks of dating, the women would be invited to visit the 'boyfriend's' family in Israel, with their boyfriends facing a last-minute trip or meeting but sending 'gifts' for their families and promising to join them a few days later (Dolnik 2007, 84). Thus disguised, the bombs were then packed in the unsuspecting women's luggage with the hope that the women, who did not fit the profile in use at the time and did not appear nervous (due to being unaware of the subterfuge), would bypass El Al employees tasked with passenger screening. The first such attack occurred on 28 July 1971, when a Dutch woman boarded an El Al plane flying from Rome to Tel Aviv with an explosive device hidden in the suitcase given to her by her 'boyfriend'; however, the device malfunctioned, and the plane reached its destination safely (Mickolus 1980, 274).

This technique was, nevertheless, employed successfully on 16 August 1971, when a bomb placed in a portable record player, replete with 200 grams of Semtex and the detonating mechanism placed ingeniously in the machine's own electrical infrastructure, detonated in the baggage compartment of an El Al flight from Rome to Tel Aviv, with 148 persons on board (Mickolus 1980). The explosion caused a crack in the aft door and a hole in the baggage compartment but failed to down the plane as a result of preventative armouring of the baggage compartment introduced on El Al planes (Dolnik 2007) in response to other bombing attempts. As in the previous case, the explosives were brought on board by two unsuspecting British women who had been given the record player by a man they met in Rome (Mickolus 1980, 336). On 3 September 1971, two different women were arrested at Lod Airport (now Ben Gurion Airport) for unwittingly taking explosives on board El Al planes from New York to Israel; once against the hidden devices appeared to have malfunctioned (Mickolus 1980, 277). Slightly more than two weeks later, explosives were discovered in the suitcase of a Peruvian woman travelling on board an El Al flight from London to Tel Aviv.[4]

While these plots largely fall outside the scope of this book, they nonetheless demonstrate changes in claim-makers' propositional knowledge – in this case awareness of changes in the security environment, notably the screening of air cargo packages heading for Israel after the simultaneous bombings of Swiss Air Flight 330 and of an Austrian Airlines Caravelle on 21 February 1970 and the introduction of security profiling for all El Al flights as a result of previous hijackings (Dolnik 2007, 83–84). The changes to this knowledge base prompted the generation of new prescriptive knowledge.

Non-Palestinian Actors

In the aftermath of the Dawson's Field hijackings, the PFLP banned attacks against non-Israeli targets. As a result, a breakaway group of the PFLP founded by Haddad, the Popular Front for the Liberation of Palestine-External Operations (PFLP-EO) was established; this group would later conduct several high profile and violent attacks against civilians, garnering much media attention. The PFLP-EO innovated further in response to the changing security environment. In particular, in response to the increasingly extensive profiling introduced by El Al and adopted by non-Israeli carriers, the PFLP-EO took the unorthodox step of accepting and training non-Palestinian volunteers, who were often motivated by a combination of sympathy for the Palestinian cause and a desire to acquire skills to achieve their own political agendas (Schweitzer 2011).

The use of non-Palestinian volunteers first occurred, on a limited scale and admittedly before the formation of the PFLP-EO, when Haddad recruited Argüello, a Nicaraguan American and a member of the Sandinista National Liberation Front,[5] to participate in the Dawson's Field hijackings.[6] As well as having realized that foreign operatives provided a tactical advantage, in that they could penetrate security measures with less scrutiny, Haddad predicted that they would also project 'an international aura and cause people to ask . . . "Why are these foreigners, with no direct stake in the Arab-Israeli conflict, conducting operations on behalf of the Palestinians?"' (Bacon 2005, 115). Such participation by non-Palestinians thus created a sense that the Palestinian cause transcended the Palestinian people and therefore kept the issue in the international spotlight. This propositional knowledge led the PFLP-EO to recruit a handful of Japanese leftists who arrived in Lebanon in 1971 seeking training and who eventually went on to perpetrate one of the deadliest attacks in the history of the State of Israel. The use of non-Palestinian operatives increased the feasibility of PFLP-EO attacks in the context of the extensive profiling happening at the time.

Indeed, on 30 May 1972, three men arriving at Lod Airport on a flight originating in Rome attacked passengers in the baggage claim area with automatic rifles and hand grenades hidden in their suitcases, killing twenty-six and injuring eighty others (Bar-Maoz 1991; Clutterbuck 1990). The PFLP-EO immediately took responsibility for this attack. However, because the surviving attacker, Kōzō Okamoto, had confirmed his nationality as Japanese and another deceased attacker had been identified as Japanese, the PFLP-EO pressed Fusako Shigenobu, the leader and founder of the Japanese Red Army (JRA), to publicly announce the involvement of the JRA (Steinhoff 2016), which he did. While foreign operatives had previously been used by Palestinian groups, this incident was unique in that the entire team of operatives was composed of Japanese attackers. Despite the death of two of the attackers, the Lod attack demonstrated the effectiveness and feasibility of foreign involvement in such campaigns, both tactically and for publicity purposes.

The role of such allies continued to expand, with Japanese operatives participating alongside their Palestinian comrades in subsequent operations. On 20 July 1973, the PFLP-EO hijacked a Japanese Airline flight using a joint Japanese-Palestinian team under the alias of the Palestinian Liberation Movement. Their demands included, for the first time, the release of a non-Palestinian prisoner – 'Kōzō Okamoto, the sole survivor of the three-man team responsible for the massacre at Tel Aviv's Lod Airport 15 months earlier' – along with 'a ransom of $5 million' (Gero 1997, 74). Consistent with prior PFLP operations, and replicating these prior successes, the unit employed the technique of aeroplane destruction, setting the aircraft ablaze after landing in Libya, once again demonstrating how well established aeroplane destruction had become within the Palestinian repertoire of contention and those of their allies.

Japanese volunteers also participated in a botched PFLP-EO attack on an oil refinery in Singapore. This led to a subsequent attack perpetrated by other PFLP-EO members on the Japanese Embassy in Kuwait to free the attackers apprehended after the refinery attempt. According to Yallop (1993, 343), Haddad's recruitment of Japanese nationals was motivated by their ability to travel across Europe without arising suspicion, thus making such spectacular attacks more feasible. As such, they became increasingly integral to Haddad's group, rather than being viewed as 'operational contractors', as they had been previously. However, JRA members, accustomed as they were to a culture of collective decision making and respect for consensus, grew increasingly frustrated by the PFLP-EO's organizational dynamic and discontented with Haddad's dogmatic management style, including his tendency to dictate decisions, issue orders, and compartmentalize information (Steinhoff 2016). Moreover, while the three PFLP-EO operations that employed JRA members were considered 'successes' from the PFLP-EO's standpoint, from the JRA perspective, all three operations had gone awry as a result of Haddad's management style (Steinhoff 2016). Faced with Haddad's unwillingness to compromise on his scrupulous operational security practices, the Japanese volunteers in the Middle East created an independent Japanese organization in 1974.

Faced with the JRA's move toward independence, the PFLP-EO increasingly drew on members of the German New Left movement, particularly Revolutionary Cells operatives. The German New Left of the 1970s was composed of three significant organizations – the Red Army Faction (RAF), the 2nd of June Movement, and the Revolutionary Cells – which were in a quasi-permanent state of in-fighting and competition.[7] Despite this in-fighting – since the actual ideological differences between these groups were largely idiosyncratic and hard to ascertain and because all three groups advocated the release of the imprisoned RAF leaders – actions taken by the 2nd of June Movement and the Revolutionary Cells are often attributed to the RAF, perhaps in part due to the higher profile of the RAF. While all three groups were allied to varying degrees with the PFLP-EO, of the three groups, the Revolutionary Cells was undeniably the most closely linked. As such, although often overshadowed by the RAF's high-profile actions and dominant personalities, the role of the Revolutionary Cells in PFLP-EO operations should not be overlooked.

For example, Revolutionary Cells' operatives assisted PFLP-EO operatives during the two failed attempts at downing El Al planes taking off from Paris' Orly Airport in January 1975. Similarly, in need of operatives who could easily operate in Austria, the PFLP-EO employed Revolutionary Cells members, along with one female member of the 2nd of June Movement, in an attack on the Organization of the Petroleum Exporting Countries (OPEC) ministers in Vienna in 1975 (Yallop 1993, 392). Subsequently, two Revolutionary Cells operatives Wilfried Böse (who had assisted in the preparation for the takeover of the OPEC headquarters in Vienna) and Brigitte Kuhlmann, along with two PFLP-EO operatives were tasked with the hijacking of Air France Flight 139 in 1976 (Kundnani 2009, 134), which will be discussed in detail in the *selection* section of this chapter.

Throughout the late 1960s and 1970s, the Popular Front for the Liberation of Palestine and its splinter groups rapidly responded to the changing security environment. Each Palestinian attack led to rapid changes in existing propositional knowledge, and as a result, Israeli and western security services and airlines sought to mediate newly exposed vulnerabilities and make previously feasible modes of attack unfeasible by instituting a range of new methods to stop such attacks. These included profiling protocols, hiring sky marshals, training pilots to conduct inflight counter-hijacking manoeuvres, ensuring check-in staff inquired about the content of passengers luggage, and armouring aeroplane's baggage compartments. In response to this changing environment, and undeterred, the PFLP and its splinter groups quickly adapted and innovated, creating 'mutations' of hijacking: using foreign actors to conduct attacks, or unknowing individuals as bomb-mules, conducting simultaneous attacks, landing hijacked planes in deserted airfields, destroying hijacked aeroplanes, and temporarily shifting their attention away from the heavily secured El Al flights towards other, comparatively more feasible, targets. In this way, the parallel to evolutionary biology emerges clearly, with both claim-makers and their adversaries caught in an evolutionary cycle, striving for competitive advantages and changing their environment as a result, thus prompting further innovations from their counterparts.

5.2 TRANSMISSION: SUCCESS AND ACCELERATED DIFFUSION

In his study of aeroplane hijackings, Holden (1986) reports that successful hijackings increase the rate of subsequent hijackings, whereas unsuccessful hijackings have no discernible effect. Holden correctly identifies the 'media coverage of hijacking incidents' (p. 874) as the mechanism by which the hijacking of planes spread between individuals, 'advertising . . . hijacking as a possible means of solving their problems' (p. 877). However, due to his reliance on statistical analysis alone, Holden (1986) does not provide a compelling narrative of the mechanism that led to the spread of innovations by Palestinian claim-makers and the wider spread of hijacking as a technique of contention among claim-makers worldwide following the late 1960s.

As aforementioned, the hijacking of El Al Flight 426 in July 1968, which eventually resulted in the release of sixteen Palestinian prisoners, was highly mediatized. In fact, according to Hoffman (2006), this incident resulted in a dramatic shift in people's understanding of hijacking and terrorism in general. Hoffman argues that, prior to the hijacking of El Al Flight 426, the public was more likely to see terrorism as something that only affected those living in specific regions and targeting those who were directly connected to the grievance(s) of the attackers. However, after July 1968, Hoffman suggests, the PFLP not only demonstrated that hijacking could be used to level specific concessions from governments, but also showed that a carefully orchestrated and executed hijacking – especially one affecting passengers with diverse nationalities – could greatly increase public exposure for claim-makers' grievances.

Holden (1986) and LaFree et al. (2015), among others, attribute a great deal of importance to the hijacking of El Al Flight 426 in the global diffusion of hijacking as a technique of contention. However, it is easy to exaggerate its importance or to strip the mechanisms by which hijacking was globally diffused of nuance. For example, the adoption of hijacking by the black nationalist social movement,[8] one of the earliest instances of aerial hijacking after July 1968, cannot be solely attributed to the hijacking of El Al Flight 426. In fact, removing the adoption of hijacking by the black nationalist movement from the wider context of hijacking in Cuba and the United States from 1958 to 1968 (as described in the previous chapter) would be counterproductive, overly simplistic, and misleading. Instead, the adoption of hijacking by the black nationalist movement, as previously demonstrated, is better understood in terms of its US and Cuban context. That being said, in other contexts, the wide media attention surrounding El Al Flight 426 did function as the key contributing factor in the adoption of hijacking as a technique of contention (Holden 1986).

Following the PFLP's deployment of hijacking as a technique of contention, other adopters of this technique emerged around the world. For example, on 8 November 1968, two Italian nationals hijacked an Olympic Airways flight en route from Paris to Athens; these men claimed that their actions were an act of opposition against the right-wing military junta in Greece and that the passengers had been targeted for flying to Greece (Avihai 2009). The following year, on 12 December 1969, members of the Eritrean Liberation Front hijacked two Ethiopian Airline flights and diverted them from Addis Ababa, Ethiopia, to Athens, Greece. In March 1970, the JRA hijacked a Japan Airlines flight originating in Tokyo. On 22 August, six members of the Palestine Popular Struggle Front, a splinter group of the PFLP, hijacked a Boeing 727 en route to Athens from Beirut, taking fifty-five passengers and crew hostage in an attack unsurprisingly similar to those perpetrated by the PFLP. In September 1970, seemingly in response to Palestinian hijackings – particularly the large-scale 'airplane operation' at Dawson's Field – two members of the Jewish Defense League (JDL) were arrested in New York as they attempted to hijack a United Arab Republic[9] airliner using firearms and explosives. This overwhelming increase in the use of hijacking by a wide range of different groups and the accelerated rate of transmission following the hijacking of El Al Flight 426, including those with a variety of grievances and identities, supports Holden's (1986) argument that the media, especially with the advent of live broadcasting, is central to the replication of techniques of contention, serving as the dominant transmission mechanism.

In addition to hijacking, the deliberate destruction of a hijacked plane – the PFLP's innovation – was also replicated by a non-affiliated individual soon after the PFLP introduced it. In January 1970, a French citizen named Christian Belon drew a pistol and commandeered TWA Flight 802 from Paris to Rome with twenty people on board. After a refuelling stop in Rome, the plane was flown to Beirut where, upon landing, Belon fired a dozen shots into the aircraft's instrument panel and surrendered. Explaining the hijacking and the damage to the plane, Belon stated: 'I did what I did to spite America and Israel, because America helps and encourages Israel and her aggression' (Newton 2002, 23). Belon's case is significant in that it demonstrates how quickly and widely the PFLP's techniques were transmitted through indirect ties outside the confines of organized Palestinian groups to the wider global Palestinian liberation movement. Indeed, while there is no evidence that Belon had received any direction or training from the PFLP or other organized groups, nor that he was even in contact with such members, he nonetheless chose to employ a technique devised by the PFLP to make his claim against Israel in support of Palestinian liberation. Belon's intentional damage to the plane prior to his surrender implies a general acceptance of the destruction of aircraft as a legitimate technique by which to advance grievances, at least by some supporters of the Palestinian liberation movement.

According to the detailed database of hijacking incidents created for this research, hijacking was deployed by at least 111 different organized groups of claim-makers or social movements in 978 distinct events worldwide between July 1968 and the events of 11 September 2001. While, tracing the entirety of the transmission process of hijacking following 1968 is impractical because of its sheer scale and complexity, it is nonetheless possible to derive several observations about the mechanisms by which hijacking was transmitted.

As addressed in the second chapter, diffusion of knowledge can occur by two primary types of linkages or channels: direct or indirect. Direct channels of diffusion 'are akin to cohesion models used by network analysts which hold that ideas diffuse most rapidly when individuals are in direct and frequent contact' (Soule 2011, 294). In other words, the rate at which knowledge diffuses varies with the level of interaction between actors. At high levels of interaction between individuals, higher rates of adoption of innovations can be expected. These direct, person-to-person contacts allow organizations to address errors in comprehension by the 'learners' but also provide the 'teachers' with the opportunity to customise the technique to match the 'learners' needs (Cragin et al. 2007, 21). However, direct contact takes significant time and effort, especially if 'learner' organizations require multiple interactions before exchange is effective (Von Hippel 1988).

The existence of alliances among terroristic groups is a well-established subject in existing literature (Chenoweth 2010; Karmon 2005; Asal and Rethemeyer 2008; Pedahzur and Perliger 2006). In relation to the diffusion of techniques of contention, these alliances facilitate direct contact among members. Indeed, Karmon (2005, 279) demonstrates that strategic incentives, especially the desire to increase their capabilities, often drives collaboration between terroristic groups.[10]

With regards to the transmission of hijacking, the PFLP established links with various leftist organizations worldwide, including the JRA members who perpetrated the Lod Airport attack. However, despite the strong evidence of collaboration between the PFLP and some leftist organizations, it is possible to exaggerate the importance of the role of operational cooperation in the transmission of hijacking.

While it is certain that members of the European New Left underwent training in, or at the very least, attended Palestinian training camps, the persistence of the notion that Palestinian liberation groups sought to create an 'international brigade' is left over from the largely discredited 'Soviet Theory' advanced by Sterling (1981). In fact, testimonies from members of the Italian Red Brigades who trained at a Palestinian training camp, along with reports from an Al Fatah training camp, seem to further discredit the notion that Palestinian groups routinely sought to conduct joint armed actions (Falciola 2016). According to one PFLP recruit, Habash warned his operatives to 'be wary of Western comrades. Most of them are agents of imperialism' (Falciola 2016, 16). While the camps were reportedly 'submerged' by Europeans, and while some foreigners participated in PFLP-EO operations, foreigners were generally rejected for service within the PFLP/PFLP-EO, and on the whole, the Palestinians did not seek 'mercenaries' who they viewed as potential turncoats (Falciola 2016, 16). Indeed, with the exception of JRA and members of the German New Left, non-Arabs rarely participated in PFLP operations. That this exclusion occurred due to a basic level of distrust, despite existing ideological overlap, cannot be overlooked (Falciola 2016, 16). Most importantly, it is crucial to recognize that, although members of the German New Left undoubtedly received PFLP training prior to the hijacking of Air France Flight 139, members of the JRA and Italian revolutionaries engaged in their own hijackings *prior* to training with the PFLP. For example, the preparation undertaken by the JRA prior to their hijacking of a Japan Airlines flight from Tokyo to Fukuaka in 1970 clearly suggests that the transmission of hijacking from the PFLP to the JRA occurred by means of indirect channels of diffusion rather than by direct contact well before they allied with the PFLP.

Indirect channels of diffusion occur when one organisation or individual learns through observation from afar. In this mode of knowledge exchange, media reports or public statements are likely to facilitate transmission of techniques. Although these reports can alert claim-makers to the use of new techniques, research indicates that media reports do not generally contain sufficient information for the technique to be replicated effectively (Rogers 1983). Instead, the 'learners' must 'figure out' any tacit requirements from whatever prescriptive knowledge is available to them about the new technique prior to enacting it. In evolutionary terms, this may well be one of the causes for the emergence of new variations of existing techniques: akin to biological copy errors in mutations. JRA efforts to decrypt the necessary prescriptive knowledge to successfully carry out a hijacking can be best exemplified by their preparation for their first hijacking; members of the JRA rented a large meeting room full of folding chairs, rearranged the room in an aeroplane seating configuration, and rehearsed the hijacking several times (Steinhoff 1989, 731).

Similarly, it seems unlikely that the transmission of the prescriptive knowledge for hijacking between the PFLP and groups such as Eritrean Liberation Front or – even more unlikely – the JDL occurred as a result of direct channels. Having observed the repeated deployment of hijackings by Palestinian claim-makers, culminating in the Dawson's Field hijackings, members of the JDL opted to employ a similar technique to advance its claims. Overall, it appears that the unprecedented media attention awarded to the hijacking of El Al Flight 426 and to other hijackings committed by the PFLP and its splinter groups, along with the highly mediatized government concessions that resulted, led to the transmission of the technique to other groups of claim-makers globally, at which point these groups could choose whether to adopt this new technique within their respective repertoires.

5.3 SELECTION: ADOPTION AND REJECTION BY VARIOUS GROUPS

One of the major advantages of hijacking passenger aeroplanes as a technique of contention was its almost certain ability to gain immediate and widespread media coverage. Indeed, as LaFree et al. (2015) argue, 'a drama in which the well-being of a large number of vulnerable people is suddenly dependent on the actions of unpredictable assailants makes for great television' (p. 174). Thus, the use of hijacking gave claim-makers substantial negotiating power with governments motivated to prevent the unnecessary and highly public death of their citizens, increasing the effectiveness of this technique as a method by which to gain concessions. As addressed previously, prior to the hijackings perpetrated by the PFLP, airlines in the West had developed a set of norms referred to as the 'Havana Rules', instructing crew to comply with hijackers to avoid endangering the lives of those on board. This improved the feasibility of hijacking as a technique of contention. As a result, the existence of the Havana Rules likely facilitated the early successes of the PFLP operations, particularly the hijacking of El Al Flight 426, which encountered no resistance from the crew. However, El Al quickly adapted to the threat of hijacking, opting for a policy of resisting hijackers by fielding armed guards and re-enforced steel cockpit doors in the aftermath of Flight 426. Indeed, the full scale of El Al's defensive stance against hijacking came to light after the attack against El Al Flight 432 in 1969, when the plane's security guard, a former Sayeret Matkal member, foiled the attack and killed one of the four attackers. The three other attackers were subsequently apprehended – alongside the plane's security guard – by Swiss police, and all four people were put on trial. This incident caused Israel to publicly admit that security personnel accompanied Israeli flights to prevent hijacking (Fitzgerald 2010, 365–66), effectively marking the end of El Al's acceptance of the Havana Rules and thereby changing the global propositional knowledge considerably. Nonetheless, other carriers were slow to adapt and respond; this resistance to change exposed these airlines to the threat posed by Palestinian hijackers seeking more feasible targets. The Dawson's Field hijackings further highlighted the vulnerability of international air travel as a target for terrorists; the fact that the attack on the one targeted El Al flight was foiled only serves to underline the effectiveness of rejecting the Havana Rules and instead using force to neutralize the threat of hijacking.

The Dawson's Field hijackings are also significant as they show that Palestinian claim-makers had found a way to achieve dual symbolism by combining the hijacking of the aircraft and holding passengers as hostages with the subsequent destruction of the planes. By repeating this with multiple planes in different locations, the claims of the Palestinian liberation movement reached a global audience. The destruction of the Pan Am Flight 93 in Cairo, during the Dawson's Field hijackings, had particular significance as the Boeing 747 had only been introduced into service eight months previously and was still viewed as a technological marvel (Evans 2001, 119).[11] As such, its destruction on the tarmac of Cairo International Airport was a symbol of contempt for both the latest US technological advances and US companies who conducted business with Israel. It seems to be no coincidence that the United States was particularly affected by the Aeroplane Operation: four of the five targeted flights were destined for New York and 107 of its citizens were eventually held hostage at Dawson's Field. In addition, another 46 US lives were jeopardized during the hijacking of Pan Am Flight 93 and the failed hijacking of El Al Flight 219. In addition to the human impact, two US planes, including a Boeing 747, were destroyed on the tarmac. It is worth noting that, as a direct result of these attacks, insurance premiums for aeroplanes substantially increased globally, which had an immediate financial impact on all airlines (Nyampong 2013). These damages, coupled with concurrent domestic hijackings within the United States, led to the most comprehensive aviation security reaction of any state up to that point, fundamentally altering propositional knowledge regarding how states respond to hijacking.

Indeed, in the aftermath of the Dawson's Field hijackings, President Richard M. Nixon stated that 'the menace of air piracy must be met – immediately and effectively' and introduced a series of significant initiatives, eschewing the Havana Rules and making hijacking far less feasible. This included the creation of a federal air marshal program, which would train and deploy 3,200 armed guards recruited and trained by the Bureau of Customs and assigned to the Federal Aviation Administration as a permanent force of sky marshals aboard commercial passenger flights. Until these marshals could be trained, an interim force composed of both military personnel and civilian agents from the Treasury Department and other agencies were organized to fulfil these duties (Preston 1998, 129). Secondly, these initiatives included the introduction of passenger screening technology to detect weapons 'by US flag carriers to all gateway airports in the US, and in other countries wherever possible' (Preston 1998, 129). Thirdly, they included 'accelerated efforts by Federal agencies to develop security measures including new methods for detecting weapons and explosive devices' (Preston 1998, 129). Fourthly, the State Department and other appropriate agencies were instructed to consult foreign governments and foreign carriers on anti-hijacking techniques. Fifth, the president 'called on the international community to suspend airline service to countries refusing to extradite or punish hijackers involved in international blackmail. He stated that it was U.S. policy to hold nations in which a hijacked plane landed responsible for appropriate steps to protect the lives and property of U.S. citizens' (Preston 1998, 129). Lastly, the president called on 'all countries to accept the multilateral convention (to be considered at a conference held under the auspices of the International Civil Aviation Organization) providing for extradition or punishment of hijackers' (Preston 1998, 129). For its part, Israel doubled down on its position that hijacking attempts should be resisted by the crew, regardless of international laws or norms. In fact, in the months after Dawson's Field, then transportation minister Shimon Peres helped pass a new law that protected Israeli pilots against foreign lawsuits resulting from their attempts to resist hijackings.

Constituency Costs and Black September

In planning a multi-airline hijacking, Haddad inarguably achieved a worldwide impact; however, the unintended effects included high constituency costs. In the aftermath of the Dawson's Field hijackings, the PFLP – until this time still operating under the umbrella of the wider PLO – enjoyed initial tactical success, but the attacks ultimately led to the splintering of the PFLP; caught up in the euphoria of their ability to stage an incident on such a large scale, the organization failed to appreciate the constituency costs they could incur. In particular, Haddad did not prepare for the response of the PFLP and the wider PLO's state supporters, namely Jordan and Lebanon, who, despite sharing their values, feared Israeli retribution similar to 'Operation Gift', when an Israeli army's elite Sayeret Matkal destroyed fourteen aeroplanes at the Beirut International Airport in response for a PFLP attack on the El Al Flight 253 in 1968.

In contrast to Haddad, the PLO seemed keenly aware of the constituency costs associated with conducting hijackings. As Morris (2011) notes, 'Arafat and the majority of the PLO opposed the hijackings, understood that the Arab states were being alienated, and moved to eject the PFLP' from the PLO (p. 372). In fact, Haddad's decision to release of the majority of the hostages prior to the established deadline was likely intended to minimize the response they expected to receive from the PLO and PFLP leadership.

However, despite this behaviour suggesting some awareness of the wider PLO's concerns, Haddad nonetheless demonstrated a complete lack of awareness of the cost of alienating their supporters and took control of swathes of northern Jordan immediately following the Dawson's Field operation. This included the town of Irbid, setting up roadblocks, and effectively marking off the area as sovereign Palestinian territory. For the Jordanian government, this behaviour by the PFLP represented the final provocation in

a series of flagrant Palestinian violations of Jordanian sovereignty and chal-
lenges to King Hussein's rule. On 17 September 1970, the Jordanian military
unleashed a full-scale assault on the wider PLO in Jordan (Morris 2011).
Over the following two weeks of pitched battle between Jordan and the
PLO – often referred to as 'Black September' – 900 PLO members and 3,500
Palestinian non-combatants were killed (Morris 2011, 347–76).

Given the severity of Jordanian reprisals and in light of a significant
global backlash, the PLO convinced the Secretary-General of the PFLP that
it was necessary to curb the PFLP's international operations and to expel
Haddad from its organization. As such, Haddad's most innovatively grandi-
ose operation ironically led to his departure from the PFLP due to the high
constituency costs incurred. This also caused the organization's centre of
hijacking operations to shift from the PFLP to Haddad's splinter organization, the PFLP-EO. In other words, the PFLP and the PLO more broadly
publicly rejected hijacking as a technique within their repertoire of contention after being confronted with the loss of support both from within the
Palestinian liberation movement and, more importantly, from their state supporters.

A Shift away from Hijackings

Internationally, it took the Palestinian resistance movement a full year to
recover from the war with Jordan. Very little action was taken during this
period, except for some retaliatory ground attacks perpetrated by the wider
Palestinian resistance movement. Two such attacks targeted the Jordanian
airline, Alia; one targeted the airline's office in Rome and the other slightly
damaged an Alia plane at Cairo Airport ("Terrorist Group Profiles" 1989,
13). However, after a period of recovery, the PFLP-EO quickly attempted to
harness a new technique, briefly shifting focus from hijacking. This emergent
technique was based on the successful appearance of man-portable air-de-
fence systems (MPADS), including anti-aircraft missiles used during the
1973 Yom Kippur War, and the fact that the technical requirements to effectively bring down modern commercial airliners were thus lowered. The
PFLP-EO attempted on three occasions to use MPADS to down El Al flights,
meeting with failure each time, but using different MPADS launchers.[12] The
change of MPADS can probably be understood as the operatives adapting,
using a more accurate weapon in light of their previous failure. While
MPADS remained a threat to commercial (and military) aviation,[13] faced
with repeated failures, neither the PFLP-EO nor any other Palestinian groups
attempted to down a commercial airliner again.

Although outside the scope of this case study, the Palestinian experiments
with MPADS demonstrate the Palestinian liberation movement's desire to
expand on their existing repertoire of contention, experimenting with new

techniques. However, faced with a succession of costly failures and undoubtedly emboldened by the illocutionary successes of the Munich Olympic hostage taking in 1972,[14] and the takeover of the OPEC headquarters in 1975,[15] among others,[16] hostage taking continued to be a favoured technique within the Palestinian liberation movement during the mid-1970s.

The shift toward non-hijacking-related hostage taking and the reduction of Palestinian hijackings by nearly half following Dawson's Field can also be attributed to the increasing difficulties getting weapons on board aircraft due to added security measures and increased cooperation between states,[17] along with the decreased capabilities of the PFLP and its splinter groups. Using the Global Terrorism Database, Hsu and Apel (2015) demonstrate that the introduction of metal detectors from 1973 onwards corresponded unsurprisingly with a statistically significant reduction in aeroplane hijacking and a corresponding increase in non-hijacking-related hostage taking. This increase was arguably linked to the emergence of new propositional knowledge: The longer an incident persisted, the more press coverage the incident garnered, and the more pressure was placed on the government to resolve it peacefully and quickly. Therefore, despite the creativity in identifying new venues in which hostage taking could occur, the prescriptive knowledge detailing the requirements for successful hostage taking – a secure yet highly visible place to keep hostages along with a form of transportation to facilitate the escape of the perpetrator – remained largely unchanged. As a result, despite its reduced usage at this time due to a reduction in feasibility, hijacking of commercial aircraft remained an important technique within the Palestinian liberation movement's repertoire of contention during the mid-1970s as, when successfully implemented, it remained highly effective.

The deployment of techniques which involved hostage taking, either in the air or on the ground, placed governments in an impossible situation: either they were deemed too brutal when violence occurred during a rescue operation or impotent if they acquiesced to claim-makers' demands. This perhaps goes some way towards explaining the increasingly aggressive responses taken to both avoid hijackings in the first place but also to resolve them swiftly before hostages were secured.

The Final Nail in the Havana Rules' Coffin

Throughout the early 1970s, the Havana Rules of the 1950s still generally held sway. However, as early as February 1969 – during the attempted hijacking of El Al Flight 432 – Israel demonstrated that it would oppose hijackings with deadly force. As hijacking incidents increased in scale, duration, and severity, and particularly with the growing threat of the systematic murder of hostages, Western governments found it difficult – and in some cases simply unacceptable – to sit idly by and watch other governments negotiate, especially given that diverting planes to countries with either sympathetic or weak or incompetent governments was a core feature of the Palestinian liberation movement's hijacking technique. Within this context, Israel escalated its policy of non-compliance with hijackers in 1976 in a fashion that fundamentally shifted the propositional knowledge of how states would react to hijackings.

On 27 June 1976, two members of the West German Revolutionary Cells (*Revolutionäre Zellen*), along with two members of the PFLP-EO, boarded Air France Flight 139 from Tel Aviv to Paris, with 258 passengers and crew, during a stopover in Athens using false passports. When the plane took off from Athens, the hijackers initially forced the pilot to divert to Libya. After refuelling, the plane continued on to Entebbe International Airport in Uganda, where they met three more members of the PFLP-EO. The hijackers were warmly welcomed by Ugandan dictator Idi Amin. Amin had been formally asked in a letter from Haddad – who represented himself as being from the PFLP, which was not privy to this plan – to accept the hijackers and then the prisoners they hoped to free (Charbel 2008, 175). Upon landing, the passengers on the flight were taken to the old terminal of Entebbe airport, after which the hijackers broadcasted their demands on the Ugandan radio: the release of fifty-four prisoners held by Israel, West Germany, and France (Kundnani 2009, 134). Two days into the incident, on 29 June, the hijackers divided the hostages into two groups. After isolating around a hundred Jewish and Israeli passengers in a separate room of the airport building, the hostage-takers released the remaining hostages. When information about the separation of Jewish and gentile hostages reached Israel, the Israeli government feigned a willingness to negotiate with the hijackers while it prepared a daring rescue operation (Byman 2011, 55). The release of the 148 non-Israeli hostages on the second day, along with the threat of executing the Israeli and Jewish hostages if the hijackers' demands were unmet, left Israeli authorities, who believed that acquiescing to the hijackers was akin to 'being asked to release potential murderers who probably will strike again', in an unacceptable position (Taillon 2002, 125).

On the night of 3 July 1976, Israel launched a rescue operation, codenamed 'Thunderbolt' and later renamed 'Operation Yonatan' in memory of the unit's leader, Lieutenant colonel Yonatan Netanyahu, who was killed during the mission. In a feat described by historian Richard Deacon (1977) as 'an astonishing epic of military adventure and enterprise carried out in a spirit of medieval buccaneering by a team trained in the arts of both the military and espionage' (p. 271), an Israeli Hercules C-130 plane carrying a twenty-nine-man assault unit composed entirely of Sayeret Matkal commandos landed without authorization in Entebbe (Smith 1976, 1, 10; Blumenau 2014, 68–69). This unit, tasked with assaulting the old terminal and rescuing the hostages, was quickly followed by three additional C-130 carrying approximately seventy more support commandos tasked with securing the civilian airport, protecting and fuelling the Israeli aircrafts, holding off hostile ground reinforcement from the city of Entebbe, and destroying a squadron of MiG fighter jets to prevent possible interception by the Ugandan Air Force. The assault unit quickly overwhelmed the Ugandan forces and the hijackers, killing all hijackers and twenty Ugandan soldiers and successfully rescuing all but four of the hostages (Choi 1994, 51).

Israel's daring rescue mission signified the beginning of a full scale abandonment of the Havana Rules, which had previously been integral to the propositional knowledge of how states would react to hijacking. States' previous compliance with the Havana Rules was conditional, based on the propositional knowledge that, if complied with, hijackers would minimize the risk to the hijacked plane's passengers and crew and, usually, to the vessel itself. Therefore, as attacks increased in scale, duration, severity, and violence, states whose citizens were at risk were no longer willing to sit idly by and allow the fate of their people and property to be negotiated by some other hapless or hostile government. As a result, countries whose nationals were singled out or those whose 'flagship' airlines were involved began eschewing the Havana Rules and responding to hijacking with bold rescue attempts.

In another such example, on 18 October 1977, West Germany took similarly decisive action when a PFLP-EO team of Palestinian and Lebanese operatives using false Iranian passports and calling itself the 'Organization of the Struggle against World Imperialism' hijacked a Lufthansa plane primarily carrying German tourists (Aust 2009, 373). Fearing repercussion from Israel, South Yemen – which had previously been permissive of PFLP-related activities – refused to allow the plane to land. The plane was eventually diverted to Mogadishu, Somalia, where, using a special operations unit created after the failed rescue attempt during the 1972 Munich Olympics, the West German government launched a mission to free the hostages. West German commandos of the *Grenzschutzgruppe 9 der Bundespolizei* (GSG 9) rescued all hostages and killed three perpetrators.[18] In addition to the obvious rewards of freeing hostages, the illocutionary impact of these successful counter-terrorism interventions had deterrent effects and reinforced the message that it was possible to successfully resolve hijacking without giving into the demands of terrorists. Indeed, speaking after the Entebbe raid, Brigadier General Dan Shomron, the commander of the rescue operation, commented: 'It resonated far and wide. . . . It showed that you could counter terrorism, and it was worth cooperating to do so' (Grunor 2005, 296). This fundamentally altered the existing propositional knowledge of both states and adversaries.

The PFLP-EO did not have another opportunity to recover from these setbacks; in April 1978, Wadie Haddad – dubbed 'the godfather of international terrorism' by *The Economist* – died in an East German hospital (*The*

Economist 1978, 66). Along with the death of several of his most highly valued deputies in recent years, Haddad's death created a prescriptive knowledge void that could not be filled, especially given his micro-management of all aspects of the group. A member of the Revolutionary Cells, who worked closely with Haddad and participated in the OPEC operation, summarized that '[w]ithout Haddad, nothing works' (*Der Spiegel* 1978). Following his death, Haddad's group splintered into several smaller offshoots, though none lived up to its predecessor, either operationally or as an alliance hub. However, the marked decline in hijackings in the late 1970s cannot be wholly attributed to Haddad's death. The change in states' responses to hijacking was also undoubtedly a key factor in its reduced feasibility (and, therefore, to some extent its effectiveness) as a technique of contention, but crucially, hijacking also lost legitimacy because the increased violence in hijackings resulted in clear constituency costs among the supporters and allies of the Palestinian liberation movement. This was particularly evident following the Entebbe raid in the public rejection of hijacking by the German New Left, who had previously strongly allied themselves with the Palestinian cause.

Entebbe and the Rejection of Hijacking

The German New Left, particularly those who turned to violence during the late 1960s, did so believing ardently that West Germany was still in the clutches of fascism, albeit a cleverly disguised version. In their opinion, the source of this concealed fascist threat was twofold: (i) West Germany's unresolved Nazi legacy – a force they perceived to still dominate and control the apparatuses of power – and (ii) the US war in Vietnam, which shattered the post-Second World War image of the United States as a liberator and replaced it with the worst kind of hypocrisy: an imperialist power trying to cover up its true nature in order to dupe the masses (Varon 2004, 132). As such, the understanding of the Vietnam War among the German New Left was inextricably bonded to the country's past, with anti-Vietnam war activists frequently evoking Nazi metaphors to describe US intervention in Vietnam.[19]

Therefore, as the 1960s progressed, anti-Zionism, which members of the German New Left conflated with anti-US imperialism, increasingly represented an integral part of the movement's creed. While the old guard of the German Left had taken a largely pro-Israeli stance in the aftermath of the Holocaust, the Six-Day War and the Vietnam War – along with growing anti-imperialism and anti-Americanism ideology among student movements – had turned the tide completely by the late 1960s: 'Israel was now identified with imperialism and placed in the same imperialist category as the U.S., which had already become the preferred object of hate among the protesting youth of Western Germany' (Erlanger 2009, 96). Israel was thus deemed to be an aggressor, an occupier, and an imperialist force responsible for subjugating the Palestinians. The intensity of the New Left's condemnation of Israel reflected the disturbing spectre of enduring anti-Semitism within their generation despite their avid condemnation of their parents' actions.[20]

However, for this highly politicized generation of students protesting and demonstrating against a perceived failure to de-Nazify West Germany, against their parents' authoritarianism, and against what they perceived as the new face of fascism and imperialism (Schlembach 2009), the shocking resemblance between the Entebbe hijackers' actions and Nazi 'selections' at Auschwitz and other concentration camps was simply too much to overlook. 'For most group members' notes Karcher, a historian of the German New Left, 'the failed kidnapping would lead to a turn away from "Anti-Zionist" attacks, which had previously constituted a central field of action' for the movement (David 2016, 362).

These uncomfortable parallels between the events at Entebbe and the memories of the Holocaust, highlighted by national and international media and felt by some members of the New Left, resonated deeply with the wider West German public as well. For example, on January 1977, Marvin J. Chomsky's melodramatic and star-studded *Victory at Entebbe* began screening in West German cinemas. The film heavily emphasized the parallels between the hijackers and guards at Nazi death camps; when the hijackers announce that they will read out the Israeli passengers' names, a Holocaust survivor is portrayed as being haunted by his memories of selection at Auschwitz. As Ebbrecht-Hartmann (2015) notes, the film also emphasizes the German background of two of the hijackers:

> the Kuhlmann character transforms from a rational political activist into a Jew-hating fanatic, which mainly manifests on an audible level. When the first name is called, dramatic music rises. The German command 'Schnell, schnell!' (Quick, quick!) mixes with instructions, despotically executed by the female German terrorist. When the Belgian Jewish couple argues her language significantly changes to German: 'Ihr seid Juden! Los, gehen Sie rechts, Schnell!' (You are Jews. Go to the right. Quick!). Over the course of the selection scene the dramatic musical score gives way to a variation of traditional Jewish tunes and melodies, which highlight the subtext of the scene and turn it, when the selected hostages are forced to walk silently into a separate room, into a movement where past and present merge. (pp. 258–59)

The New Left was painfully aware of the impact of Chomsky's film on the public perception of their alliance with the Palestinian liberation movement and their adoption of some Palestinian liberation movement techniques. Therefore, New Left groups called for protests against the screening of the film, going so far as to plant explosive devices in cinemas screening the film.[21]

Despite these attempts to curtail screenings, some parts of the German Left had already started discussing the legitimacy and impact of hijacking in general – particularly reports of the 'selection' of passengers (Claussen 1976). Events at Entebbe with Jewish passengers specifically slated for execution should the hijackers' demands be ignored had a profound effect on members of the New Left such as Joschka Fischer, the future foreign minister and a former associate of Böse, one of the two German hijackers at Entebbe. According to Fischer, he began soul-searching upon realizing how compulsively the members of the New Left were obsessed with the primal shock of Auschwitz, which played a key part in his *Desillusionierung* with the New Left. Fischer recounted that 'the "selection" of passengers, Jews on one side, non-Jews on the other, with the Jews slated for execution' led him to believe that the New Left's anti-Zionism was in fact simply a new version of the despicable ideologies of his parents' generation, despite his generation ostensibly claiming to expunge these views (Berman 2006, 57). Berman (2006), summarizes this view by stating that Entebbe led to soul-searching within West Germany's New Left:

> It was a worried suspicion that New Left guerrilla activity, especially in its German version, was not the struggle against Nazism that everyone on the New Left had always intended. It was a suspicion that, out of some horrible dialectic of history, a substantial number of German leftists had ended up imitating instead of opposing the Nazis—had ended up intoxicating themselves with dreams of a better world to come, while doing nothing more than setting out to murder Jews on a random basis: an old story. (pp. 59–60)

Although a small portion of the New Left felt that, despite Entebbe, they should continue to participate in armed conflict around the globe, this subset of the movement became increasingly isolated from the majority of the German New Left, who avoided further attacks against Israeli targets and rejected hijacking as a whole, instead focusing on local struggles and new social movements such as the anti-nuclear movement and the women's movement in West Germany (David 2016, 363). Building on this understanding, that the excesses of Entebbe delegitimized hijacking among the German New Left and led the movement to reject it as a technique of contention, it is useful to consider the roles of feasibility and effectiveness – which essentially represent two sides of the same coin – in the adoption and, in some cases, rejection of hijacking by various groups of claim-makers.

As addressed previously, Holden (1986) and Dugan et al. (2005) claim that successful hijackings generate additional attempts, an assertion which is supported by consideration of several early adopters of the hijacking technique, as detailed throughout this book. Like the PLFP (and its splinter groups), which continued to deploy hijacking in an attempt to replicate its initial successes, hijacking entered the Eritrean Liberation Front's repertoire of contention in full force after its two successful hijackings of Ethiopian Airlines flights. On the other hand, my analysis found that those whose initial forays with hijacking failed, such as the JDL and the Provisional Irish Republican Army (PIRA), quickly abandoned the technique. For example, in 1974 the PIRA attempted two attacks, one attacking a police station and another targeting an army base. The aim was to drop milk churns filled with explosives out of hijacked aircraft. However, in the first attempt the bombs missed their target and failed to explode, and in the second attempt the first bomb struck the wing of the plane, causing the hijackers, now unable to drop the other bombs, to abandon the attack (Mickolus 1980, 481). These incidents, highlighting to the PIRA the unfeasibility of such attacks, marked the first and the last time the PIRA employed such a technique. In contrast, the PFLP-EO largely abandoned hijacking as a result of incurring serious losses as the Havana Rules were abandoned; the resultant change in propositional knowledge led to this technique of contention losing its effectiveness and, therefore, being winnowed out of the group's repertoire. Added to this, the death of Haddad led to a serious lack of the required prescriptive knowledge, making such attacks likely less feasible, even had the environment remained constant; in this way similarities in these cases begin to emerge.

Overall, it can be seen that the driving forces behind the selection of hijacking as a technique of contention are its perceived effectiveness, feasibility, and legitimacy – which includes the constituency costs incurred. While the PFLP-EO, PIRA, and JDL all abandoned hijacking either as a result of a perceived lack of feasibility or effectiveness, the German New Left and the PLO proved more sensitive to questions surrounding the legitimacy of the techniques, particularly with regards to constituency costs. The reasons why different groups are affected more by some factors than others are harder to ascertain.

Overall, it seems clear that when a lack of perceived legitimacy arises, the rejection of a technique is a relatively slow process arising largely from internal factors, rather than being due to intervention by a claim-maker's adversary, especially if the technique has already been adopted and become established within a group's repertoire. In contrast, techniques seen to be either unfeasible or ineffective are quickly abandoned or never fully enter the claim-makers' repertoires of contention; in other words, a group may foster a technique without ever fully adopting it. Indeed, it seems that the calculation of a technique's feasibility and effectiveness is ever changing and intrinsically tied to the existing propositional knowledge of a group or movement, which is largely dependent on external factors such as their interactions with their adversaries and their adversaries' actions.

NOTES

1. Numerous excellent works have addressed the Palestinian national movement, including those by O'Neill (1978), Khalaf (1991), Khalidi (2007), and Pearlman (2011).

2. These attacks against Israeli targets did not cease in 1970; for example, on 9 April 1973, a Land Rover and another car crashed through the gate at Nicosia Airport. The occupants then riddled an El Al Viscount with machine gun fire (*Times* 1973), and on 27 April, 'an Italian employee of El Al, the Israel airline, was shot dead in a busy street' by a man who 'claimed to belong to the Palestinian Black September organization' ("Chronology February 16, 1973–May 15, 1973" 1973, 356–57).

3. An event not to be confused with the bombing of TWA Flight 840 on 2 April 1986.

4. A similar ruse was at the centre of the Hindawi affair, another attempted bombing of an El Al flight. On 17 April 1986, a week before Passover, Anne-Marie Murphy, a thirty-two-year-old Irish woman attempting to board El Al Flight 016 from London to Tel Aviv, was discovered to be the unwitting carrier of a bomb set to destroy the Boeing 747 carrying 375 passengers. Travelling to Israel to meet the parents of her Jordanian fiancé, Nezar Hindawi, the father of her unborn child, Murphy was using a wheeled carry-on suitcase provided by Hindawi. After failing to detect anything untoward in her bag, El Al screeners, suspicious of the weight of the bag, opted to do a hand search and uncovered a false bottom containing a half-inch-thick sheet of Semtex. The suitcase also contained a Commodore scientific calculator, ostensibly a present from Hindawi to a friend in Israel. The calculator, the main mechanism of which remained functioning should it be tested by security, had been modified with a circuit board timer and 10.7 ounces of Semtex, serving as initiator for the larger load of explosives. According to Scotland Yard, the bomb, given its sophistication, was almost certainly manufactured by Syrian intelligence officers. During the trial, Hindawi retracted his confession, instead claiming he was being scapegoated by Israeli agents. Furthermore, his legal counsel argued that Hindawi was being manipulated by Israeli intelligence, seeking to humiliate the Syrian government. The jury was unconvinced by this and dismissed such interpretations as entirely lacking in evidence, convicting Hindawi and imposing a sentence of forty-five years in prison (Seale 1993, 249).

5. In 1969, the Sandinistas sent the first of several contingents to train at a PLO camp, probably run by Fatah ("The Sandinistas and Middle Eastern Radicals" 1985). However, the trainees were disappointed with their experience, which consisted of developing skills that were of little use in their environment in South America: a complaint also made by West Germans who trained with Fatah in the 1970s (Aust 2009, 67–68). Indeed, Fatah was not overly concerned with building the capability of its partners but, rather, on the generation of propaganda through cooperation. As such, the Sandinistas, after a short cooperation with the Fourth International, a Trotskyite group based in Paris, received training instead from the PFLP, which sought to fulfil one of its emerging organisational needs: that the PFLP would provide training if the Sandinistas assisted the PFLP with its operations.

6. Hoffman (2006) has questioned whether Argüello's participation was of his own volition and thus indicative of an individual-level relationship or as a result of an order by his superiors, which would instead imply an organizational-level alliance. However, in addition to the absence of indications that Argüello was particularly committed to PFLP objectives, an organizational-level relationship had been forged between the PFLP and the Sandinistas at this time, which strongly suggests that Argüello was acting in his capacity as a representative of this group. Moreover, the Sandinistas' spokesman embraced the hijacking operation, telling the *al-Watan* newspaper: 'A number of Sandinistas took part in the operation to divert four aircraft which the PFLP seized and landed at a deserted airfield in Jordan. One of our comrades was also wounded in a hijack operation in which Leila Khaled was involved. She was in command of the operation and our comrades helped her carry it out' ("The Sandinistas and Middle Eastern Radicals" 1985, 3).

7. The RAF openly distained the 2nd of June Movement's laissez-faire lifestyle and attitude towards drugs and sex, accusing its members, along with those of the Revolutionary Cells, of not being fully committed to the revolution (Alexander and Pluchinsky 1992, 80; Bougereau and Klein 1981, 56). For their part, the 2nd of June Movement and the Revolutionary Cells

found the RAF to be arrogant, overly hierarchical and rigid. In fact, in 1976, the Revolutionary Cells sent an open letter to the RAF challenging them to define their current tenets and justify several recent actions, statements and failures (Moncourt and Smith 2009, 460).

8. On 4 November 1968, a National Airlines flight from New Orleans to Miami was diverted to Cuba by Raymond Johnson, a civil rights activist at Southern University in Louisiana, who, upon landing in Cuba, christened the aircraft 'the Republic of New Africa' (*United States v. Raymond Johnson*, 1978, 14–20).

9. The United Arab Republic was a short-lived political union between Egypt and Syria, which dissolved in 1961.

10. One of the best documented alliances between terroristic organizations is the relationship between Hezbollah and Hamas. Despite their ideological differences, scholars have documented the extent to which Hezbollah taught Hamas and Palestinian Islamic Jihad (PIJ) about the operational nuances of suicide terrorism during this period (Pedahzur 2007; Ricolfi 2005, 91–92) and how Hamas apparently used connections and funding from Hezbollah to buy precursor technologies for crude mortars and Qassam rockets ("Hezbollah Increasing Terror Activity" 2004). Similarly, the links between the Provisional Irish Republican Army (PIRA) and the Revolutionary Armed Forces of Colombia (FARC) came to light after James Monaghan, Martin McCauley, and Niall Connolly, three experienced PIRA operatives, were captured in Colombia while training and working with the FARC (Horowitz and Potter 2014). Moreover, during one raid, the Colombian army found FARC-operated mortars with similar design principles to those used by the PIRA in Northern Ireland (Murphy 2005, 81), leading a 2002 committee report from the US House of Representatives to remark that, after interacting with the PIRA, the FARC began to employ new techniques initially developed by the PIRA. Specifically, the FARC adopted the PIRA tactic of 'car bombings which target police explosives teams and other first-responders whose job is to dismantle or neutralize these deadly devices' (Horowitz and Potter 2014, 207).

11. Heralded as the replacement for the Boeing 707, the Boeing 747 provided a 10 percent speed advantage, carried three times as many passengers, and was slated to become the icon of a new generation of wide-bodied airliners (Evans 2001, 108–19).

12. The first attempt occurred on 13 December 1975, when two men fired two RPG-7 rockets at an El Al 707 scheduled to fly from Paris to Montreal and New York, missing the El Al plane and instead hitting the fuselage of a parked Yugoslav DC9 scheduled to fly to Zagreb. Six days later, once again at Orly Airport in Paris, police engaged in a firefight with three men as they attempted to mount a MPADS on a tripod to fire at a scheduled El Al flight to Tel Aviv. The MPADS used during the second attack was probably an SPG-9, a tripod-mounted recoilless rifle that fired RPG-7 rounds. The PFLP-EO once again attempted to down an El Al flight in 1976 as the flight touched down in Nairobi Kenya. However, the attempt was thwarted when Kenyan authorities, apparently acting on information provided by Israel, arrested the entire cell (Schweitzer 2011).

13. Since 1978, ten civilian aircraft have been targeted by non-Palestinian groups using MPADS (Jaffe 2016, 208).

14. During the 1972 Olympic Games in Munich, Germany, eight members of Fatah's auxiliary force, the Black September Organization, killed two members of the Israeli Olympic team and then took nine others hostage, demanding their exchange for the release of 234 prisoners jailed in Israel and the German-held founders of the Red Army Faction (Andreas Baader and Ulrike Meinhof). A rescue mission launched by the West Germans at the airport went awry and ended tragically with the death of all of the hostages (Byman 2011, 46).

15. On 21 December 1975, the takeover of the Organization of the Petroleum Exporting Countries (OPEC) headquarters in Vienna resulted in the seizure of sixty OPEC officials and staff members. The following day, the hostage takers, along with forty-two hostages, were provided an airliner and flown to Algiers where thirty hostages were freed; the DC-9 then flew on to Tripoli where additional hostages were freed before returning to Algeria, where the remaining hostages were freed 'for a sum believed to have been in the tens of millions of dollars – perhaps as much as $50 million' (Koerner 2013, 368).

16. Some of the higher profile hostage taking perpetrated by Palestinian resistance groups in the aftermath of the Black September include: the Kiryat Shmona massacre, where three mem-

bers of the PFLP-GC, another PFLP splinter group, killed eighteen civilians in the Israeli town of Kiryat Shmona on 11 April 1974; at Orly airport in Paris on 19 January 1975, ten hostages were seized in a terminal bathroom; at the Savoy Hotel in Tel Aviv on 4–5 March 1975, eight members of the PLO seized then civilian hostages; and on 21 December 1975, the OPEC headquarters in Vienna were taken over by the PFLP-EO.

17. There appears to be a clear association between the adoption of The Hague Hijacking Convention (formally the Convention for the Suppression of Unlawful Seizure of Aircraft) and the Convention for the Suppression of Unlawful Acts against the Safety of Civil Aviation (sometimes referred to as the Montreal Convention), and the significant decline in international hijackings.

18. For a detailed discussion of the operation, see Taillon (2002, 107–48).

19. For example, protesters regularly asserted that they refused to be 'good Germans' and idly stand by while this 'travesty' took place, as their parents had done a generation before (Klimke 2010, 137). Moreover, a banner placed on the Dachau concentration camp memorial site in 1966 crudely declared that 'Vietnam is the Auschwitz of America' (Varon 2004, 35).

20. For example, the attempted bombing of a Jewish Community Centre in West Berlin in 1969 by a German New Left group, the Tupamaros West Berlin, coincided with the anniversary of *Kristallnacht* (Hoffman 2006, 230).

21. In Frankfurt, leftist groups planned to prevent the screening of the film, forcing police to close off the area around the cinema (Ebbrecht-Hartmann 2015); in Berlin, police officers had to prevent members of the New Left from interrupting screenings (Bröhl 1977); in Munster and Mainz, showings took place under police protection (*Die Welt* 1977). The situation further escalated when two explosive devices, manufactured by members of the Revolutionary Cells, were found in two cinemas in Dusseldorf and Aachen (Ebbrecht-Hartmann 2015).

Chapter Six

Criminal Innovations

Prior to the 1968–1973 period, air travel had a long history of being targeted by criminals[1] and insurance fraudsters;[2] however, running parallel to the 'hijacking for transportation' and the 'Palestinian' strains of hijacking, this period saw the emergence of what can best be understood as 'criminal innovations'.[3] Criminal innovation, much like innovation by claim-makers, seeks to outwit authorities but, in this case, for financial reward. Therefore, for the purposes of this chapter, 'criminal(s)' shall refer to those motivated primarily by financial or other personal gain, while 'claim-maker(s)' continues to refer to those motivated to advance a particular political claim; by no means is this distinction meant to deny the criminal nature of politically motivated hijacking.

The main changes that hijacking underwent at the hands of those motivated by greed were demands for ransom money in exchange for the safe passage of crew, passengers, and aircraft and the daring use of parachutes as a means of escape. Like the hijackings perpetrated by black nationalists during this period, little attention has been dedicated to criminally motivated hijacking within the existing aviation security and terrorism literature. To address this lacuna, in the *variation* section of this chapter I demonstrate the twofold importance of these incidents for a wider consideration of the evolution of hijacking. Firstly, while the acts of these individuals can hardly be understood as claim-making, their innovations were influenced by knowledge gleaned from hijackings committed by political claim-makers and state responses to these acts. Secondly, and perhaps most importantly, these criminal innovations quickly became part of the existing propositional and prescriptive knowledge surrounding hijacking in the United States, coming to represent an important facet of security threats airlines and law enforcement faced. Therefore, in the *transmission* section, I address the role of media in spreading knowledge of these techniques; within the United States in particular, criminal hijackers received almost cult status after their endeavours were detailed in publications with mass appeal and high readership, and in turn, their innovations were increasingly replicated, not only by other criminals, but also by claim-makers both nationally and internationally as a means of funding additional operations.

Finally, in the *selection* section, I explore how both criminally motivated hijackers and security officials entered into a circle of innovation and counter-innovation. While the US government and public had previously tolerated hijackings under the guise of the 'Havana Rules' as a nuisance but one that was usually benign, the brutality and disregard demonstrated by criminally motivated hijackers forever changed the existing propositional knowledge and led, for the first time, to collaborative efforts between Cuba and the United States to curb hijackings and to severely prosecute hijackers. In many ways, it is argued, the actions of criminally motivated hijackers and the subsequent responses of some states proved to be one of the most significant driver to aviation security reforms prior to 9/11.

6.1 VARIATION: HIJACKING AS A MEANS OF EXTORTION

During the summer of 1970, national headlines in the United States announced the emergence of a new phenomenon: hijacking for extortion. On 4 June, Arthur Gates Barkley, who had been entangled in near-constant litigation since 1963 with the Internal Revenue Services, including an unsuccessful attempt to have his appeal heard in the Supreme Court, boarded a TWA flight from Phoenix to Ronald Reagan Washington National Airport. As a result of a defective magnetometer and overwhelmed ticket agents, he was able to smuggle aboard a pistol, a straight razor and a steel can full of gasoline. Over Albuquerque, Barkley entered the cockpit and demanded the plane be diverted to Dulles International Airport, about 50 km away from its intended destination, along with a ransom of $100 million in small-denomination, non-sequential bills taken from the coffers of the Supreme Court. Barkley vowed that, if these demands were not met, he would set the plane and its passengers ablaze.

TWA officials were caught unprepared by Barkley's demand for a ransom, based on the existing propositional knowledge that hijackers on US soil were solely interested in obtaining passage to a foreign nation rather than exchanging passengers for money. However, cognizant of the murder of an Eastern Air Lines co-pilot during a hijacking three months previously, TWA opted to comply – so far as was feasible – and delivered $100,000 in ransom. The incident ended when police marksmen shot out the plane's tires and stormed the plane, injuring Barkley, who was eventually declared incompetent to stand trial in November 1971 and committed to a psychiatric hospital in Georgia.

Despite his spectacular failure, Barkley's ambitious revenge against the US government and the Supreme Court represented one of the year's most captivating media spectacles. Dozens of cameras had captured the money exchange from the tarmac to the plane, and a photojournalist who happened to be a passenger had taken five pictures of the firefight inside the plane. Moreover, *Life* magazine ran a major spread on Barkley's life, featuring the blurry photographs taken aboard the plane (Koerner 2013). Given the potential gain, and the apparent lack of punishment Barkley received, it is not surprising that this highly publicized incident was followed by a string of similar acts of financial extortion.

Arguably the most long-lasting and noteworthy criminal innovation related to hijacking was that proposed by Paul Joseph Cini. Inspired by a television news segment about Barkley's failed hijacking, Cini had surmised that a hijacker could escape with his ransom if he then took to the skies once more and parachuted from the plane. In the autumn of 1971, Cini – who falsely claimed membership of the Provisional Irish Republican Army (PIRA) – seized an Air Canada plane flying from Vancouver to Toronto and set out to test his innovative idea, bringing on board a parachute he had purchased from a Chicago skydiving shop, which he would use to facilitate his escape with the $1.5 million he demanded in ransom. After having received only $50,000 in ransom, Cini's plan came to a halt when he 'put his shotgun down to use a fire axe to cut open the parachute pack'. Immediately, the captain kicked 'the gun down as far as [he] could and grabbed his throat', after which another crew member 'grabbed an axe and hit the hijacker on the head', fracturing his skull (*Times* 1971). While unsuccessful, Barkley's and Cini's innovations – ransom demands and the use of parachutes, respectively – quickly became part of the prescriptive knowledge surrounding criminally motivated hijacking in the United States and came to represent a new manner of security threat.

6.2 TRANSMISSION: THE ROLE OF THE MEDIA

The transmission of hijacking for ransom was facilitated by media attention. Although crew members foiled Cini's attempt, the event received international attention and, only twelve days later, Cini's innovation was replicated in what arguably became the most infamous US criminal hijacking.

On 24 November 1971, Northwest Airlines Flight 305, a Boeing 727 flying from Washington, DC, to Portland, Oregon, was hijacked by an individual calling himself Dan Cooper, who claimed to have a bomb in his briefcase. After requesting and receiving a ransom of $200,000 in cash and two parachutes, he asked to be flown to Mexico City, with a refuelling stop in Reno, Nevada; he subsequently bailed out of the aft stairs en route to Reno. While some of the ransom money was later recovered along the banks of the Columbia River in 1980, the hijacker was never apprehended despite a massive search. It is unlikely that 'Cooper' survived the jump having apparently had very limited knowledge of skydiving, as evidenced by the fact that he jumped without a reserve chute or protective gear. Moreover, the speed at which the plane was travelling, roughly 195 miles per hour, would most likely have rendered him unconscious immediately after jumping, meaning he likely fell to his death without ever having a chance to deploy his parachute.[4] Even if Cooper had survived the jump, it is likely that he would have succumbed to the elements, having jumped into the darkness at a temperature of −15C, without any equipment to survive in the wilderness. Nonetheless, the incident generated widespread interest and was immortalized in US folklore. For example, a Portland lounge singer Thom Bresh scored a minor hit with his 1972 popular country-and-western song titled *D.B. Cooper, Where Are You?* (Kingsbury 1998, 32). This hijacking also provided the plot lines for a made-for-TV movie titled *In Search of D.B. Cooper* (1979), a 1981 adventure movie titled *The Pursuit of D.B. Cooper* starring Treat Williams as Cooper and Robert Duvall as an insurance investigator pursuing him, and countless articles and books.[5]

More importantly, a wave of similar criminal hijackings – involving demands for ransoms and parachutes – ensued, with seventeen such similar events occurring within the next six months (Preston 1998, 137). In three additional cases, a parachute was not identified as part of the ransom demand, but the hijackers did parachute out of the hijacked aircraft. Although parachutes were part of the ransom demanded in seventeen cases, the jump was only made by the hijacker in five of these cases. In the first case, the hijacker jumped off the aircraft over Denver, Colorado, where he was later captured and sent to prison for forty years (*Times* 1972a, 5). Another hijacker parachuted from a jet over Provo, Utah, but was apprehended soon after his jump and sentenced to forty-five years in prison (*New York Times* 1972a, 1; *United States v. Richard Floyd McCoy* 1973, 14–20). A third hijacker parachuted over Honduras but was shortly captured and received a life sentence (*Times* 1972b; 1972c). The fourth hijacker jumped off a hijacked jet near Lake Washoe, Nevada, and was apprehended within two hours of his jump and sentenced to prison for thirty years (*New York Times* 1972b). The final hijacker jumped from the aircraft over Peru, Indiana, was captured five days after the hijacking, and sentenced to life in prison (*Chicago Tribune* 1972; *United States v. Martin J. McNally* 1973). Despite the general failure of such hijackings, this trend prompted the Federal Aviation Administration (FAA) to order airlines to modify the tail and central exit doors of the relevant aircraft so that they could not be opened in flight (Kraus 1973).

Mass media's role in spreading new technical innovations for criminal gains during this period is exemplified by the patterns observed by the FAA in relation to airings of the television program *Doomsday Flight* and subsequent hijackings. The plot of this 1966 disaster program involved an extortionist calling and threatening airline officials by revealing that a pressure sensitive bomb would explode aboard the plane should it descend below five thousand feet. The FAA observed that there was a correlation between broadcasts of the film and bomb threats; as a result FAA officials urged TV stations not to air the film on the basis that it seemed to inspire similar extortion attempts (*Byran Times* 1971). This rather extraordinary request, well beyond the scope of the FAA's powers, was prompted by the diversion of a British Airways Boeing 747 from Montreal to London, following a threat that almost exactly followed the script of the film: an extortionist threatened that a bomb would explode if the plane dropped below five thousand feet. This threat – which turned out to be a hoax – occurred less than a week after a screening of the film in Canada (*Byran Times* 1971).

Mindful of their potential role in spreading pertinent information (namely prescriptive knowledge about hijacking that could be used by others) and showing uncharacteristic restraint, media outlets in the United States began to black out the details of successful hijackings and generally abstained from publishing the names of hijackers. This initiative was largely motivated by the generally held belief that hijackers were dangerously psychotic but logically brilliant in working out and executing their plans, possessing the capability to quickly innovate on previous attempts (Rogers 2005, 185). FAA officials reasoned that the continuous emergence of new variations of hijacking made the control of aerial piracy an especially difficult task; therefore, an important aspect to curbing this trend was to make it impossible for would-be hijackers to learn from the trial-and-error process of others (Rogers 2005, 183–85).

The Diffusion of Hijacking for Financial Gain

On an international scale, and likely learning from the well-publicized innovations of criminals in the United States, claim-makers rapidly adopted hijacking for the purpose of extortion to fund their claim-making exercises. For example, Palestinian claim-makers, who continued to innovate in parallel to criminal innovators, began incorporating demands for financial ransom into their hijacking techniques during the same time period, as did a number of other groups.

As discussed in the previous chapter, during the late 1960s, the PFLP and splinter groups had successfully deployed the deliberate destruction of aircraft, along with hostage taking, as means of obtaining concessions from governments. However, emboldened by their previous successful negotiations with various Western and Middle Eastern governments, and likely inspired by events in the United States, the Popular Front for the Liberation of Palestine-External Operations (PFLP-EO) introduced hijacking for ransom as part of their repertoire of contention in 1972. On 22 February, Lufthansa Flight 649, a Boeing 747 airliner en route from New Delhi to Athens, was hijacked and, mimicking the technique employed successfully two years previous during the Dawson's Field hijackings, diverted to an unprepared airstrip in the Arabian Desert. Arguing that landing at this unkempt airfield would be too dangerous, the crew managed to convince the hijackers to land elsewhere. The plane was thus diverted to Aden International Airport, in what was then South Yemen, and the hijackers, having threatened to destroy the aircraft, demanded and received a ransom of $5 million, which, according to the West German magazine *Der Spiegel*, was later used to fund the joint PFLP-EO and Japanese Red Army's (JRA's) Lod Airport massacre, detailed in the previous chapter (*Der Spiegel* 1972). The hijacking of Lufthansa Flight 649 represents the first time the PFLP demanded a monetary ransom in exchange for the safe return of a hijacked aircraft, instead of a political concession such as the release of prisoners. Hijacking thus no longer represented only a means to make a symbolic point or gain political concessions but emerged as part of the logistics of claim-making, allowing groups to fund other activities.

6.3 SELECTION: AUTHORITY INNOVATION AND THE ABANDONMENT OF HIJACKING

Criminal hijackings by Barkley, Cini, 'Cooper', and their contemporaries in the early 1970s demonstrate the continued importance of the Havana Rules – which prior to the rescue operations in Entebee (1976) and Mogadishu (1977) had not yet been totally abandoned – as the basis for propositional knowledge about how authorities would and should react to hijackings. Indeed, while sky marshals were used during the 1960s in the United States (such programs have already been instituted onboard Soviet and Israeli airlines in response to the freedom flights and Palestinian operations respectively), this was met with resistance from pilots at first.

The US government initially instituted a small programme of sky marshals, but by the end of the decade this programme had been replaced by FAA peace officers; these were generally former pilots deputized by the Justice Department and trained in the use of firearms. However, the FAA programme only involved a small number of plain-clothes officers, who travelled on domestic flights randomly and infrequently, usually after receiving a tip about a potential hijacking (Phillips 1973, 233). This programme existed despite resistance from the majority of professional US pilots, who opposed any armed presence on their planes: 'You will find most crew would rather fly the aeroplane to Cuba than get their fuel line or control shot out', remarked a FAA official (Phillips 1973, 233). This attitude was also reflected in airlines' guidance to crew, which was directly influenced by the Havana Rules:

> The most important consideration under the act of aircraft piracy is the safety of the lives of the passengers and crew. Any other factor is secondary. In the face of an armed threat to *any* crew member, comply with the demands presented. Do not make an attempt to disarm, shoot out, or otherwise jeopardize the safety of the flight. . . . To sum up: Going on past experience, it is much more prudent to submit to all the gunman's demand than to attempt action which may well jeopardize the lives of all on board. (Phillips 1973, 233)

Given that the propositional knowledge encompassed in the Havana Rules was arguably well understood by both crews and perpetrators, the latter generally avoided using lethal force during takeovers prior to the later escalation in violence committed by Palestinian hijackers and their supporters. As a result, the public perception in the United States of hijacking for ransom remained largely similar to feelings about planes hijacked for transportation to Cuba. Hijacking for ransom was deemed a mild inconvenience for those victimized, and, while potentially dangerous, it was not taken overly seriously when it ended without physical harm to planes or passengers, as it did in the majority of cases. Reflecting on this somewhat laissez-faire attitude, an editorial in the *Pittsburgh Press* reported: 'It seems the best we can do is add airplane hijacking to the list of things we don't like, along with sin and high taxes . . . and pray there are no tragedies' (Koerner 2013, 49).

Indeed, hijackings in the United States were initially seen as little more than an inconvenience to those affected, including airlines, crew, and passengers. Newspapers were somewhat sympathetic but downplayed any threats of violence by portraying hijackers as an unwelcome nuisance to travellers, not unlike lost baggage or a weather-related delay (Latner 2015, 24). In fact, some publications made light of the phenomena and went so far as to offer tongue-in-cheek advice to passengers lest their plane was taken over. For example, *The Sun*'s (1969) coverage of the first hijacking of 1969 featured a photograph of a flight attendant with the caption, 'Coffee, tea or – Castro?' on its front page. Furthermore, a cartoon published in the *Bangor Daily News* (a Maine-based publication) depicted US tourists boarding a passenger aeroplane asking the Captain, 'Do you think we can get a side trip to Cuba or someplace?' Similarly, a December 1968 *Time* magazine article, 'What to Do When the Hijackers Come?' – published in the travel section of the magazine – provided travel tips for passengers diverted to Cuba, encouraging them to enjoy their overnight stay at the Havana Libre Hotel or the Varadero Internacional, courtesy of the Cuban government. Furthermore, they were urged to take advantage of the shopping opportunity for high-quality cigars and rum, and to 'bring your bathing suit' to enjoy the '15-mile-long-ribbon of white sand' at Varadero Beach. The guide predicted: 'You will probably be treated to a nightclub, complete with daiquiris, a chorus line and an audience of gaping Eastern Europeans', and advised that 'The shopping downtown is better: in addition to cigars and rum, bargains include East German cameras and beautifully embroidered Czech peasant blouses' (Koerner 2013, 49–50). Indeed, diverted passengers and crew often received extravagant treatment on their arrival, including entertainment from a live Cuban band and gourmet dinners of steak and shrimp. Others were given cigars and photos of Che Guevara while they waited on the airport tarmac, the bills for which were often sent to the airlines (*New York Times* 1969, 1967).

However, media coverage of hijacking sobered somewhat in the early 1970s, partly as a result of increased violence and the lethal nature of aeroplane hijackings, as the technique was increasingly appropriated by criminals looking for financial gain and less concerned by optics or constituency costs, rather than claim-makers whose behaviour was chiefly influenced by the propositional knowledge of the Havana Rules and an understanding that the effectiveness of their technique depended in part on perception of legitimacy. The rise in violence and lethal hijacking-related attacks in the United States is best exemplified by two incidents at the end of 1972, one of which included the first threat of deliberately crashing a hijacked aeroplane into a building, foreshadowing the events of 9/11 some three decades later.

On 29 October 1972, four fugitives, a father and three sons, killed a ticket agent and injured a member of ground crew while forcing their way aboard an Eastern Boeing 727 in Houston bound for Atlanta, before forcing the pilot to fly them to Cuba. This was followed by an even more sensational incident two weeks later when, on 10 November 1972, three wanted men – two of whom were out on bail accused of rape and the other an escaped convict – hijacked a Southern Airways DC-9 flying from Birmingham to Montgomery, Alabama, and perpetrated the first, in several, recorded credible threats of using an aircraft as a weapon:

> Fearing that male passengers might be concealing weapons, the hijackers made them all strip down to their underwear. After refuelling at Jackson, Mississippi, the plane circled Detroit, and the hijackers demanded a ransom of $10 million and threatened to crash the plane into the atomic plant at Oak Ridge, Tennessee, if the ransom was not paid. The plane circled the nuclear plant until deteriorating weather conditions forced it to land at Cleveland with only eight minutes of fuel left. The plane [refuelled and] took off for Toronto with the threat that unless the $10 million was handed over to them there, they would return to crash the plane into the Oak Ridge [nuclear] plant. (St John 1991, 20)

In addition to the money, the hijackers demanded parachutes, bulletproof vests, amphetamines, and food, as well as a document bearing a US official seal that stated that the ransom was a federal grant (Phillips 1973). In Toronto, authorities gave the hijackers $500,000, reporting that an additional $1,500,000 was on its way to Toronto in a Lear executive jet chartered by Detroit City officials. Deeming this sum insufficient, the hijackers ordered that the plane take off again in the direction of Oak Ridge, where it circled for five hours as the hijackers threatened to 'make this thing look worse than Munich', a reference to the Munich massacre during the 1972 Summer Olympics only three months earlier, when eleven Israeli athletes had been killed by the Black September Organization (Phillips 1973, 91). The Atomic Energy Commission evacuated more than two thousand employees and shut down three nuclear reactors. The plane then landed at Lovell Field airport in Chattanooga, Tennessee, to collect the additional $1,500,000 in ransom from the chartered Lear jet along with ten parachutes, crash helmets, bullet-proof vests, amphetamines, fifty packaged meals, and a (worthless) declaration typed up by a federal court clerk in Knoxville on parchment paper bearing a US Attorney seal and tied with a ribbon, stating that the ransom was a grant. The plane then took off for Cuba, where, upon arrival, the hijackers were refused asylum but permitted to re-board the aircraft and take off again. With a US Navy DC6 plane containing Federal Bureau of Investigation (FBI) agents and sharpshooters tailing the flight, the hijackers announced they would fly to Switzerland and landed in Orlando to refuel and to collect navigation aids. After the plane refuelled, the FBI opted to end the hijacking by shooting out its tires, prompting the hijackers to shoot the co-pilot in the shoulder and threaten to shoot all the passengers, one by one, unless the aircraft was allowed to take off. The plane, now with the additional issue of overheating engines caused by pieces of shot-away tires, circled President Richard M. Nixon's home in Key Biscayne for approximately an hour and demanded to speak to the president – a request that was denied by his staff – before once again heading to Cuba. After a dramatic landing, the hijackers were finally arrested by Cuban authorities. The hijacking lasted a total of twenty-nine hours, included nine forced stops, and involved three countries (*Times* 1972d, 6; 1972e, 9).

Authorities' prescriptive and propositional knowledge dramatically changed as a result of this event. First, shooting out tires while a plane was taxiing was no longer considered a safe procedure; in fact, this FBI reaction seriously undermined the aviation community's confidence in the bureau as a hijacking intervention force. Second, 'a serious threat to an American nuclear reactor had been made . . . and the vulnerability of the whole airport system had been mercilessly exposed' (St John 1991, 21). Lastly, the event prompted a growing recognition of the catastrophic potential of ceding control of a commercial airliner to hijackers. As a result of these changes to propositional knowledge, authorities undertook a series of reactive measures.

On 5 December 1972, all US airport operators were given sixty days to arrange for armed local law enforcement officers to be stationed at passenger checkpoints during boarding and re-boarding. As of 5 January 1973, it became mandatory for all US commercial airports be equipped with walk-through metal detectors (Phillips 1973, 266). Following their introduction in the United States, the use of airport metal detectors spread fairly rapidly to other industrialized countries, before being gradually adopted by most other nations of the world in a short time period. Moreover, the aforementioned event led directly to the negotiation of a hijacking agreement between the Nixon administration and Cuba, the *Cuba-United States Memorandum of Understanding on Hijacking of Aircraft and Vessels* (MOU) – discussed in chapter 4 – which facilitated the extradition or punishment of a person 'who seizes, moves, appropriates, or diverts from its normal route or activities an aircraft or vessel' (*Cuba-United States: Memorandum of Understanding on the Hijacking of Aircraft and Vessels* 1973).

These new measures were effective in that no airliner was successfully hijacked in the United States the following year, due to the reduced feasibility of such action given that it was increasingly difficult to get weapons on board. In fact, it would be more than three years before there was another successful hijacking in the United States, and the number of diverted US flights never returned to a level as high as that in the pre-1973 period. In its efforts to suppress further aircraft seizures, Cuba took the unprecedented step of beginning to extradite hijackers of US aircraft in May 1975 (*New York Times* 1975, 10; *Washington Post* 1975, 11). Within eight days, three perpetrators from separate hijackings in 1970 and 1971 were handed over to US authorities and, during the next year, eleven hijackers whose offences had been committed between 1961 and 1973 were returned to the United States to face prosecution (Evans and Murphy 1978, 26).

The main explanation for the sharp drop in hijackings in the United States between 1973 and 1980 is threefold. First, the technique significantly lost feasibility and effectiveness after the introduction of deterrence measures that decreased the probability that a hijacking would get off the ground. Second, the likelihood of incarceration implies a change in the perceived legitimacy of the technique; while less applicable to criminal actors, for claim-makers the mutual extraditions of hijackers between Cuba and the United States signalled that these countries' perception of hijacking as a legitimate technique had ceased. Third, and perhaps most significant when discussing hijacking as a technique of contention, the severity of sanctions – with the Cuba-US agreement to extradite hijackers back to the flight's country of origin – made the effectiveness of the technique almost non-existent for those who wished to leave their home country because they were no longer granted refuge abroad. Supporting this, Dugan et al. (2005) contends that the introduction of the *Cuba-United States Memorandum of Understanding* significantly decreased the hazard of Cuba-diverted and US-origin hijackings, arguing that manipulating the costs and benefits – in other words the effectiveness and feasibility – of hijacking led to crime prevention in this case.

Addressing the innovations brought about by hijackers attempting to derive financial profit is significant to gaining an understanding of the outcomes of both the intense one-upmanship among perpetrators and the responses of airlines and law enforcement officials to such actions. Most importantly, the so called 'criminal innovations' addressed in this chapter – and indeed the change in response by states – significantly influenced the wider propositional and prescriptive knowledge surrounding all strains of hijacking in the United States. In many ways, some of the most innovative changes to hijacking during this period were not the product of political struggle but rather the brainchild of greedy individuals seeking money, fame, and notoriety. However, irrespective of their motives – and perhaps because of their highly ambitious, dramatic, and daring feats – their innovations were quickly transmitted by the media and then replicated by others, both criminals and claim-makers alike. The survey of criminal innovations serves to clearly illuminate the indisputably important role of the media in accelerating the spread of a given technique.

Finally, the importance of criminal innovations can be seen by the response they provoked; the unquestionably selfish nature of these people's motives, alongside their brutality and disregard for the safety of passengers finally pushed the US government into preventative action after many years of accepting, if not encouraging, those who used hijacking as a means to escape the yoke of communism. Ultimately, the significance of this strain of hijacking to the development of hijacking over time is how completely they altered the security environment, and for that reason, criminal innovation should not be ignored.

NOTES

1. On 28 March 1933, a G-AACI travelling between Brussels and London plummeted to the ground after suffering a catastrophic fire on board. In the absence of discovered technical failures in the aircraft, it has been suggested that fire was a result of a botched robbery (Gunston 2001, 305). On 16 July 1948, the 'Miss Macau', a Cathay Pacific Catalina flying boat, was commandeered by a four-man robbery team and crashed after the pilot and co-pilot were shot. All twenty-five people on board the flight died (Gero 1997; Phillips 1973, 269).

2. As mentioned in chapter 5, a DC-3 disintegrated in flight outside of Quebec, killing all twenty-three individuals aboard, as a result of a bomb placed by a jeweller in his wife's luggage in a plot to kill her, avoid a divorce, collect a $10,000 life-insurance policy, and elope with his mistress. Three people were named as beneficiaries of the life-insurance policy: the husband, his mistress, who airmailed the bomb, and her brother, a clockmaker, who helped make the

timing mechanism (Gero 1997, 12). Similarly, on 1 November 1955, a bomb made of dynamite exploded on a Denver to Seattle flight, killing forty-four people. The bomb had been placed on the plane by John Graham, who sought to kill his mother to collect a large life-insurance payout (Gero 1997, 94).

3. For more on the concept of criminal innovation, see Furnell et al. (2005), Lacoste and Tremblay (2003), Nagin (1998), and Jacobi and Kind (2005).

4. Experienced skydivers have raised serious doubts that Cooper could have survived his jump. In fact, no professional skydivers attempted to jump out of a Boeing 727 until the 1992 World Freefall Convention. One of the jumpers, who jumped at an airspeed of 155 miles per hour, 40 miles per hour slower than Cooper, was amazed by the violence of the experience, stating: 'The first thing you noticed after exit was the heat from the jet engines and the smell of jet fuel . . . there was a dead void, then a blast from the jet stream. It felt like I was being tackled from behind' (Koerner 2013, 84).

5. See Rhodes and Calame (1991), Collins (2013), Gray (2012), and Tosaw (1984).

Chapter Seven

Aeroplanes as Weapons of Destruction

On 11 September 2001, four passenger airliners, operated by two major US air carriers, were hijacked by 19 al-Qaeda operatives planning to crash the planes into salient landmarks, and effectively employing the hijacked aircraft as weapons of destruction. At 8:13 am, fourteen minutes after departure from Logan International Airport in Boston, American Airlines Flight 11, was hijacked and diverted to New York, where it was deliberately crashed into the World Trade Center's North Tower at 8:46. Upon impact, the plane, travelling at 470 mph and filled with 10,000 gallons of fuel, exploded with the estimated force of 480,000 pounds of TNT. Sixteen minutes later, United Airlines Flight 175 – on route to Los Angeles from Logan International Airport – struck the South Tower. With steel beams supporting the upper floors literally buckling in the heat, the entire South Tower collapsed at 9:59, with the North Tower succumbing and collapsing at 10:28. Meanwhile, American Airlines Flight 77, from Dulles International Airport en route to Los Angeles, was hijacked at 8:50, diverted from its scheduled flight path, and deliberately flown into the Pentagon at 9:45. The last flight, United Airlines Flight 93, from Newark International Airport to San Francisco, was hijacked and then crashed into a field in Somerset County, Pennsylvania, to thwart an attempt by the passengers and crew to regain control (Cauchon 2001). In total, 2,996 died during the attacks, including the 19 hijackers, making it the single deadliest terror attack in history.

Although the use of aircraft as weapons only achieved notoriety after the events of 9/11 and despite the fact that – in the words of Dolnik (2007), the 'execution and planning in this case was superb' (p. 38) – the idea of deliberately flying an aircraft into a building to cause destruction was far from new. Indeed, the antecedent events of 9/11 emerged first in the 1970s. As such, the purpose of this chapter is threefold. First, in the *variation* section I demonstrate that this technique existed long before its adoption by al-Qaeda. I begin by situating the emergence of technique within the long history of using the kinetic energy of maritime and aerial vessels to damage a target by ramming them during warfare, contending that the propositional knowledge that formed the epistemic base for the technique was therefore widely available by the time it first emerged as a form of political contention. In fact, the first concrete plot to advance a political claim can be found in 1974, when a man with a personal vendetta against the Internal Revenue Service attempted to hijack a plane with the intent of crashing it into the White House. However, despite the existence of up to twenty-one such plots – culminating in the hijacking of Air France Flight 8969 that the hijackers intended to deliberately destroy over Paris – officials in the United States appear to have failed to take the existence of this threat seriously, and no change to existing security regimens occurred to counter this emerging technique, an oversight that would later have tragic consequences. Second, in the *transmission* section I argue that prior to the attacks of 9/11, both the propositional knowledge providing the epistemic base for this technique and a rudimentary form of the prescriptive knowledge about it already existed within works of fiction and in the minds of some claim-makers. The diffusion of this technique therefore was not entirely facilitated by the media – though the media's coverage of other hijacking events certainly continued to play a role – but works of literary fiction and films appear to have also played a seminal role in spreading prescriptive knowledge. Lastly, in the *selection* section of this chapter, I argue that al-Qaeda's adoption of aeroplanes as weapons is best understood as the result of a lengthy trial-and-error process by several groups; the 9/11 plot was, in fact, designed explicitly to attack weaknesses in air travel security and hijacking response policies produced as a result of a fixation with preventing the post-1968 style of hijackings.

While al-Qaeda's attacks on 11 September 2001 were undeniably novel in terms of the magnitude of infrastructure destruction and loss of life caused, I argue that, ultimately, they should be understood as a mutation, just one among many variations, of the technique of aircraft hijacking along an evolutionary path that started in Peru in the 1930s. Further, it will be demonstrated that within the cat-and-mouse game many states engaged in with claim-makers, they failed to take seriously the emergence of aeroplanes as weapons and, instead, focused on disrupting hijacking for transport, hostage taking, or bomb plots, failing to adapt to new propositional knowledge about hijacking as a possible technique of contention.

7.1 VARIATION: NOT SUCH AN ORIGINAL IDEA AFTER ALL

The prescriptive knowledge at the root of using aeroplanes as weapons of destruction has a long history that far predates aviation. In its basic form, the prescriptive knowledge that one can damage a target by ramming a vessel into it is centuries old and was a common feature of naval warfare for thousands of years. For instance, as early as the eighth century BCE, galleys were equipped with heavy bronze rams, and records of the Persian Wars in the early fifth century BCE, written by the ancient historian Herodotus (c. 484–425 BCE), show that ramming tactics had emerged by this time. Centuries later, at the battle of Hampton Roads during the US Civil War, the armoured Confederate warship *Virginia* purposefully rammed the Union frigate *Cumberland*, sinking her almost immediately (Mark 2008). Furthermore, during both World War I and II, naval ships often rammed other vessels, and in the air, both conflicts saw pilots routinely ramming other aircraft as a last-ditch tactic in combat (Quinlivan 1986).

In fact, the Japanese practice of *kamikaze* during the Second World War is clearly an example of ramming, although the primary mode of destruction was not the physical impact itself but rather the explosives carried. Japan's Kamikaze Special Attack Force sent many young men with limited military or flying skills to mount between three and five thousand suicide missions from 1944 to 1945, resulting in between fifteen and sixteen thousand Allied deaths along with more than forty thousand wounded (Dower 1993, 331; Stern 2010, 329–30). In the Battle of Okinawa, some two thousand Kamikaze pilots rammed fully fuelled planes into more than three hundred ships, killing five thousand Americans, alongside the two thousand Kamikaze pilots, in the costliest naval battle in US history (Madsen 2004). These attacks are important in the examination of hijacking because they were the first examples of aeroplanes being used intentionally as weapons in such a way that made the death of the pilots inevitable and, as such, can be seen to be the bridge between ramming and using aircraft themselves (rather than the armaments they could carry) as a weapon of destruction.

While some scholars have attempted to draw – at times rather spurious – comparisons between the Empire of Japan's ideological use of the native folk traditions of Shinto and the ideologies of al-Qaeda,[1] such analyses tend to miss the most salient point: The widespread mediatization and construction of mythical narratives around kamikaze attacks had a profound influence on diffusing both propositional and prescriptive knowledge at the root of using aeroplanes as weapons of destruction. In fact, despite the apparent absence of kamikaze-style suicide attacks in the 1950s and 1960s, the propositional knowledge of planes as weapons of destruction arguably persisted through mythical war stories and films, a point I will explore in greater depth in the *transmission* section of this chapter.

In non-military settings, the technique of deliberately crashing an aircraft into a building to cause its destruction also has a history that predates 9/11. In fact, prior to 9/11, there were at least twenty-one occasions,[2] compiled in this study's hijacking database, where an aeroplane was deliberately flown into a building or where a concrete plan to fly an aeroplane into a building was curtailed.

The earliest recorded concrete attempt to employ a hijacked aircraft as a weapon of destruction in a non-military setting for political purposes occurred on 22 February 1974 when Samuel Byck attempted to hijack a Southern Airways flight. While, admittedly, a similar threat was made (as discussed in the previous chapter) in the case of the 1972 Southern Airways Flight 49 hijacking where the hijackers threatened to fly the plane into a nuclear facility, the hijackers did not seem to seriously intend to follow through on these threats – given that their primary motive was to escape prosecution. In contrast, in the aftermath of Byck's attempted hijacking of a Delta flight to Atlanta at Baltimore/Washington International Airport, the full scale of his plan was uncovered when a series of public figures and journalists received audio cassettes sent by Byck in the days prior to the attempted hijacking, in which he detailed his plan to hijack a commercial airline, force the pilot to fly it to Washington, then grab hold of the controls, and crash it into the White House to kill President Richard Nixon as retribution for the Watergate scandal ("Summary Statement of Facts: The September 12, 1994 Plane Crash" 1995). However, Byck's plan was foiled on the ground, as – after he killed a guard at the security check point and the co-pilot and wounded the pilot – police outside the plane initiated a firefight after failing to shoot out the tires; Byck killed himself after sustaining an injury (Clarke 1990). Byck had previously been investigated by the Secret Service in 1972 on the basis of reports that he had threatened President Nixon, which lent credence to his recorded messages, as did his eventual suicide.

How exactly Byck developed the idea of deliberately crashing a plane into a building to conduct a political assassination is unclear, especially given that relatively little attention has been devoted to Byck and his intentions in comparison with other would-be presidential assassins such as John Hinckley, Jr.[3] However, it appears that Byck might have been influenced by the actions of Robert Preston, whose aerial joyride a week previously in the exclusion zone around the White House highlighted the site's vulnerability to aerial attacks.

On 17 February 1974, Robert Preston, a private in the US Army, stole a US Army Bell UH-1 Iroquois helicopter from Fort Meade, Maryland, and flew it to the White House complex, ostensibly to demonstrate his piloting skills to his superiors, less than a week prior to Byck's attempted hijacking. Passing over the building, he returned to the south grounds, where he hovered for approximately six minutes and touched down briefly about 150 feet away from the West Wing. Members of the Executive Protective Service (EPS) – now called the US Secret Service Uniformed Division – seemingly unaware that the helicopter was stolen, made no attempt to engage the pilot or bring down the helicopter. Preston then left the area and flew back to Fort Meade, pursued by two Maryland State Police helicopters, one of which was forced to abort the pursuit due to Preston's erratic manoeuvres. Preston then returned to the White House; this time, as the helicopter hovered ten metres above the south grounds, EPS officers engaged with shotgun and submachine gunfire, forcing a slightly injured Preston to land the aircraft (Brogan 1974, 1; *Times* 1974, 10).

Preston's and Byck's actions demonstrate a number of important features, particularly if we assume that news reports of Preston's actions may have partly inspired Byck's actions five days previously – a likely proposition given the close temporal proximity of both incidents and the identical chosen 'staging area'. Indeed, while both Preston and Byck had profoundly different objectives, both events are connected by the lure of national symbols as a place of high visibility. In the case of Preston, the White House was chosen as an eye-catching venue for showing off his flying ability, while for Byck, it was selected to increase the visibility and, therefore, effectiveness of an attack against the president. Moreover, Preston's joyride showed the feasibility of using an aircraft as a means of access to symbolically important structures, and Byck attempted to put that prescriptive knowledge into action to make a political point. Indeed, if Byck was inspired by Preston, it further demonstrates how the actions of criminals (as described in the previous chapter) can have a profound impact on the emergence of techniques of contention, especially in the presence of media attention.

In addition to the impact Preston's joyride may have had on Byck, I argue that various previous events had an impact on the general propositional knowledge forming the epistemic base on which Byck conceived his seemingly innovative technique of contention. First, throughout the 1960s, individuals seizing planes and deliberately destroying them – often causing significant loss of life – became widespread. For example, on 22 May 1962, a passenger purposefully destroyed Continental Airlines Flight 11 en route from O'Hare Airport to Kansas City, killing himself, along with forty-five crew and passengers on board to commit insurance fraud to benefit his widow (Gero 1997, 49, 98). Similarly, on 7 May 1964, Francisco Paula Gonzales shot and killed both the pilot and co-pilot of a Pacific Airlines Flight 773 flying from Stockton Metropolitan Airport to San Francisco, causing the plane to crash, killing himself and all forty-four aboard (*New York Times* 1964, 1). These events served as the basis for the story of the 1970 Academy Award winning film *Airport*. Moreover, the catastrophic potential of aircraft crashes was well understood, as demonstrated by the fact that the hijackers of the 1972 Southern Airways Flight 49, who threatened to attack a nuclear plant, claimed that the outcome would be 'worse than Munich' (Phillips 1973, 91) if their demands were not met.

In addition to the propositional knowledge of the destructive potential of aircraft formed by these events, it would be unwise to dismiss the importance of the kamikaze tradition on propositional knowledge concerning the use of planes as weapons. This propositional knowledge persisted, after the Second World War, through war stories and films that had a long-lasting legacy in Japan and elsewhere. The influence of these narratives is possibly best illustrated by an attack against Yoshio Kodama, a multi-millionaire Japanese right-wing politician accused of accepting more than $7 million from the Lockheed Corporation to bribe Japanese officials. On 23 March 1976, Mitsuyasu Maeno, a Japanese actor dressed in the uniform of a kamikaze pilot, announced over his aircraft's radio that Kodama had betrayed both Japan and the Samurai spirit and then deliberately crashed his rented Piper Cherokee into Kodama's house while shouting 'Long live the Emperor!' Maeno's plane smashed into the veranda, killing Maeno and setting the building ablaze (*The Naples Daily News* 1976, 2). Maeno's attack clearly demonstrates the enduring influence kamikaze attacks had on the propositional knowledge of claim-makers.

Between 1973 and 2001, government intelligence officials around the world reported numerous plots to crash aeroplanes deliberately into targets as a means of claim-making (Dolnik 2007). In fact, in 1993, the Pentagon commissioned an expert panel to discuss how aeroplanes might be used to destroy national landmarks and indicated their concerns regarding the deployment of such techniques, directly referencing the 1974 Preston and Byck incidents. However, detailed scenarios identified in the $150,000 study for the Department of Defense's Office of Special Operations and Low-Intensity Conflict were not published, 'partly out of a fear that it could give terrorists ideas' (Warrick and Stephens 2001). Despite the decision not to publish this report, prescriptive knowledge relating to the use of an aircraft as a weapon had existed long before the report was conducted, as shown by the replication of kamikaze-style attacks, and partly thanks to novelists and screenwriters, which I will address further in the *transmission* section of this chapter.

Despite the Office of Special Operations and Low-Intensity Conflict report, the threat posed by this technique does not appear to have been taken seriously until 1994, when the White House was once again targeted. On 12 September 1994, Frank Eugene Corder, a thirty-eight-year-old man apparently troubled by a 'wide array of financial, marital, and legal problems', broke into the Aldino Airport in Churchville, Maryland, stole a single-engine Cessna P-150 aircraft, and flew to Washington, DC, with the intention of using it as a weapon ("Summary Statement of Facts: The September 12, 1994 Plane Crash" 1995). After circling over the western part of the District of Columbia, the Cessna turned 'over the Ellipse and dove directly towards the White House at a steep angle of descent' (Harding 2006, 283) before crashing onto the White House lawn, skidding across the ground, hitting a tree and then the southwest corner of the building. While there was minimal damage to the building itself, Corder died from multiple, massive, blunt-force injuries ("Summary Statement of Facts: The September 12, 1994 Plane Crash" 1995).

Although Corder had previously articulated discontent with the policies of the Bill Clinton administration and expressed dislike toward President Clinton, there was no evidence that the aim of the flight was to injure or kill the president or any other Secret Service protectee. Indeed, prior to this incident, Corder had not come to the attention of the Secret Service as a potential threat; therefore, it appears that by crashing onto the White House lawn, he was attempting to fulfil an ambition he had previously expressed to friends: to kill himself 'in a big way' ("Summary Statement of Facts: The September 12, 1994 Plane Crash" 1995). Nonetheless, the incident highlighted the real threat posed by the use of civil aircraft as weapons of destruction and prompted questions among security officials about the adequacy of defence for the nation's capital, reinforcing concerns that had already been expressed in the 1993 report.

Furthermore, this event, as well as the hijackings by Preston and Byck, underscored the longstanding attraction of national symbols as targets of hijacked aeroplane attacks ("Summary Statement of Facts: The September 12, 1994 Plane Crash" 1995). In fact, after the crash, intelligence sources initially theorised that the flight was most likely flown as a deliberate 'proof of concept' attack designed to test Washington's air defence strategy and to expose potential flaws. Intelligence sources argued that if the Cessna 150L had struck the White House wall directly, the concept would have been considered proven and perhaps paved the way for later attacks using heavier aircraft, potentially loaded with explosives (Harding 2006, 283). While the initial assessment of Corder's flight was refuted once information about the perpetrator became known to authorities (Harding 2006, 283), the incident nonetheless did unintentionally function as a proof of concept despite intelligence sources believing otherwise; whereas Byck had failed, Corder showed it was indeed feasible to hijack a plane and to deliberately crash it into the White House before security forces could interfere. If anything, the attack showed that Corder's poor piloting skills appeared to have been the White House's best line of defence against such an attack.

Perhaps the clearest indication that the use of aircraft as a weapon of destruction had truly entered claim-makers' repertoire of contention came on Christmas Eve 1994, during the hijacking of Air France Flight 8969 from Algiers to Orly Airport in Paris. The plane was seized on the ground by members of the Groupe Islamique Armé, a group briefly supported by Osama bin Laden[4] and one of the two main insurgent groups fighting against the

Algerian government during the Algerian Civil War. Imitating the 1986 hijacking of Pan Am Flight 73 by members of the Abu Nidal Organization – a Palestinian nationalist militant group – the hijackers were disguised in uniforms of the Algerian presidential police (Sancton 1995).[5] This operational detail further evidences the claim that successful techniques are transmitted across repertoires of contention and emulated.

After a thirty-nine-hour standoff in Algiers, during which three passengers were killed, the flight departed; however, because of the use of the auxiliary power unit during the standoff, the aircraft had insufficient fuel to reach Paris and was diverted to Marseille (Riding 1994a, A1). In Marseille, the hijackers demanded twenty-seven tons of fuel to fly to Paris, three times the amount required for that route. In response, and believing that the fuel-laden plane could easily be used as a weapon, the French government deployed its specialized counterterrorist paramilitary unit, the *Groupe d'Intervention de la Gendarmerie Nationale* (GIGN), to the airport. Having practiced its rescue manoeuvres on an identical Airbus (Sancton 1995), the GIGN team boarded Flight 8969 and freed all 173 hostages, killing all four terrorists. The subsequent investigation, along with reports from released passengers, concluded that the hijackers had indeed most likely intended to either crash the aeroplane into the Eiffel Tower or blow it up over Paris (Riding 1994b, A3).

The hijacking of Flight 8969 represents the most salient documented use of this combination – the hijacking of a commercial airliner with the intention to use it as a weapon and the targeting of a national symbol to advance a political claim – prior to 9/11. In fact, this case served as a learning tool for the 9/11 attackers. Indeed, although the hijackers of Flight 8969 exhibited a high degree of innovation in their plan to use the aircraft itself as a weapon, they also exhibited major shortfalls in planning and made numerous mistakes in executing their plan. For example, they clearly exhibited a lack of familiarity with the fuel load and the range of the aircraft, communicating the necessity of interference while also creating opportunities for the French security services to storm the plane. Moreover, they failed to maintain the operation's security in front of their hostages, allowing the state new insight into the group's prescriptive knowledge. Potentially more importantly, the incident represented a learning experience for those seeking to employ the technique: Seizing an aircraft was one thing, but any would-be hijackers faced the fundamental problem of forcing airline crews to crash the plane deliberately, given that the threat of death could hardly be seen as persuasive in such circumstances. Therefore, astute observers would recognize that for the technique to be feasible, future attempts would require at least one hijacker to be capable of and willing to steer a plane into a target. Highlighting the fact that this was not an unreasonable or particularly difficult conclusion to come to, the French government warned other governments in early 1995 that the hijackers of Flight 8969 had intended to fly into the Eiffel Tower and cautioned that the next step for terrorists would be to train as pilots (*CBS News* 2004). However, US intelligence officials instead viewed this incident as part of what was – at that time – an ongoing but isolated bombing campaign in France to protest its intervention in Algeria. The Federal Aviation Authority (FAA) meanwhile viewed it as a foiled hijacking rather than a failed use of an aeroplane as a weapon of destruction (Karber 2005, 1382). As a result of these assessments, neither the US government, nor the FAA introduced any new security measures in response to the deployment of this innovative technique. Despite this somewhat nonchalant attitude within the United States, the hijacking of Air France Flight 8969 served, at least in part, as a source of inspiration for the Bojinka plot, which would eventually materialize into 9/11 attacks.

7.2 TRANSMISSION: FROM FICTION TO REALITY

In October 2001, in direct response to the 9/11 attacks, a three-day summit was held at the University of Southern California Institute for Creative Technology, which brought together counter-terrorism officials and Hollywood screenwriters, directors, and producers.[6] The stated purpose of this meeting was 'to brainstorm about possible terrorist targets and schemes in America' (Frank 2017, 1). Frank (2017) contends that the genesis of this meeting was the widespread belief among intelligence officials that the success of the 9/11 attack largely represented a failure of imagination on the part of the US security establishment:

> According to this line of reasoning, counterterrorism cannot confine itself to the accumulation of data concerning the goals, strategies, and means of terrorist networks; it also depends on ingenuity in the imagination of future events. In addition to analyzing facts, it must speculatively work through possibilities, think in the subjunctive. . . . The pivotal task here is to anticipate – on the basis of both fact and conjecture – who could strike when and where and how. Screenwriters and directors seem particularly well equipped for this challenge; after all, they have been tirelessly imagining attacks on domestic targets for several decades. Doubtless, this was the understanding that prompted Washington to seek the advice of Hollywood, in the hope of being able 'to devise plausible ways in which terrorists might launch new attacks against the US'. (Frank 2017, 3–4)

In other words, to prevent future terroristic attacks, counter-terrorism stakeholders deemed it necessary to put the creative imagination to work in devising potential terroristic scenarios. Simply put, as introduced in my framework, innovation is the creative use of propositional knowledge to develop new prescriptive knowledge; in the context of a post-9/11 security environment, professional creative thinkers were called on in hopes of anticipating what the next attack would look like. Later, the 9/11 Commission (National Commission on Terrorist Attacks upon the United States 2004) would reinforce this epistemic reorientation, showing a understanding of the difficulty in anticipating innovation and suggesting that: 'It is therefore crucial to find a way of routinizing, even bureaucratising, the exercise of imagination' (p. 340).

The implication was that Hollywood screenwriters and directors could, and previously had, envisaged techniques that might be employed by claim-makers and identified targets they might select. For example, in March 2002, in an episode of the BBC current affairs television program *Panorama* titled 'Warning from Hollywood', retired US Army Lieutenant Colonel Ralph Peters dramatically stated that 'Hollywood's take on terrorism . . . was absolutely more accurate than virtually any intelligence report I read when I was in the Pentagon' (Frank 2017, 5). The documentary then goes on to contend that, by imagining future techniques employed by terrorists, literary works of fiction, along with television and film, could inspire attacks like 9/11. For example, Tom Clancy's 1994 novel *Debt of Honor* chronicles a Japanese-American war and ends with a Japanese airline pilot crashing his Boeing 747 into the US Capitol Building during the State of the Union Address. Clancy's book is merely one of several works of fiction that depicted events similar to the 9/11 attacks before they occurred. For example, an early scene of the 1977 movie *Telefon* shows the pilot of a small floatplane deliberately crashing into an oil refinery. He is, the film later reveals, a Soviet agent who was planted in the United States to carry out acts of sabotage. The desperate hero of *The Running Man*, a 1982 novel by Stephen King, takes his final revenge on a corrupt corporation by flying an explosive-laden airliner into its headquarters. Moreover, the cover of the paperback edition of Dean Ing's novel *Soft Targets* (1979) depicts a small plane intentionally crashing into the Statue of Liberty.

My argument is not that these works of fiction necessarily did inspire – or were even seen or read by – the 9/11 masterminds but, rather, to prove the previous existence of this technique – at least within the realm of film and literature. The original inspirations for these works of fiction are particularly hard to ascertain, but whether these authors where inspired by early use of ramming as a technique of contention (such as Byck's and Maeno's flights) or by other events such as the Japanese use of kamikaze attacks during the Second World War is somewhat irrelevant; the important fact is that by the mid-1970s and later, the propositional knowledge that underpinned this technique was already widespread and had been furthered by works of fiction. While it is not clear whether the writers of such works were inspired by real-life events, it has been clearly shown that criminals and claim-makers alike often derive their inspiration from fiction. Indeed, Timothy McVeigh, the perpetrator of the 1995 Oklahoma City bombing was inspired by *The Turner Diaries* (1978),[7] whose fictional plot he partly re-enacted. More significantly for this study, the Department of the Treasury's report on Corder's 1994 attack against the White House suggested that he was influenced by Tom Clancy's fictional work, showing that not only was the propositional knowledge providing the epistemic base for this technique widely spread well prior to 9/11, but also, that a rudimentary form of the prescriptive knowledge about this technique already existed within works of fiction and in the minds of some claim-makers.

Although there is no readily accessible evidence of the 9/11 plotters being directly influenced by works of fiction or by the actions of Byck, Maeno, or Corder, their inspiration for the attack did not come out of thin air. That the necessary propositional and prescriptive knowledge already existed – as evidenced by the nineteen previous events in the years between 1972 and the 1994 hijacking of Flight 8969 some of which were inspired by works of fiction and many of which received significant media attention globally – cannot be dismissed. In fact, there is clear evidence Khalid Sheikh Mohammed, 'the principal architect of the 9/11 attacks' (National Commission on Terrorist Attacks upon the United States 2004, 145), was directly influenced by the well-publicized 1994 hijacking of Flight 8969 – and the failed plot to crash it into the Eiffel Tower – when planning the Bojinka Plot, which evolved into the plan for 9/11. Of obvious significance for transmission is that the perpetrators of this hijacking were a group that had previously received support from bin Laden.

7.3 SELECTION: THE RESULT OF TRIAL AND ERROR

Mohammed's final blueprint for the 9/11 plot evolved directly out of the Bojinka plot, which never fully materialized but which in many ways represented an early draft of the fateful attacks against the United States. The Bojinka plot is frequently described as a complex and convoluted assortment of subplots: to assassinate President Clinton and the Pope, to blow up eleven airliners, to bomb movie theatres in Manila, and most importantly for the subject of this research, to crash a small plane or commercial aircraft deliberately into the Central Intelligence Agency (CIA) headquarters in Langley or even to hijack ten airliners and use them as weapons against targets in the United States.[8] While this vast and impractically complex plot appears to represent 'ill-conceived ideas' with improbable chances of success 'pursued by ill-equipped or unprepared men' (McDermott 2002), it was nonetheless based on a specific timetable and involved three phases of sequential and simultaneous attacks, foreshadowing the event of 9/11. Moreover, it demonstrates that the use of aircraft as weapons in and of themselves was seen as both feasible and effective means by which to exploit an existing vulnerability in security arrangements. Further, it shows that Mohammed considered the use of aircraft as weapons of destruction as more effective and more feasible compared to conventional bombings, a lesson he claimed to have learned from the 1993 World Trade Center Bombing (Ilardi 2009).

Phase I of the Bojinka plot involved the assassination of Pope John Paul II during his visit to the Philippines for World Youth Day in 1995. The attack sought to target the Pope using a suicide bomber disguised as a priest during the planned papal visit to the Asian Bishops' Conference at the San Carlos Seminary in Makati City. The assassination of the Pope was intended to divert attention from the next phase of the operation, namely the destruction of eleven US airliners flying across the Pacific on 21 January 1995. The success of this phase hinged on the manufacture of 'microbombs' or 'Mark II', which would be carried on board without being detected by screening machines. The 'microbombs' had timers composed of modified Casio digital watches that could still be worn in a normal manner, undetectable quantities of nitro-glycerine as the primers, and an explosive charge. The testing of these bombs occurred two months prior to the operations (*United States v. Ramzi Yousef, Eyad Ismoil, also known as Eyad Ismail, and Abdul Murad* 2003) when a prototype was placed under a seat in the Greenbelt Theatre in Manila on 1 December 1994 and successfully showed what would happen if a bomb exploded under an airline seat, exploding and injuring several patrons.

On 10 December 1994, in preparation for the Bojinka plot, Ramzi Yousef – one of the main perpetrators of the 1993 World Trade Center bombing, long-time accomplice of Mohammed and co-conspirator of the Bojinka plot – boarded Philippine Airlines Flight 434, a B747-200 flying from Manila to Tokyo with a stopover in Cebu. During the flight, Yousef assembled a microbomb, which he then placed in the life-vest pocket under a seat, after which he disembarked the plane during the stopover in Cebu. Two hours into the final leg of the flight, the bomb detonated, killing one passenger, damaging controls, depressurising the hull, and forcing the pilot to make an emergency landing in Okinawa (*Reuters* 1994). Phase II of the plot envisaged at least five operatives assembling and arming bombs while on board eleven different US-bound flights during the first leg of two-leg flights and then disembarking before the final leg. Placed under seats directly above the fuselage fuel tanks, the relatively small charges were intended to ignite the fuel tanks, causing catastrophic secondary detonations, with potential casualty estimates reaching as high as four thousand (*United States v. Ramzi Yousef, Eyad Ismoil, also known as Eyad Ismail, and Abdul Murad* 2003). The notion of employing a second-order effect strategy to maximize the destructive energy produced by blowing up a fuel-laden plane, while minimizing the size of the explosive charge to avoid detection, was perhaps best exemplified by al-Qaeda operative Richard Colvin Reid, who later attempted to detonate explosives packed into his shoes while on American Airlines Flight 63 from Paris to Miami on 22 December 2001.

The last phase of the plot, which was in its infancy when the Bojinka plot was eventually uncovered and subsequently thwarted, involved the use of aircraft as a deliberate weapon of destruction and represents the most significant part of the plot for the case study at hand. According to the detailed confession of Abdul Makim Murad,[9] Phase III involved Murad renting, buying, or hijacking a small plane, preferably a Cessna, filling it with explosives and crashing it into the CIA headquarters at Langley. In the same vein, Murad also discussed an alternative plan of hijacking a commercial airliner and using it as a weapon against the CIA headquarters: 'What the subject has in his mind is that he will board any American commercial aircraft pretending to be an ordinary passenger. Then he will hijack said aircraft, control its cockpit and dive it at the CIA headquarters' (Lance 2005, 277–78). This alternative plan – which was revealed in a 20 January 1995 memo from Filipino investigator Colonel Rodolfo Mendoza to the United States – favoured an airliner instead of a small aircraft loaded with explosives. This was probably due to the frustration the Manila cell encountered while manufacturing and testing explosives, a dangerous exercise that greatly increased chances of detection, as evidenced by the eventual discovery of the plot as a result of such efforts, when, nine days prior to Pope John Paul II's visit to the Philippines, an apartment fire in Manila drew the attention of authorities. Upon searching the flat, authorities uncovered bomb-making materials and manuals, fake passports, priest clothing, and a laptop with four floppy disks containing details of the Bojinka plot (*United States v. Ramzi Yousef, Eyad Ismoil, also known as Eyad Ismail, and Abdul Murad* 2003). In addition to these items, a copy of a *Time* magazine article detailing the hijacking of Flight 8969 was found in the apartment, which was shared by Ramzi Yousef and three other Bojinka conspirators: Abdul Murad, Mohammed Jamal Khalifa (bin Laden's brother-in-law), and Mohammed. The presence of this particular edition of the publication clearly demonstrates both their awareness of and interest in the failed 1994 attack and, once more, highlights the role of the media in transmitting prescriptive knowledge.

The Bojinka plot also evidences the notion that the process leading to the adoption of planes as weapons of destruction by al-Qaeda was long and complex, and is best understood as a trial-and-error process spanning several years, in which Mohammed and Ramzi Yousef refined a plan to conduct a major operation involving multiple airliners. They conducted various trials to improve their techniques, while suffering several significant setbacks that helped build their prescriptive knowledge base and understanding of their adversaries.

According to the 9/11 Commission report, Abu Hafs al Masri, better known as Mohammed Atef, al-Qaeda's chief of military operations, also began exploring the potential use of commercial aviation as a means of advancing al-Qaeda's claims while he and bin Laden were still in Sudan between 1991 and 1996:

> [Atef] concluded that hijacking operations did not fit the needs of al-Qaeda, because such hijackings were used to negotiate the release of prisoners rather than to inflict mass casualties. The study is said to have considered the feasibility of hijacking planes and blowing them up in flight, paralleling the Bojinka concept. Such a study, if it actually existed, yields significant insight into the thinking of al-Qaeda's leaders: (1) they rejected hijackings aimed at gaining the release of imprisoned comrades as too complex, because al-Qaeda had no friendly countries in which to land a plane and then negotiate; (2) they considered the bombing of commercial flights in mid-air – as carried out against Pan Am Flight 103 over Lockerbie, Scotland – a promising means to inflict massive casualties; and (3) they did not yet consider using hijacked aircraft as weapons against other targets. (National Commission on Terrorist Attacks upon the United States 2004)

The 9/11 Commission believed that al-Qaeda initially rejected hijacking because it would not 'inflict mass casualties'. Put in the terms of the framework of this book, it was believed that hijacking had not yet entered al-Qaeda's repertoire of contention, and not because of concerns about the feasibility of such acts but, rather, because it would be 'ineffective' in accomplishing the group's perceived aims of maximal casualties.

According to the 9/11 Commission Report (2004), Mohammed had started contemplating the use of aeroplanes in the aftermath of the 1993 World Trade Center bombing and, when he was not yet a member of al-Qaeda, supporting the notion that the technique had not yet been adopted by al-Qaeda. Faced with the failure to bring down the World Trade Center using a truck bomb, Mohammed realized that 'bombs and explosives could be problematic' (p. 155). This belief was almost certainly reinforced after the discovery of the Bojinka plot due to issues with manufacturing explosives, and Mohammed subsequently identified a need to 'graduate to a more novel form of attack' (p. 155).

Demonstrating this line of thinking, and evidencing their underlying understanding of the technique's potential, Mohammed and his co-conspirators initially considered a much more ambitious option for the final act of the Bojinka plot: The hijacking of ten aircraft, nine of which would be crashed into targets on both US coasts, including the US Capitol, the White House, the World Trade Center, the Pentagon, the CIA and FBI headquarters, nuclear power plants, and the tallest buildings in California and the state of Washington. The remaining hijacked plane would land at a US airport, where, after 'killing all adult male passengers on board and alerting the media', Mohammed would 'deliver a speech excoriating U.S. support for Israel, the Philippines, and repressive governments in the Arab world' (National Commission on Terrorist Attacks upon the United States 2004, 54). However, there were apparently no overt preparations to enact this idea. Significantly, the enactment of this ambitious version of the plan was likely impeded by resource limitations, which – as I have previously argued – is of the core variables that influences a technique's feasibility and, therefore, its likelihood of being selected. Since no commercial pilot could be expected to fly his plane deliberately into such targets – the same problem the hijackers of Air France Flight 8969 faced – the deployment of this technique would require the training of pilots capable of flying the aeroplanes after they were acquired; a problem that al-Qaeda would later devote considerable time and resources to overcome.

Despite its overall failure, the Bojinka plot – particularly in the use of liquid explosives – demonstrates the co-conspirators' recognition of the necessity to innovate to circumvent existing screening procedures and destroy several airliners simultaneously, as well as their willingness and ability to do so. Moreover, by the end of 1995, the use of planes as weapons was clearly established within numerous groups' repertoires of contention, as was the illocutionary impact of targeting high-profile national landmarks. The importance of having hijackers capable of flying aircraft once they were seized was also becoming increasingly apparent based on the propositional knowledge derived from previous failures. While these innovations and realizations are significant in and of themselves, they also demonstrate the tendency of claim-makers to learn from their previous actions and those of others; they innovate on and refine existing techniques, adjusting them based on structural preconditions and resource limitations. Simply put by 1996, the propositional knowledge, and much of the prescriptive knowledge, required to enact an attack like 9/11 existed, though it was not necessarily readily available to al-Qaeda at this stage. What was lacking were the resources required – namely trained pilots – which al-Qaeda would eventually develop.

Following the dismantling of the Bojinka plot and the arrest of Yousef in Pakistan on 7 February 1995, Mohammed attempted to push ahead with a less ambitious version of the second phase of Bojinka, using shoe bombs, before relocating to Afghanistan in mid-1996. There, according to the 9/11 Commission Report (2004), he 'arranged a meeting with Bin Laden in Tora Bora', where he briefed him and Mohammed Atef 'on the first World Trade Center bombing, the Manila airport, the cargo carriers plan, and other activities' he and his colleagues in the Philippines had pursued (pp. 148–49). Unable to realize his plan of carrying out an operation involving the use of aircraft as a weapon on his own, Mohammed allegedly first proposed to bin

Laden at this meeting that they join forces to use hijacked airliners to attack targets in the United States:

> This proposal would eventually become the 9/11 operation. [Khalid Sheikh Mohammed] knew that the successful staging of such an attack would require personnel, money, and logistical support that only an extensive and well-funded organization like al-Qaeda could provide. He thought the operation might appeal to Bin Laden, who had a long record of denouncing the United States. (National Commission on Terrorist Attacks upon the United States 2004, 149)

According to Mohammed,[10] despite its emphasis on targets with high illocutionary impact, the ambitious proposal initially received only a lukewarm response from the al-Qaeda leadership in view of the proposal's scale and complexity (National Commission on Terrorist Attacks upon the United States 2004, 154). Nonetheless, this meeting seems to represent the point at which prescriptive knowledge surrounding the adoption of using aircraft as weapons of destruction was transmitted to al-Qaeda's leaders.

In early 1999, bin Laden summoned Mohammed to Kandahar to tell him that his proposal to use aircraft as weapons now had al-Qaeda's full support (National Commission on Terrorist Attacks upon the United States 2004, 149). According to an article published in *Al-Masrah* (the weekly magazine of al-Qaeda in the Arabian Peninsula) bin Laden's *volte-face* was prompted by the destruction of Egypt Air Flight 990 on 31 October 1999; according to the National Transportation Safety Board, Flight 990 was deliberately crashed into the Atlantic Ocean by the relief first officer, Gameel Al-Batouti[11] (Lathem 1999; Malnic, Rempel, and Alonso-Saldivar 2002; Wald 2002a; 2002b). After hearing about this event, bin Laden supposedly asked: 'why didn't he crash it into a nearby building?' Although the credibility of *Al-Masrah* is questionable, it is nonetheless plausible that bin Laden was informed of and influenced by the 1999 plane crash. Moreover, the media attention stimulated by this event would have further publicized the effectiveness of deliberately destroying an aircraft, while the event itself would have, at least partly, demonstrated the feasibility of Mohammed's plan.

Over a series of meetings, bin Laden, Mohammed, and Mohammed Atef, among others, decided on an initial list of targets, including the White House, the US Capitol, the Pentagon, and the World Trade Center (National Commission on Terrorist Attacks upon the United States 2004, 155). The decision to revisit previously targeted sites, such as the World Trade Center, demonstrates the existence of normative preferences. Moreover, according to later findings, reported in the 9/11 Commission Report (2004, 493), the idea of simultaneous attacks was a major factor in Mohammed's operational design – a remnant of the Bojinka Plot – and played an important role in the selection of targets. While the specifics of this discussion, and whether other targets were considered and subsequently rejected, are unknown. The 9/11 Commission Report lists, among other potential targets: The Empire State Building in New York City, the Statue of Liberty, and the Pan American Skyscraper and the Sears Tower, the tallest buildings in San Francisco and Chicago, respectively (National Commission on Terrorist Attacks upon the United States 2004, 155). It is, however, possible that the technique employed precluded the need for in-depth consideration about which targets to select, as large commercial aircraft could, at least theoretically, reach any potential US target. In other words, the difficulties associated – especially in terms of ground security – with conventional bombing methods, which were previously favoured by al-Qaeda, could also be overcome through the use of aircraft (Ilardi 2009). Al-Qaeda's leadership was thus free to choose whichever targets it wanted, guided almost entirely by the statement and impact they wished to make through the attacks. Simply put, once the plot was deemed feasible, al-Qaeda's target selection was informed by the perceived legitimacy and the effectiveness of any given target versus another.

By April 2000, operatives assigned to operations by bin Laden began applying for US visas, a process that posed little difficulty for the Saudi nationals but proved more difficult for Yemeni volunteers. However, by the late spring of 2000, all future team leaders had arrived in the United States and were engaged in flight training; al-Qaeda had learned from the failed attempts of the past hijackers and actively worked to overcome the largest remaining stumbling block for this sort of aerial ramming attack. Replicating conditions most likely to be encountered on the day of the attacks, al-Qaeda operatives in the United States successfully identified impediments not anticipated by the al-Qaeda leadership at the time of target selection. For example, the indecision over whether to strike the White House or the Capitol arose only after the hijackers' intelligence activities made it clear that attacking the White House would be more difficult than initially predicted. Evidently, bin Laden was determined to attack the White House, emphasizing his preference on a number of occasions (National Commission on Terrorist Attacks upon the United States 2004, 155, 243, 248). However, Mohamed Atta, one of the leaders of the attacks, informed Ramzi bin al-Shibh, a key facilitator, on at least two separate occasions that he believed the White House too difficult a target for navigational reasons (National Commission on Terrorist Attacks upon the United States 2004, 244, 288). This demonstrates the intense level of reconnaissance and planning undertaken to refine the target lists to maximize the likelihood of operational success.

Overseas, al-Qaeda started selecting 'muscle hijackers', a term used to describe those who would storm the cockpit and control the passengers on the four hijacked planes armed with small dual-use weapons, retractable utility knives ('box-cutters' or 'Stanley' knives), which could get through security. The hijackers began assembling the body of prescriptive knowledge needed to make the attack possible. The operatives received initial training at the Mes Aynak camp in Afghanistan and in Karachi, Pakistan, where Mohammed taught the future hijackers how to use basic English, 'read phone books, interpret airline timetables, use the Internet, use code words in communications, make travel reservations and rent apartments' (National Commission on Terrorist Attacks upon the United States 2004, 157–58). According to one attendee at such a training camp, recruits were trained using flight simulator computer games to become familiar with aircraft models and functions (National Commission on Terrorist Attacks upon the United States 2004, 157–58). They also viewed videos that featured hijacking scenes and discussed conducting the surveillance of flights. Although rudimentary in nature, these activities provided prescriptive knowledge of critical importance in the deployment of this new technique because it encouraged the operatives to probe for vulnerabilities in the routine behaviour of flight crews. For example, Mohammed recommended that the team 'watch the cabin doors at take-off and landing, to observe whether the captain went to the lavatory during the flight, and to note whether the flight attendants brought food into the cockpit' (National Commission on Terrorist Attacks upon the United States 2004, 157–58).

These preparations, according to Ilardi (2009) 'were intended to achieve a high level of calculability of results by identifying security arrangements they could expect to encounter on the day of the operations' (p. 175). This propositional knowledge about the environment in airports and aboard aeroplanes would, in turn, be used to facilitate the effective circumvention or negation of existing security arrangements and, therefore, further advance the prescriptive knowledge surrounding the use of aeroplanes as weapons of destruction. Bin al-Shibh would subsequently convey the meticulousness of these intelligence activities when he commented that the hijackers studied 'the security arrangements that [were] adopted at all the airports and establish[ed] a comprehensive picture about the procedures at all the airports and also unravel[ed] the security loopholes that exist at these airports' (Mowbray 2002, 37). The first reconnaissance flights took place with the purpose of uncovering such weaknesses in airport security measures and establishing the feasibility of deploying such a technique. For example, Walid bin Attash, one of bin Laden's bodyguards, flew from Bangkok to Hong Kong early in January 2000 on board a US airliner, seating himself in first class. The flight proved instructive as he identified several issues not envisaged by the architect of the attack, namely that al-Qaeda operatives would be unable to view the cockpit door from certain first-class seats. Attash also surveyed airport security by carrying a box cutter onto the aircraft in his toiletry bag (National Commission on Terrorist Attacks upon the United States 2004, 158–59).

By summer 2001, the pilots began conducting additional flight training and reconnaissance flights, travelling 'first class, in the same type of aircraft

[they] would pilot', some travelling along the Hudson Corridor, a low-altitude 'hallway' along the Hudson River that passed several New York landmarks, including the World Trade Center (National Commission on Terrorist Attacks upon the United States 2004, 242). These reconnaissance flights were seemingly designed to familiarize the attackers with the conditions they would most likely encounter on the day of the attack. In further preparation, Mohammed Atta travelled to Spain in mid-July and informed bin al-Shibh that he, Marwan al-Shehhi, and Ziad Jarrah had carried box cutters onto their surveillance flights, similarly encountering no problems. He also reported to al-Qaeda that operatives in the United States 'had been able to carry box cutters onto their test flights' and observed that the 'best time to storm the cockpit would be about 10–15 minutes after take-off, when they noticed that cockpit doors were typically opened for the first time' (National Commission on Terrorist Attacks upon the United States 2004, 245). These surveillance flights were so successful that Atta informed bin al-Shibh that he would not need other weapons and that he was so confident the cockpit doors would be opened that he did not consider contingency plans (National Commission on Terrorist Attacks upon the United States 2004, 245).

As aforementioned, aviation security experts and intelligence personnel in the United States appeared to have had a difficult time imagining or believing that planes could be employed as weapons for ramming, instead favouring mitigation measures to counter 'traditional' hijackings (National Commission on Terrorist Attacks upon the United States 2004, 348). Indeed, the apparent disregard for the seriousness of the threat before 9/11 was also evident in the lack of security response in light of the hijacking of Flight 8969, despite explicit warnings from French authorities of this potential security threat. The many changes to air travel security after 9/11[12] provide further evidence of a belated acceptance of the feasibility of aeroplanes being used as ramming weapons only after this fateful day. However, prior to these events, although some effective security measures were put in place by the authorities in the United States as a result of hijackings for transportation and extortion, these were woefully insufficient to counter such an attack. Therefore, the 9/11 plotters and hijackers were able to find and exploit existing loopholes in the security environment in their favour during the preparation and the execution of the attacks.

In addition to the existing security weakness, the planning and training for 9/11 was meticulous, which undeniably contributed to the successful deployment of this technique, as did the in-depth reconnaissance and training undertaken by the operatives involved in the execution of the plot. Once operatives were selected, those who would fly the planes went through hours of flight training – largely in the United States – to ensure that they would each be able to pilot their aircraft to their desired targets, thus overcoming one of the major challenges with the Air France Flight 8969 plot. Moreover, although other groups and individuals, including those affiliated with al-Qaeda, had previously considered employing similar techniques, the 9/11 attacks were something of a departure from al-Qaeda's previous behaviour and normative preference for ground attacks involving suicide bombers, thus catching US authorities by surprise. Al-Qaeda's normative preference behaviour also provides a satisfactory explanation as to why the organization's leadership continued to attempt to target the airline industry, even after the introduction of enhanced security measures in the aftermath of 9/11.[13] Moreover, Omar Farouk Abdulmutallab's failed attempt to detonate plastic explosives hidden in his underwear during a Northwest Airlines flight from Amsterdam to Detroit on Christmas Day 2009 also suggests that al-Qaeda's normative preference for targeting the airline industry had also been diffused to some of its affiliates, in this case al-Qaeda on the Arabian Peninsula.

Above all, this chapter highlights the importance of situating even those events that on the surface may seem novel and extraordinary within the context of an evolutionary trajectory. Neglecting to situate these attacks within their wider context – including numerous historical antecedents of aeroplanes being deployed as weapons and, indeed, in the longer history of the use of planes to express contention and gain political concessions – results in an incomplete story. Moreover, the insights gleaned from examining antecedent events and subsequent behaviour of states, when considering any technique is vital in understanding how the environment may shape a technique's evolution, including the innovative behaviour of claim-makers, the transmission of propositional and prescriptive knowledge, and the likelihood of adoption by others. Only by paying close attention to the changes techniques of contention undergo over time and, by employing some creative thought, can states and their apparatus hope to form any meaningful approach to mitigate the effectiveness and feasibility of emerging threats.

NOTES

1. See, for example, Neria et al. (2005) and Mizuta (2013).
2. This list of pre-9/11 incidents is largely derived from Dolkin (2007). In addition to the 10 November 1972 hijacking and threat to crash into the atomic plant at Oak Ridge addressed in the previous chapter, in 1973, Israel claimed that numerous threats had been made by the Black September Organization to hijack airliners and crash them into Tel Aviv. On 22 February 1974, Byck attempted to hijack a flight from Baltimore/Washington International Airport bound for Atlanta, with the ultimate aim to crash it into the White House. In 1975, according to Dolkin (2007) 'an individual in the US' attempted to seize an aircraft and 'later claims that he intended to crash [it] into a terminal tower as a protest against abortion'. A year later, on 23 March 1976, Mitsuyasu Maeno deliberately crashed a rented Piper Cherokee into the home of Yoshio Kodama, a multi-millionaire right-wing leader and a leading figure in the Lockheed bribery scandals. In 1984, after observing suspicious movements of light planes and helicopters in Iran, Syria and Lebanon, the Pentagon – fearing kamikaze-like attacks – deployed FIM-92 Stinger MPADS on board US Navy ships in the region. The same year, Interpol warned that an Iranian group planned to fly a small aeroplane laden with explosives into the US embassy in

Cyprus, prompting the United States to install anti-aircraft weapons on the embassy roof. The CIA also warned the Ronald Reagan administration of similar plots against US targets in the Middle East, and in 1985, media in Cyprus reported the existence of similar plots against the US and Israeli embassies. In 1985, a Lebanese hijacker threatened to crash a plane into the presidential palace in Beirut during negotiations. The same year, the Austrian government warned Israel about a plot to hijack an El Al flight and crash it into Tel Aviv. The following year, in the aftermath of the hijacking of Pan American World Airway Flight 73 on 5 September 1986, the hijackers confessed that they planned on blowing up the aircraft over an Israeli city following the completion of a prisoner exchange, and one of the twenty-one Libyan students whose release they secured from the United Kingdom was a pilot trainee who vowed to carry out a 'kamikaze-like' raid against US installations. Columnists in the US press also reported in 1986 the existence of a training programme in Iran in preparation for such attacks against US targets. In 1988, a Brazilian police spokesman announced that, during a recent hijacking, the hijacker had planned to crash the plane into a building in Brasilia. In 1989, the *Washington Post* reported that it had received a credible warning that an Iranian-trained pilot might be planning to crash an explosive-rigged plane into the White House. In 1990, Hamburg police reported that 'the Palestinian Liberation Front of Abu Abbas [was] preparing an attack with light aircrafts' (Dolnik 2007, 39–40). On 7 April 1994, Federal Express Flight 705 was nearly hijacked by Auburn Calloway, who the prosecution argued was attempting to commit suicide. However, FedEx employees have contended that he intended to deliberately crash the plane into the FedEx superhub to take revenge upon the company. In the same year on 12 November, Frank Eugene Corder crashed a stolen single-engine Cessna 150 into the South Lawn of the West Wing of the White House. Intelligence reports also indicate that the perpetrators of the Christmas Eve 1994, hijacking of Air France Flight 8969 intended to deliberately destroy the plane over Paris. In 1998, the Turkish government detained twenty-three individuals who planned to crash an explosive-laden plane into the Ankara mausoleum of Mustafa Kemal Ataturk on the seventy-fifth anniversary of the republic.

3. See for example Abrams (1992), Wilber (2012), Dershowitz (2004), or Bill O'Reilly and Martin Dugard's rather dubious but best-selling *Killing Reagan: The Violent Assault That Changed a Presidency* (2015).

4. Groupe Islamique Armé (GIA) was supported in the early 1990s by Osama bin Laden, who provided them with weapons left over from the Afghan war and smuggled through Sudan. However, bin Laden reportedly withdrew his support because he felt that the massacres by the GIA of Muslims in Algeria would have a negative effect on his objectives of unifying the *ummah* under his umbrella organization (Elias 2010, 46).

5. Similarly, the hijackers of Pan Am Flight 73 managed to evade airport security and seize the aircraft with its 360 passengers and nineteen crew by wearing airport security uniforms and driving a van that had been modified to resemble an airport security vehicle through a security checkpoint and up to one of the boarding stairways to Pan Am Flight 73.

6. For an incisive analysis of this fascinating meeting, see Frank (2017, 1–9).

7. Published though the US neo-Nazi organization National Alliance, the novel describes the overthrow of the US government by rural white supremacists who destroy the FBI headquarters with a truck bomb, instigating a race war against Jews and African Americans (Zulaika and Douglass 1996, 9–10).

8. The details of the Bojinka plot became widely publicized in 1997 during the trial of Ramzi Yousef, one of the main perpetrators of the 1993 World Trade Center bombing and the bombing of Philippine Airlines Flight 434 and a co-conspirator in the Bojinka plot (*United States v. Ramzi Yousef, Eyad Ismoil, also known as Eyad Ismail, and Abdul Murad* 2003).

9. It should be noted that Murad's confession was obtained under torture, which raises questions about the accuracy of information (Moher 2003).

10. It should be noted that Khalid Sheikh Mohammed's confession was obtained under torture, which raises to questions about the accuracy of information (*The Senate Intelligence Committee Report on Torture: Committee Study of the Central Intelligence Agency's Detention and Interrogation Program* 2014).

11. There remains much speculation about what motivated Al-Batouti to deliberately crash Flight 990 into the Atlantic Ocean. However, the dominant hypothesis is that he sought to take

revenge against an Egypt Air executive onboard, who had recently demoted Al-Batouti (Wald 2002a; 2002b).

12. These changes included but, were not limited to, cockpit doors on many aircraft being reinforced and made bulletproof; passengers being prohibited from entering the cockpit during flights; pilots trained and licensed to carry firearms being allowed to do so; smalls knives and other sharp items being prohibited in hand luggage; and new body scanners being introduced as well as new complex procedures to verify the identity of passengers.

13. Shortly after the 9/11 attacks, for example, the group dispatched two operatives, Richard Reid and Saajid Badat, to detonate improvised explosive devices hidden in their shoes when aboard aeroplanes. In August 2006, more than twenty people, mostly British citizens of Pakistani extraction, were arrested in London on suspicion of plotting to blow up between ten and a dozen airliners over the Atlantic Ocean and American cities, using liquid explosives.

Chapter Eight

Conclusion

The approach presented in this book outlines a framework grounded in evolutionary theory to facilitate the examination of the emergence of claim-making techniques associated with terrorism. The argument herein rests on the central argument that evolutionary theory, as postulated by Charles Darwin, is not inherently biological but is rather a logical framework that rests on a set of three assumptions explaining change within any given population. Indeed, as Orr (2009) recently argued, 'Darwinism was revolutionary not because it made arcane claims about biology but because it suggested that nature's underlying logic might be surprisingly simple' (p. 44). Essentially, Darwinian evolutionary thought aims to move past simple proximate explanations describing the current utility or nature of a given entity. Instead, the theory addresses how that specific entity came about, and – perhaps most interestingly – which factors influenced or applied pressure on it, and thus led to its current incarnation. In other words, in its biological setting, Darwinian evolutionary thought provides a framework by which to explain the processes that led to the immense variety of life on Earth. In non-biological applications, I argue that the same set of three underlying assumptions can be successfully employed to explain the development of socially constructed entities based on their shared traits and can explain the presence of variation within a subject population. These three assumptions can be distilled to the *principle of variation* – which explains why and how differences amongst the populace emerge; the *principle of transmission* – which essentially is the mechanism by which these differences are passed on or spread; and lastly, the *principle of selection* – which explains why certain variations are retained while others are eliminated, based on defined external forces.

However, to apply evolutionary insights to a non-biological topic such as terrorism, it was necessary to identify and define the unit of inheritance;

scilicet the entity whose observable characteristics or traits are being studied must be selected. Given the highly contested nature of terrorism and the ongoing definitional debate surrounding the concept of terrorism, an approach rooted in social movement theory was employed to argue that the appropriate unit of analysis is not terrorism as a distinct and holistic phenomenon in and of itself but, rather, individual violent techniques of contention that fall outside the forms of claim-making deemed legitimate by authorities in the sociohistorical context in which they occurred. This approach focuses on the characteristics of acts of political violence rather than on the underlying motivations or ideologies of the individuals who perpetrate them, and thereby refocuses the study of political violence on 'terrorism' rather than on 'terrorists', thus allowing for the tracing of genealogical influences and historical lines of descent that a fixation on selected instances of violence or their perpetrators might otherwise obscure.

As aforementioned, the framework proposed within this book is based on the Darwinian principles of *variation, transmission,* and *selection.* In the biological world sources of *variation* are generally 'blind' or random mutations; in contrast, when considering techniques of political violence, variations are consciously developed by claim-makers responding to the changing body of propositional knowledge held within a society. In this way, humans actively create variation and then knowingly select from the resulting self-made variants. Propositional knowledge – which is conceptualized as a given society's understanding of their social, cultural, economic, political, or religious context and of the nature of the relationships between claim-makers and their adversaries – provides the necessary epistemic base on which new techniques can be developed or existing techniques can be innovated upon. Pondering the nature of changes in existing propositional knowledge, along with the sources of new propositional knowledge, thus provides developmental explanations as to how and why a new technique of contention, or variant thereof, came about.

Due in part to this conscious choice, the mechanisms of *transmission* by which techniques of contention are spread from one repertoire to another is much more rapid than the slow intergenerational process of inheritance within the biological world, involving a rapid, flexible, and continuous process of imitation across the ever-proliferating avenues of human communication. It is proposed within the framework of this book that because repertoires of contention are inherently flexible, claim-makers observing other groups' techniques of contention may choose to imitate said techniques to gain tactical advantages over their adversary. This process occurs along two main channels, either through relational ties (or direct transmission) or nonrelational ties (or indirect transmission). Contemplating the exact channels by which a technique – or its variants – is transmitted from one repertoire to another provides another layer of developmental explanations, allowing researchers to understand not only how a technique 'came about' but also 'where' it came from and whether it differs in some significant way from the original iteration.

Departing from developmental explanations, the third Darwinian principle, *selection*, provides a functional account of the evolutionary processes through which a given technique of contention is adopted or rejected by various claim-makers. Three distinct – but interrelated – selection pressures that act on any given technique of contention are proposed within this framework: (i) Whether the structural barriers or costs which must be overcome by an actor wishing to adopt said technique allow the technique to be deemed feasible, (ii) whether a technique is deemed legitimate, in other words whether it is 'just', 'right', or 'appropriate', from the viewpoint of those who are to employ it or their constituents, and lastly, (iii) the technique's perceived effectiveness, namely the belief by the claim-makers that the technique will be successful and lead to their desired outcome.

To demonstrate the potential application of this framework, and the insights that can be derived from it, the case study chapters of this book survey the evolution of aeroplane hijacking, focusing particularly on the various adaptions the technique has undergone since its inception, the means by which it has spread, and the factors leading to its adoption or rejection by claim-makers operating in different environments and seeking to advance different claims. To achieve this aim, a database comprised of 1,084 incidents of successful or thwarted hijackings, ranging from 1930 until 11 September 2001, was compiled – arguably representing the most comprehensive database on aeroplane hijacking to date – and examined to create an empirically rich account of the technique's history.

The genesis of hijacking as a technique of contention is traced to two highly troubled periods of intense and accelerated nationalism in South and Central America, first in Peru during the 1930s and, subsequently thirty years later, during the Cuban Revolution. In both cases, the most salient factors leading to the emergence of hijacking appear to be a belief among claim-makers that airpower or, at least the semblance of uncontested control of airspace, could be conflated with political legitimacy, leading to conscious campaigns to deprive the ruling regimes of their monopoly over the skies. Undoubtedly, the most fascinating aspect of the Peruvian and Cuban cases is the conspicuous lack of evidence of transmission of the technique between the two, meaning that hijacking was essentially 'invented' twice by separate sets of claim-makers operating in relatively similar environments and possessing similar understandings of the relationship between airpower and political legitimacy. Although there is no clear evidence of transmission between the Peruvian and Cuban cases, in contrast, the exploits of the June 26th of July Movement in Cuba were quickly and clearly transmitted between revolutionaries and counter-revolutionaries in Cuba. These hijackings, coupled with those from behind the Iron Curtain in the aftermath of the Second World War, have become known as 'freedom flights' or 'hijackings for transportation'; this misnomer that strips the hijackers of any political agency and the hijackings of their status as claim-making events. Indeed, as demonstrated in chapter 4, the existing literature's tendency to dismiss these early hijackings as the irrelevant acts of desperate souls seeking freedom and liberty, is shown to be problematic in two respects: First, exit from a repressive regime cannot be divorced from a wider political meaning. In fact, Western states consciously sought to politicize the dramatic escapes from the Soviet Union to challenge the legitimacy of communist regimes worldwide. Secondly, by doing so, and by establishing the set of implicit norms known as the 'Havana Rules' – whereby hijackers originating from communist states would only receive nominal sanctions – Western states enabled new prescriptive knowledge about hijackings to be spread to an audience that far exceeded Cuba and the Soviet Union. As a result, hijacking found new adopters among the black nationalist movement in the United States. Indeed, the general acceptance within the Western world of hijacking as a legitimate means of political activity served to augment its appeal to others who, in turn, emulated the same techniques against Western states, until Western governments began engaging in multilateral security efforts to curb hijackings. These multilateral security efforts were not only introduced as a result of the increasing number of hijackings committed by black nationalists in the United States but also as a result of the emergence of hijacking for extortion and co-occurring events in the Middle East that forever transformed global aviation security and the way hijacking was understood.

Akin to the hijackings perpetrated by black nationalists, little attention has been dedicated to criminally motivated hijacking. However, while departing from a singular focus on techniques of contention, criminally motivated hijackings provide an extraordinarily clear picture of the role of mass communication and, particularly that of the media, in spreading knowledge about successful hijackings, which thus increase the likelihood of subsequent attempts by others. Moreover, this period is also noteworthy as one of intense competition between would-be hijackers and law enforcement officials, in which each party attempted to respond quickly to counter the other's party actions. This phenomenon is also extremely clear in the discussion about hijackings committed by groups linked to the Palestinian liberation movement, where the adoption of hijacking by these Palestinian groups led to a period of intense variation in aeroplane hijacking, as the Popular Front for the Liberation of Palestine (PFLP) and other splinter groups introduced increasingly innovative means of hijacking in response to various counterterrorism measures. The application of the proposed framework highlights both the impact of high-profile hijackings carried out by Palestinian groups in spreading the technique to other social movements worldwide and the selection factors that led to other groups either adopting or rejecting the technique to advance their own movements.

In concluding the case study section of the book, the events surrounding the 9/11 attacks are scrutinized to trace the history of the use of aeroplanes as weapons of destruction – a history that long predates the 11 September 2001 attacks. This allows for an understanding of the process by which al-Qaeda came to use hijacked aircraft to attack targets in New York and Virginia; the examination of these events uncovers a long process of trial and error, replete with failures and setbacks in the lead up to 9/11. The application of the framework described in chapter 2 and its use in the study of other strains of hijacking shows that the techniques employed on 9/11 – while at first sight representing a departure from previous hijackings – were nothing more than one mutation along a long evolutionary path that began in the jungles of Peru nearly ninety years ago. Neglecting to situate the 9/11 attacks within the wider context of the long history of using hijacking as a means of expressing contention and to gain political concessions would not only tell a partial story but wrongly reinforce the notion of the exceptionality of 9/11.

Policy Implications

The application of evolutionary insights to the study of hijacking also provides several important lessons for counter-terrorism practitioners, particularly those concerned with the proliferation of new techniques such as vehicle-ramming attacks and the use of new technologies such as commercial drones, three-dimensional (3-D) printing, and autonomous vehicles to wreak havoc. As demonstrated throughout this book, terroristic innovation does not occur within a vacuum but rather is largely the product of changes in existing propositional knowledge either as a result of (i) changes in social, cultural, economic, technological, political, or religious contexts or (ii) changes in the nature of the relationships between claim-makers and their adversaries (and thus the status quo). One of the most salient recent examples of the latter is exemplified by the innovative use of leaf blowers to counter police use of lachrymator agents (tear gas), and Apple devices' AirDrop feature to subvert censorship efforts during the 2019 Anti-Extradition Law Amendment Bill protests in Hong Kong. As such, counter-terrorism officials must remain keenly aware (and ideally begin cataloguing) not only proven cases of 'terroristic innovation' but also changes to existing technologies and techniques developed by non-violent claim-makers and non-political actors such as hobbyists or criminals. After all, some of the most innovative changes to hijacking did not emerge from the minds of politically motivated individuals but (as demonstrated in chapter 6) were the inventions of greedy men who sought fame and fortune. Such data can then be situated within the framework presented in this book to track noteworthy developments and, therefore, better understand the evolution of new techniques that may pose a threat to the public. Such a resource could be created and maintained with minimal resources and would pay dividends in years ahead, undoubtedly helping government officials make more informed resourcing and regulatory decisions; in particular, this type of data – and the potential to observe patterns therein – would allow governments to consider carefully the impact of decisions made in terms of intentionally altering the feasibility, effectiveness, and perhaps perceived legitimacy, of certain emerging techniques of contention. The nature of the terroristic innovation cannot fully be understood by looking at developments solely by those we label 'terrorists'; evaluating terroristic threats is also about paying attention to innovation that occurs in private industries, academia, and by creatively minded hobbyists. As such, those involved in thwarting terroristic innovation need to monitor several spheres and need to include terror specialists, technologists, and industry experts in their efforts.

Counter-terrorism practitioners also must remain keenly aware of the wider impact of new policies and initiatives; throughout this book, I have demonstrated not only how claim-makers react to changes in the existing security environment and, on occasion, appear to have drawn inspiration directly from state techniques but also how claim-makers appear to have distinctive evolutionary advantages. Unencumbered by bureaucracy and other such constraints, claim-makers appear to innovate at a much quicker speed, thus leaving idle states, or states whose approach to terroristic innovation is solely reactive, particularly vulnerable. When considering efforts to thwart hijacking, past innovations by claim-makers reacting to Western security efforts illustrate the importance of imagination on the part of those responsible for reducing the threat of terrorism. Therefore, the US government's openness to consulting Hollywood screenwriters, directors, and producers should not be ridiculed; these efforts in the aftermath of 9/11 attacks to discern the existing propositional knowledge and how it could be harnessed into new claim-making techniques exemplifies a recognition of the importance of creative approaches to red-teaming – the practice of challenging plans, policies, and systems by adopting an adversarial approach – as a counter-terrorism tool. Governments must remain open minded and creative about the structures it creates, who they bring in to serve as advisers and facilitate the meaningful exchange of ideas.

Finally, governments must be mindful of the potential outcomes of such new measures in terms of creating new opportunities or leaving openings that may then be exploited; the introduction of metal detectors at US airports – while effective in the short term – prompted Marielitos' use of flammable liquids in hijackings, a potentially more dangerous innovation. Similarly, El Al's use of profiling – while proven effective on several occasions – led to the use of unwitting carriers and foreign operatives, the latter of which may have as a result strengthened ties between dangerous groups. Moreover, governments also need to recognize in any action they take, new propositional and prescriptive knowledge is generated. Indeed, claim-makers have shown on multiple occasions their capacity and willingness to learn from and replicate their adversaries; hijacking first emerged in Peru as a direct duplication of government techniques, with Peruvian revolutionaries taking control of Panagra flights to airdrop propaganda as the government had previously done; Israel's retributive action against PFLP supporting states during 'Operation Gift', led the PFLP to later systematically destroy hijacked aeroplanes.

Future Research Avenues

The framework presented also offers several promising possibilities to further the academic research agenda on terroristic innovation. First, this book illustrates the potential of reconstructing the evolutionary pathway of claim-making techniques by distinguishing among variation, transmission, and selection. As demonstrated, this reconstruction allows us to examine whether connections exist between one enactment of a technique of contention and another, but it requires intensive historical investigations, beyond simple classification and enumeration. Having demonstrated that almost all acts of hijackings belong to a single lineage, future research should investigate whether the use of this framework can illuminate similar insights into other (violent or non-violent) claim-making techniques. For example, did the sit-down strikes, which emerged on a massive scale in Europe in North America in the 1920s and 1930s, constitute a series of variations and adoptions descending from a single invention? Or were they invented numerous times in response to similar propositional knowledge? The framework proposed in this thesis could also be generalized beyond techniques of contentions to observe collective actions frames.

The second avenue for further research is directly linked to one of the limitations of the case study, namely the case study's inclination towards a focus on hijackings in the United States, Central America, and Western Europe – a choice that was largely dictated by linguistic access. Thus, although the database includes all known hijacking events, the book does not thoroughly explore the presence of this technique in, and the mechanisms by which it spread to, non-Western settings. However, there is no reason why the framework presented could not be employed to expand the current study of techniques of contention to include the voices and perspectives and behaviours of those in the Global South, for example. While there has been a marked improvement in the reduction of 'orientalist' prejudices in social science, political violence committed by non-Western social movements often continues to be interpreted as driven by 'irrationality, tribal primitivism, ideological fanaticism, or charismatic leaders' and, therefore, these actors are often framed as lacking 'either the agency or the structural context that Western movements are assumed' to inherently possess (Gunning 2009, 172). However, the framework proposed herein can serve to overcome this bias by placing non-Western social movements into the same conceptual space as Western social movements, subject to the same pressures and dynamics. Moreover, it can serve to de-essentialize the role of ideology and culture, thus returning the focus to the structure of contention and the techniques employed. Indeed, this approach offers distinct advantages for the inclusion of non-Western examples and subjects: at the very core of the framework is the recognition that political systems and sociocultural norms differ significantly; thus, by providing a thematic framework which focuses and organizes the types of questions one should ask, this framework should have no difficulty in accommodating and accounting for regional or systemic differences in non-Western contexts. Moreover, the framework does not presume a particular political or socioeconomic system, or a particular type of movement organization, but instead encourages researchers to survey the impact these systems and organizations have on the formation of new techniques of contention, irrespective of whether the societies in which these techniques emerge are democratic or totalitarian or whether organizations are formal, clan-based, or class-based, for example.

A third avenue of potential research derived from this book deals with the nature of the interactions between claim-makers and governments. Much progress has been made toward conceptualizing groups employing 'terroristic' violence as rational and strategic actors, and researchers have developed useful notions regarding how violent techniques of contention fit within larger strategies aimed at achieving defined political goals (Enders and Sandler 1993; Sandler, Tschirhart, and Cauley 1983; Atkinson, Sandler, and Tschirhart 1987; Li 2005; Aksoy and Carter 2014). However, theoretical ideas about interactions between claim-makers and governments have rarely been directly modelled. One area where future research is needed surrounds the understanding of how claim-makers strategically anticipate government actions. As demonstrated, claim-makers appear to have an intrinsic evolutionary advantage over governments, innovating and replicating successful techniques at a much quicker rate than governments, who tend to act in response rather than in anticipation of innovation. A better understanding of this cat-and-mouse interaction, along with a wider understanding of the incremental evolution of techniques of contention, could be co-opted by counter-terrorism officials and policy makers; insights from evolution could indeed be exploited to reduce claim-maker innovations and to improve the government's own potential to innovate.

This book's development of an evolutionary framework and the subsequent creation of an accurate and contextually appropriate understanding of the history of hijacking represents the first step in the endeavour to understand how techniques of contention spread, endure, and sometimes, disappear altogether. This understanding is vital if we hope to reduce the impact of seemingly endless torrents of terrorist innovation, whether it be the threat of armed drones, vehicle ramming attacks, 3-D printed weapons, or the malevolent use of gene-editing technology.

Bibliography

Abrams, Herbert L. 1992. *"The President Has Been Shot": Confusion, Disability, and the 25th Amendment in the Aftermath of the Attempted Assassination of Ronald Reagan.* 1st ed. New York: W. W. Norton.

Aggarwala, N. 1971. "Political Aspects of Hijacking." *International Conciliation* 585: 7–27.

Aksoy, Deniz, and David B. Carter. 2014. "Electoral Institutions and the Emergence of Terrorist Groups." *British Journal of Political Science* 44 (1): 181–204. https://doi.org/10.1017/S0007123412000282.

Aldrich, Howard E., Geoffrey M. Hodgson, David L. Hull, Thorbjørn Knudsen, Joel Mokyr, and Viktor J. Vanberg. 2008. "In Defence of Generalized Darwinism." *Journal of Evolutionary Economics* 18 (5): 577–96. https://doi.org/10.1007/s00191-008-0110-z.

Alexander, George. 1991. "Discipline of Terrorology." In *Western State Terrorism*, edited by Alexander George, 76–101. Cambridge: Polity Press.

Andrews, Kenneth T., and Michael Biggs. 2006. "The Dynamics of Protest Diffusion: Movement Organizations, Social Networks, and News Media in the 1960 Sit-Ins." *American Sociological Review* 71 (5): 752–77.

Araj, Bader. 2008. "Harsh State Repression as a Cause of Suicide Bombing: The Case of the Palestinian–Israeli Conflict." *Studies in Conflict & Terrorism* 31 (4): 284–303. https://doi.org/10.1080/10576100801925273.

Arey, James A. 1972. *The Sky Pirates.* New York: Scribner.

Arizona Republic. 1980. "Cuban Hijackers Ignored Castro's Warning," September 18, 1980.

Asal, Victor, and R. Karl Rethemeyer. 2008. "The Nature of the Beast: Organizational Structures and the Lethality of Terrorist Attacks." *The Journal of Politics* 70 (2): 437–49. https://doi.org/10.1017/S0022381608080419.

Atkinson, Scott E., Todd Sandler, and John Tschirhart. 1987. "Terrorism in a Bargaining Framework." *The Journal of Law & Economics* 30 (1): 1–21.

Aunger, Robert, ed. 2000. *Darwinizing Culture: The Status of Memetics as a Science.* New York: Oxford University Press.

———. 2006. "What's the Matter with Memes." In: Richard Dawkins, *How a Scientist Changed the Way We Think; Reflections by Scientists, Writers, and Philosophers*, edited by Alan Grafen, 176–90. Oxford: Oxford University Press.

Aust, Stefan. 2009. *Baader-Meinhof: The Inside Story of the R.A.F.* New York: Oxford University Press.

Avihai, Hillel. 2009. *Aviation Terrorism: Evolution, Motivation, and Escalation.* Saarbrücken, Germany: VDM Verlag.

Avise, John C. 1998. *The Genetic Gods: Evolution and Belief in Human Affairs.* Cambridge, MA: Harvard University Press.

Bacon, Tricia L. 2005. Strange Bedfellows or Brothers-in-Arms: Why Terrorist Groups Ally. PhD diss, Georgetown University, Washington DC.

Bar-Maoz, Danny. 1991. *International Terrorism Threats and How to Combat It.* Carlisle Barracks, PA: US Army War College.

Beissinger, Mark R. 1998. "Nationalist Violence and the State: Political Authority and Contentious Repertoires in the Former USSR." *Comparative Politics* 30 (4): 401. https://doi.org/10.2307/422331.

Bennett, Mary-Jane. 2014. "Nationalism in the Skies and the Bête Noire of the 21st Century." Frontier Centre For Public Policy. March 18, 2014. https://fcpp.org/2014/03/18/nationalism-in-the-skies-and-the-bete-noire-of-the-21st-century/.

Berman, Paul. 2006. *Power and the Idealists.* New York: Turnaround.

Bettinger, Robert L, Robert Boyd, and Peter J. Richerson. 1996. "Style, Function, and Cultural Evolutionary Processes." In: *Darwinian Archaeologies*, edited by Herbert Donald Graham Maschner, 133–64. Interdisciplinary Contributions to Archaeology. Boston, MA: Springer US. https://doi.org/10.1007/978-1-4757-9945-3.

Biggs, Michael. 2013. "How Repertoires Evolve: The Diffusion of Suicide Protest in the Twentieth Century." *Mobilization: An International Quarterly* 18 (4): 407–28.

Black, Jeremy. 2016. *Air Power: A Global History.* Lanham, MD: Rowman & Littlefield.

Blackmore, Susan J. 2000. *The Meme Machine.* Oxford: Oxford University Press.

Blumenau, Bernhard. 2014. *The United Nations and Terrorism: Germany, Multilateralism, and Antiterrorism Efforts in the 1970s.* New York: Palgrave Macmillan.

Bohstedt, John, and Dale E. Williams. 1988. "The Diffusion of Riots: The Patterns of 1766, 1795, and 1801 in Devonshire." *The Journal of Interdisciplinary History* 19 (1): 1–24. https://doi.org/10.2307/204221.

Bowler, P. J. 1984. *Evolution: The History of an Idea.* Berkeley: University of California Press.

Brachet de Márquez, Viviane. 2014. *Contention and the Dynamics of Inequality in Mexico, 1910–2010.* New York: Cambridge University Press.

Brent, William Lee. 2000. *Long Time Gone: A Black Panther's True-Life Story of His Hijacking and Twenty-Five Years in Cuba.* San Jose: ToExcel.

Brock, Lisa, and Digna Castañeda Fuertes, eds. 1998. *Between Race and Empire: African-Americans and Cubans before the Cuban Revolution.* Philadelphia, PA: Temple University Press.

Brogan, P. 1974. "White House Guards Open Fire on Helicopter." February 18, 1974.

Bröhl, Beate. 1977. "Viele Kinos Müssen Angst Vor Bombenterror Haben." Neue Rhein Zeitung, January 6, 1977.

Buffonge, A. E. Gordon. 2001. "Culture and Political Opportunity: Rastafarian Links to the Jamaican Poor." *Research in Social Movements, Conflict and Change* 23: 3–35.

Byman, Daniel. 2011. *A High Price: The Triumphs and Failures of Israeli Counterterrorism.* New York: Oxford University Press.

Byran Times. 1971. "TV Stations Asked to Ban 'Doomsday Flight.'" August 11, 1971.

Cardwell, Donald. 1994. *The Fontana History of Technology.* Fontana History of Science. London: Fontana Press.

Caren, Neal. 2007. "Political Process Theory." In *The Blackwell Encyclopedia of Sociology*, edited by George Ritzer. Oxford, UK: John Wiley & Sons, Ltd.

Carruthers, Susan L. 2005. "Between Camps: Eastern Bloc 'Escapees' and Cold War Borderlands." *American Quarterly* 57 (3): 911–42. https://doi.org/10.1353/aq.2005.0043.

Cauchon, Dennis. 2001. "The World Trade Center Was Only Half-Full When the First Jet Struck at 8:46." *USA Today*, December 20, 2001.

Caute, David. 2008. *The Dancer Defects: The Struggle for Cultural Supremacy during the Cold War.* Repr. Oxford: Oxford University Press.

Cavalli-Sforza, L. L., and Marcus W. Feldman. 1981. *Cultural Transmission and Evolution: A Quantitative Approach.* Monographs in Population Biology 16. Princeton, N.J: Princeton University Press.

CBS News. 2004. "'Terror Clues', Timeline: September 11 Investigation, American Under Attack." 2004.

Chabot, Sean. 2010. "Dialogue Matters: Beyond the Transmission Model of Transnational Diffusion between Social Movements." In *The Diffusion of Social Movements: Actors, Mechanisms, and Political Effects*, edited by Rebecca K. Givan, Kenneth M. Roberts, and Sarah A. Soule, 99–124. Cambridge: Cambridge University Press.

Chamberlin, Paul. 2011. "The Struggle against Oppression Everywhere: The Global Politics of Palestinian Liberation." *Middle Eastern Studies* 47 (1): 25–41. https://doi.org/10.1080/00263201003590300.

Charbel, Ghassan. 2008. *Asrâr Al-Sundûq al-Aswad (The Secrets of the Black Box)*. Translated by Nate Wilson. Beirut: Riyad El-Rayyes Books.

Chenoweth, Erica. 2010. "Democratic Competition and Terrorist Activity." *The Journal of Politics* 72 (1): 16–30. https://doi.org/10.1017/S0022381609990442.

Chicago Tribune. 1972. "Submachine Gun, Hijacking Loot Recovered in Indiana," 1972.

Choi, Jin-Tai. 1994. *Aviation Terrorism*. London: Palgrave Macmillan UK. https://doi.org/10.1007/978-1-349-23175-1.

"Chronology February 16, 1973–May 15, 1973." 1973. *Middle East Journal* 27 (3): 353–71.

Clarke, James W. 1990. *American Assassins: The Darker Side of Politics*. Rev. ed. Princeton, NJ: Princeton University Press.

Clarke, Liam, and Kathryn Johnston. 2001. *Martin McGuinness: From Guns to Government*. Edinburgh: Mainstream Publishing.

Claussen, Detlev. 1976. "Terror in Der Luft, Konterrevolution Auf Der Erde." Links, 1976.

Clutterbuck, Richard L. 1990. *Terrorism and Guerrilla Warfare: Forecasts and Remedies*. Routledge Revivals. London: Routledge.

Collier, David. 1998. "Comparative Method in the 1990s." *American Political Science Association – Comparative* 9 (1): 1–5.

Collins, Bradley. 2013. *My Father Was DB Cooper: An American Story*. London: Austin Macauley Publishers.

Commons, John R. 1936. "Institutional Economics." *The American Economic Review* 26 (1): 237–49.

Cooley, John K. 2015. *Green March, Black September (RLE Israel and Palestine): The Story of the Palestinian Arabs*. Hoboken: Taylor and Francis.

Cragin, Kim, Peter Chalk, Sara Daly, and Brian Jackson. 2007. Sharing the Dragon's Teeth: Terrorist Groups and the Exchange of New Technologies. RAND Corporation. https://doi.org/10.7249/MG485.

Crenshaw, Edward, and Kristopher Robison. 2010. "Political Violence as an Object of Study: Thee Need for Taxonomic Clarity." In *Handbook of Politics*, edited by Kevin T. Leicht and J. Craig Jenkins, 235–46. Handbooks of Sociology and Social Research. New York: Springer New York. https://doi.org/10.1007/978-0-387-68930-2.

Cuba-United States: Memorandum of Understanding on the Hijacking of Aircraft and Vessels. 1973.

Darwin, Charles. 1964 [1859]. *On the Origin of Species*. Cambridge, MA: Harvard University Press.

Darwin, Charles, and Amit Hagar. 2017 [1859]. *On the Origin of Species*. Knickerbocker Classics. Minneapolis: Race Point Publishing. http://ezproxy.gsu.edu/login?url=http://search.ebscohost.com/login.aspx?direct=true&db=nlebk&AN=1611973&site=eds-live&scope=site.

David, Paul A. 1994. "Why Are Institutions the 'Carriers of History'?: Path Dependence and the Evolution of Conventions, Organizations and Institutions." *Structural Change and Economic Dynamics* 5 (2): 205–20. https://doi.org/10.1016/0954-349X(94)90002-7.

David, Saul. 2016. *Operation Thunderbolt: Flight 139 and the Raid on Entebbe Airport, the Most Audacious Hostage Rescue Mission in History*. New York: Little, Brown, and Company.

Davies, R. E. G. 1983. *History of the World's Airlines*. New York: AMS Press.

Dawkins, Richard. 1976. *The Selfish Gene*. New ed. Oxford: Oxford University Press.

———. 1982. *The Extended Phenotype: The Gene as the Unit of Selection*. Repr. Oxford: Oxford University Press.

———. 1996. *The Blind Watchmaker: Why the Evidence of Evolution Reveals a Universe without Design.* New York: Norton.

Day, Beth. 1976. *Glacier Pilot: The Story of Bob Reeve and the Flyers Who Pushed Back Alaska's Air Frontiers.* New York: Holt.

De La Pedraja Tomán, René. 2006. *Wars of Latin America, 1899–1941.* Jefferson, NC: McFarland & Co.

Deacon, Richard. 1977. *The Israeli Secret Service.* London: Hamilton.

Della Porta, Donatella. 1995. *Social Movements, Political Violence, and the State: A Comparative Analysis of Italy and Germany.* Cambridge Studies in Comparative Politics. Cambridge, UK: Cambridge University Press.

Dennett, D. C. 1996. *Darwin's Dangerous Idea: Evolution and the Meanings of Life.* New York: Touchstone.

Der Spiegel. 1972. "Weißer Kreis." June 5, 1972.

———. 1978. "A Terrorist's Story: German Guerrilla Who Turned in His Gun After Raid Now Fears His Former Comrades as Well as Police." September 11, 1978.

Dershowitz, Alan M. 2004. *America on Trial: Inside the Legal Battles That Transformed Our Nation.* New York: Warner Books.

Diamond, Jared M. 1978. "Niche Shifts and the Rediscovery of Interspecific Competition: Why Did Field Biologists so Long Overlook the Widespread Evidence for Interspecific Competition That Had Already Impressed Darwin?" *American Scientist* 66 (3): 322–31.

Die Welt. 1977. "Entebbe-Film Unter Polizeischutz." January 7, 1977.

Dierikx, Marc, and Bram Bouwens. 1986. *Building Castles of the Air: Schiphol Amsterdam and the Development of Airport Infrastructure in Europe, 1916–1996.* The Hague: SDU Publishers.

Dietl, Gregory P. 2008. "Selection, Security and Evolutionary International Relations." In: *Natural Security: A Darwinian Approach to a Dangerous World*, edited by Rafe Sagarin and Terence Taylor, 86–101. Berkeley: University of California Press.

Dobzhansky, Theodosius. 1937. *Genetics and the Origin of Species.* Columbia Classics in Evolution Series. New York: Columbia University Press.

Dolnik, Adam. 2007. *Understanding Terrorist Innovation: Technology, Tactics and Global Trends.* London: Routledge.

Dower, John W. 1993. *War without Mercy: Race and Power in the Pacific War.* 7. printing, corr. By the author. New York: Pantheon Books.

Dugan, Laura, Gary Lafree, and Alex R. Piquero. 2005. "Testing a Rational Choice Model of Airline Hijackings." *Criminology* 43 (4): 1031–65. https://doi.org/10.1111/j.1745-9125.2005.00032.x.

Durand, Rodolphe. 2006. *Organizational Evolution and Strategic Management.* Sage Strategy Series. Thousand Oaks, Calif: Sage.

Durham, William H. 1991. *Coevolution: Genes, Culture, and Human Diversity.* Stanford, CA: Stanford University Press.

Ebbrecht-Hartmann, Tobias. 2015. "The Missing Scene: Entebbe, Holocaust, and Echoes from the German Past." In: *Jahrbuch Des Simon-Dubnow-Instituts*, edited by Raphael Gross, Romain Brethes, and Jean-Philippe Guez, 243–64. Göttingen: Vandenhoeck & Ruprecht Gm.

Eerkens, Jelmer W., and Carl P. Lipo. 2005. "Cultural Transmission, Copying Errors, and the Generation of Variation in Material Culture and the Archaeological Record." *Journal of Anthropological Archaeology* 24 (4): 316–34. https://doi.org/10.1016/j.jaa.2005.08.001.

Eggertsson, Thráinn. 2009. "Knowledge and the Theory of Institutional Change." *Journal of Institutional Economics* 5 (02): 137. https://doi.org/10.1017/S1744137409001271.

Eldredge, Niles. 1995. *Reinventing Darwin: The Great Debate at the High Table of Evolutionary Theory.* New York: Wiley.

Eldredge, Niles, and Stephen Jay Gould. 1972. "Punctuated Equilibira: An Alternative to Phyletic Gradualism." In *Models in Paleobiology*, edited by Thomas J. M. Schopf, 82–115. San Francisco: Freeman, Cooper.

Elias, Bartholomew. 2010. *Airport and Aviation Security: U.S. Policy and Strategy in the Age of Global Terrorism.* Boca Raton, FL: CRC Press.

Enders, Walter, and Todd Sandler. 1993. "The Effectiveness of Antiterrorism Policies: A Vector-Autoregression- Intervention Analysis." *The American Political Science Review* 87 (4): 829–44. https://doi.org/10.2307/2938817.

Enders, Walter, Todd Sandier, and Jon Cauley. 1990. "UN Conventions, Technology and Retaliation in the Fight against Terrorism: An Econometric Evaluation." *Terrorism and Political Violence* 2 (1): 83–105. https://doi.org/10.1080/09546559008427052.

English, Richard. 2009. *Terrorism: How to Respond.* Oxford: Oxford University Press.

———. 2012. *Armed Struggle: The History of the IRA.* London: Pan.

Erlanger, Simon. 2009. "'The Anti-Germans' - The Pro-Israel German Left." *Jewish Political Studies Review* 21: 1–2.

Evans, Alona E, and John F Murphy. 1978. *Legal Aspects of International Terrorism.* Lexington, MA: Lexington Books.

Evans, Anthony A. 2001. *The Timechart of Aviation History.* Ann Arbor, MI: Lowe & B. Hould Publishers.

Falciola, Luca. 2016. "Wearing a Keffiyeh in Rome: The Transnational Relationships Between the Italian Revolutionary Left and the Palestinian Resistance."

Falk, Richard A. 1969. "The Beirut Raid and the International Law of Retaliation." *American Journal of International Law* 63 (3): 415–43. https://doi.org/10.2307/2198865.

Fischer, Louis. 1949. *Thirteen Who Fled.* New York: Harper.

Fitzgerald, P. Paul. 2010. "Air Marshals: The Need for Legal Certainty." *Journal of Air Law and Commerce* 75: 357.

Frank, Michael C. 2017. *The Cultural Imaginary of Terrorism in Public Discourse, Literature, and Film: Narrating Terror.* Routledge Interdisciplinary Perspectives on Literature 76. New York: Routledge.

Fried, Richard M. 1998. *The Russians Are Coming! The Russians Are Coming! Pageantry and Patriotism in Cold-War America.* New York: Oxford University Press.

Friedersdorf, C. 2015. "Why It Matters That the Charleston Attack Was Terrorism: The Term Clarifies What Took Place Last Week, But Not What the Response Should Be," June 22, 2015. https://www.theatlantic.com/politics/archive/2015/06/was-the-charleston-attack-terrorism/396329/.

Gamson, William A. 1990. *The Strategy of Social Protest.* 2nd ed. Belmont, CA: Wadsworth Pub.

Gamson, William A., and David S. Meyer. 1996. "Framing Political Opportunity." In: *Comparative Perspectives on Social Movements,* edited by Doug McAdam, John D. McCarthy, and Mayer N. Zald, 275–90. Cambridge: Cambridge University Press. https://doi.org/10.1017/CBO9780511803987.014.

García, María Cristina. 1996. *Havana USA: Cuban Exiles and Cuban Americans in South Florida, 1959–1994.* Berkeley: Univ. of California Press.

Gearty, C. A. 1991. *Terror.* London: Faber and Faber.

Gelb, Joyce, and Vivien Hart. 1999. "Feminist Politics in a Hostile Environment: Obstacles and Opportunities." In: *How Social Movements Matter,* edited by Marco Giugni, Doug McAdam, and Charles Tilly, 149–81. Minneapolis: University of Minnesota Press. http://sro.sussex.ac.uk/17411/.

Gero, David. 1997. *Flights of Terror: Aerial Hijack and Sabotage since 1930.* Somerset, UK; Newbury Park, CA: Haynes Pub.

Ghiselin, Michael T. 1997. *Metaphysics and the Origin of Species.* SUNY Series in Philosophy and Biology. Albany: State University of New York Press.

Gidwitz, Betsy. 1980. *The Politics of International Air Transport.* Lexington, MA: Lexington Books.

Gilbert, Paul. 1995. *Terrorism, Security and Nationality: An Introductory Study in Applied Political Philosophy.* London: Routledge.

Givan, Rebecca K., Kenneth M. Roberts, and Sarah A. Soule. 2010. "Introduction: The Dimensions of Diffusion." In: *The Diffusion of Social Movements: Actors, Mechanisms, and Political Effects,* edited by Rebecca K. Givan, Kenneth M. Roberts, and Sarah A. Soule, 1–18. Cambridge: Cambridge University Press.

Golder, Ben, and George Williams. 2004. "What Is 'Terrorism'? Problems of Legal Definition." *University of New South Wales Law Journal* 27 (4): 270–95.

Gould, Stephen Jay. 1980. *The Panda's Thumb: More Reflections in Natural History.* 1st ed. New York: Norton.

———. 1989. *Wonderful Life: The Burgess Shale and the Nature of History.* 1st ed. New York: W.W. Norton.

———. 2002. *Full House: The Spread of Excellence from Plato to Darwin.* Cambridge, MA: Belknap Press of Harvard University Press.

Gourevitch, Alexander. 2003. "Body Count: How John Ashcroft's Inflated Terrorism Statistics Undermine the War on Terrorism." *Washington Monthly*, June 1, 2003.

Grant, Verne. 1985. *The Evolutionary Process: A Critical Review of Evolutionary Theory.* New York: Columbia University Press.

Gray, Geoffrey. 2012. *Skyjack: The Hunt for D. B. Cooper.* New York: Broadway Paperbacks.

Gray, Peter W. 2016. *Air Warfare: History, Theory and Practice.* London: Bloomsbury Academic.

Groll, Elias. 2015. "Was the Charleston Massacre An Act of Terrorism?" *Foreign Policy*, June 18, 2015. https://foreignpolicy.com/2015/06/18/was-the-charleston-massacre-an-act-of-terrorism/.

Grooch, William Stephen. 1938. *Winged Highway.* New York: Longmans, Green.

Grunor, Jerry A. 2005. *Let My People Go: The Trials and Tribulations of the People of Israel, and the Heroes Who Helped in Their Independence from British Colonialization: A Non-Fiction Account Based on Actual Correspondence of the Heroes Who Made This Possible.* iUniverse.

Guelke, Adrian. 1995. *The New Age of Terrorism and the International Political System.* London: I. B.Tauris.

Gunning, Jeroen. 2009. "Social Movement Theory and the Study of Terrorism." In: *Critical Terrorism Studies: A New Research Agenda*, edited by Richard Jackson, Marie Smyth, and Jeroen Gunning, 156–77. London: Routledge.

Gunston, Bill, ed. 2001. *Aviation Year by Year.* New York: DK.

Guridy, Frank Andre. 2010. *Forging Diaspora: Afro-Cubans and African Americans in a World of Empire and Jim Crow. Envisioning Cuba.* Chapel Hill: University of North Carolina Press.

Harding, John. 2006. *Flying's Strangest Moments: Extraordinary but True Stories from over 1000 Years of Aviation History.* London: Robson.

Hedström, Peter, Rickard Sandell, and Charlotta Stern. 2000. "Mesolevel Networks and the Diffusion of Social Movements: The Case of the Swedish Social Democratic Party." *American Journal of Sociology* 106 (1): 145–72. https://doi.org/10.1086/303109.

Heres, Celestino. 2010. *Unpardonable Crimes: The Legacy of Fidel Castro: Untold Tales of the Cuban Revolution.* Bloomington, IN: Trafford Publishing.

Herf, Jeffrey. 2016. *Undeclared Wars with Israel: East Germany and the West German Far Left, 1967–1989.* New York: Cambridge University Press.

"Hezbollah Increasing Terror Activity." 2004. *Middle East Intelligence Bulletin*. March 2004. https://www.meforum.org/meib/articles/0402_l2.htm.

Hiatt, Willie. 2016. *The Rarified Air of the Modern: Airplanes and Technological Modernity in the Andes.* New York: Oxford University Press.

"Hijacking. Operation Center, Situation Report [Sitrep] #4." 1970. Department of State.

Hilton, James. 1933. *Lost Horizon.* London: MacMillan and Co.

Hirschman, Albert O. 1970. *Exit, Voice, and Loyalty: Responses to Decline in Firms, Organizations, and States.* Cambridge, MA: Harvard University Press.

———. 1992. *Rival Views of Market Society and Other Recent Essays.* Cambridge, MA: Harvard University Press.

Hoffman, Bruce. 2006. *Inside Terrorism.* Rev. and Expanded ed. New York: Columbia University Press.

Hoffman, Bruce, and Gordon H. Mccormick. 2004. "Terrorism, Signaling, and Suicide Attack." *Studies in Conflict & Terrorism* 27 (4): 243–81. https://doi.org/10.1080/10576100490466498.

Holden, Robert T. 1986. "The Contagiousness of Aircraft Hijacking." *American Journal of Sociology* 91 (4): 874–904.

Horowitz, Michael C., and Philip B. K. Potter. 2014. "Allying to Kill: Terrorist Intergroup Cooperation and the Consequences for Lethality." *Journal of Conflict Resolution* 58 (2): 199–225. https://doi.org/10.1177/0022002712468726.

Hsu, Henda Y., and Robert Apel. 2015. "A Situational Model of Displacement and Diffusion Following the Introduction of Airport Metal Detectors." *Terrorism and Political Violence* 27 (1): 29–52. https://doi.org/10.1080/09546553.2014.962989.

Hudson, Rex A. 1999. *Who Becomes a Terrorist and Why: The 1999 Government Report on Profiling Terrorists.* Guilford, CT: The Lyons Press.

Hull, David L. 1998. *Science as a Progress.* Chicago: University of Chicago Press.

Hull, David L., Rodney E. Langman, and Sigrid S. Glenn. 2001. "A General Account of Selection: Biology, Immunology, and Behavior." *Behavioral and Brain Sciences* 24 (3): 559–69. https://doi.org/10.1017/S0140525X0156416X.

Ilardi, Gaetano Joe. 2009. "The 9/11 Attacks—A Study of Al Qaeda's Use of Intelligence and Counterintelligence." *Studies in Conflict & Terrorism* 32 (3): 171–87. https://doi.org/10.1080/10576100802670803.

Illing, S. 2015. "We Must Call Him a Terrorist: Dylann Roof, Fox News and the Truth about Why Language Matters." Salon.Com (blog). June 21, 2015. https://www.salon.com/2015/06/21/we_must_call_him_a_terrorist_dylann_roof_fox_news_and_the_truth_about_why_language_matters/.

Im, Eric Iksoon, Jon Cauley, and Todd Sandler. 1987. "Cycles and Substitutions in Terrorist Activities: A Spectral Approach." *Kyklos* 40 (2): 238–55. https://doi.org/10.1111/j.1467-6435.1987.tb02674.x.

"Incoming Telegram." 1958a. Embassy of the United States, Havana: Department of State.

"Incoming Telegram." 1958b. Embassy of the United States, Havana: Department of State.

International Civil Airport Association. 1971. "Hijacking." Doc. 711-Gen/15. Montreal: International Civil Airport Association.

"Investigation of Cubana Crash and Other Matters." 1958. Embassy of the United States, Havana: Department of State.

Jablonka, E., and M. J. Lamb. 1995. *Epigenetic Inheritance in Evolution.* Oxford: Oxford University Press.

Jablonka, Eva, Marion J. Lamb, and Anna Zeligowski. 2006. *Evolution in Four Dimensions: Genetic, Epigenetic, Behavioral, and Symbolic Variation in the History of Life.* Cambridge, MA: MIT Press.

Jackson, R. 2007. "The Core Commitments of Critical Terrorism Studies." *European Political Science* 6 (3): 244–51.

Jacobi, Tonja, and Jonah Kind. 2005. "Criminal Innovation and the Warrant Requirement: Reconsidering the Rights-Police Efficiency Trade-Off." *William and Mary Law Review* 56: 761–831.

Jaffe, Steven. 2016. *Airspace Closure and Civil Aviation: A Strategic Resource for Airline Managers.* London: Routledge.

Johnson, Allen W., and Timothy Earle. 2006. *The Evolution of Human Societies: From Foraging Group to Agrarian State.* 2nd ed. Stanford, CA: Stanford University Press.

"Jordan, Vol. V, July 1/70-September 30/70." 1970. Cable to Department of State. United States Embassy, Amman: Department of State. NSC, CO: Middle East, Box 615. NMP-NARA.

Josephson, Matthew. 1999. *Empire of the Air: Juan Trippe and the Struggle for World Airways. Literature and History of Aviation.* North Stratford: Ayer Co. Publishers.

Joyner, Nancy Douglas. 1974. *Aerial Hijacking as an International Crime.* Gobbs Ferry, NY: Oceana.

Kalyvas, Stathis N., and Ignacio Sánchez-Cuenca. 2005. "Killing Without Dying: The Absence of Suicide Missions." In: *Making Sense of Suicide Missions,* edited by Diego Gambetta, 209–32. Oxford University Press. https://doi.org/10.1093/acprof:oso/9780199276998.001.0001.

Karber, Phillip A. 2005. "Bad Men V. Soft Laws: Transnational Terrorism and the Global Aviation Security Regime: An Exploration into the Theoretical Contribution of 'Speech Acts' Constructivist Jurisprudence." PhD diss., Georgetown University, Washington DC.

Karmon, Eli. 2005. *Coalitions between Terrorist Organizations: Revolutionaries, Nationalists, and Islamists.* Leiden: Martinus Nijhoff.

Kearns, Erin M., Allison E. Betus, and Anthony F. Lemieux. 2019. "When Data Do Not Matter: Exploring Public Perceptions of Terrorism." *Studies in Conflict & Terrorism* 0 (0): 1–22. https://doi.org/10.1080/1057610X.2018.1543145.

Keller, Evelyn Fox. 2002. *The Century of the Gene.* Cambridge, MA: Harvard University Press.

Ketchley, Neil. 2014. "'The Army and the People Are One Hand!' Fraternization and the 25th January Egyptian Revolution." *Comparative Studies in Society and History* 56 (01): 155–86. https://doi.org/10.1017/S0010417513000650.

Keynen, Nik, and Jason Rhodes. 2012. "Organizing for Survival: From the Civil Rights Movement to Black Anarchism through the Life of Lorenzo Kom'boa Ervin | ACME: An International Journal for Critical Geographies." *An International E-Journal for Critical Geographies* 11 (3): 393–412.

Khalaf, Issa. 1991. *Politics in Palestine: Arab Factionalism and Social Disintegration, 1939–1948.* SUNY Series in the Social and Economic History of the Middle East. Albany: State University of New York Press.

Khalidi, Rashid. 2007. *The Iron Cage: The Story of the Palestinian Struggle for Statehood.* Boston, MA: Beacon Press.

Kingsbury, Paul. 1998. *The Encyclopedia of Country Music: The Ultimate Guide to the Music.* New York: Oxford University Press.

Kitcher, Philip. 1985. *Vaulting Ambition: Sociobiology and the Quest for Human Nature.* Cambridge, MA: MIT Press.

Klimke, Martin. 2010. *The Other Alliance: Student Protest in West Germany and the United States in the Global Sixties. America in the World.* Princeton, NJ: Princeton University Press.

Koerner, Brendan I. 2013. *The Skies Belong to Us.* New York: Broadway Books.

Koo, Hagen. 2001. *Korean Workers: The Culture and Politics of Class Formation.* Ithaca, NY: Cornell University Press.

Kraus, Douglas M. 1973. "Searching for Hijackers: Constitutionality, Costs, and Alternatives." *The University of Chicago Law Review* 40 (2): 383. https://doi.org/10.2307/1599119.

Krause, Peter. 2017. *Rebel Power: Why National Movements Compete, Fight, and Win.* Ithaca, NY: Cornell University Press.

Kriesi, Hanspeter. 2004. "Political Context and Opportunity." In: *The Blackwell Companion to Social Movements*, edited by David A. Snow, Sarah A. Soule, and Hanspeter Kriesi, 67–90. Blackwell Companions to Sociology. Malden, MA: Blackwell.

Krinsky, John, and Ann Mische. 2013. "Formations and Formalisms: Charles Tilly and the Paradox of the Actor." *Annual Review of Sociology* 39 (1): 1–26. https://doi.org/10.1146/annurev-soc-071312-145547.

Kundnani, Hans. 2009. *Utopia or Auschwitz: Germany's 1968 Generation and the Holocaust.* Oxford: Oxford University Press.

Kuznets, Simon. 1955. "Economic Growth and Income Inequality." *The American Economic Review* 45 (1): 1–28.

Labov, William. 2006. *Principles of Linguistic Change.* Vol. 2: Social Factors. Digital print. Language in Society 29. Malden, MA: Blackwell.

Lacoste, Julie, and Pierre Tremblay. 2003. "Crime and Innovation: A Procedural Analysis of Patterns in Check Forgery." In: *Theory for Practice in Situational Crime Prevention*, edited by Martha J. Smith and Derek B. Cornish, 169–96. Crime Prevention Studies 16. New York: Criminal Justice.

LaFree, Gary, Laura Dugan, and Erin Miller. 2015. *Putting Terrorism in Context: Lessons from the Global Terrorism Database.* Contemporary Terrorism Studies. Abingdon, Oxon: Routledge, Taylor & Francis Group.

Lance, Peter. 2005. *1000 Years for Revenge: International Terrorism and the FBI—the Untold Story.* New York: Harper Collins.

Laqueur, Walter. 1977. *Terrorism.* 1st ed. Boston: Little, Brown.

———. 1999. *The New Terrorism: Fanaticism and the Arms of Mass Destruction.* Oxford: Oxford University Press.

———. 2001. *A History of Terrorism.* New Brunswick, NJ: Transaction.

Lathem, Niles. 1999. "FBI Profilers Dig into Co-Pilot's Past." *New York Post*, November 18, 1999. https://nypost.com/1999/11/18/fbi-profilers-dig-into-co-pilots-past/.

Latner, T. A. 2015. "Take Me to Havana! Airline Hijacking, U.S.-Cuba Relations, and Political Protest in Late Sixties' America." *Diplomatic History* 39 (1): 16–44. https://doi.org/10.1093/dh/dht129.

Li, Quan. 2005. "Does Democracy Promote or Reduce Transnational Terrorist Incidents?" *The Journal of Conflict Resolution* 49 (2): 278–97.

Life. 1948. "The Mystery of the Kidnapped Russian," August 1948.

Lissitzyn, Oliver J. 1971. "International Control of Aerial Hijacking: The Rôle of Values and Interests." *American Journal of International Law* 65 (04): 80–86. https://doi.org/10.1017/S0002930000261642.

Livingstone, Neil C. 1983. "The Wolves Among Us: Reflections on the Past Eighteen Months and Thoughts on the Future." *World Affairs* 146 (1): 7–22.

Loescher, Gil, and John A Scanlan. 1986. *Calculated Kindness: Refugees and America's Half Open Door, 1945 to the Present.* New York: Free Press.

Loy, Frank E. 1970. "Some International Approaches to Dealing With Hijacking of Aircraft." *The International Lawyer* 4 (3): 444–52.

MacDonald, Andrew. 1978. *The Turner Diaries.* Washington, DC: National Alliance.

Maddison, Angus. 1982. *Phases of Capitalist Development.* Oxford: Oxford University Press.

Madsen, Julian. 2004. "Suicide Terrorism: Rationalizing the Irrational." *Strategic Insights* 3 (8).

Mahnaimi, Uzi, and Bassām Abū Sharīf. 1995. *Tried by Fire: The Searing True Story of Two Men at the Heart of the Struggle between the Arabs and the Jews.* London: Warner Books.

Malnic, Eric, William C Rempel, and Ricardo Alonso-Saldivar. 2002. "EgyptAir Co-Pilot Caused '99 Jet Crash, NTSB to Say - LA Times." *Los Angeles Times*, March 15, 2002. https://www.latimes.com/archives/la-xpm-2002-mar-15-mn-32955-story.html.

Maloney, Ed. 2002. *A Secret History of the IRA.* New York: W.W. Norton.

Mark, Samuel. 2008. "The Earliest Naval Ram." *International Journal of Nautical Archaeology* 37 (2): 253–72. https://doi.org/10.1111/j.1095-9270.2008.00182.x.

Masud-Piloto, Felix. 2014. "Cuban Exiles, the Cold War and the Politics of Immigration." In: *Exile & the Politics of Exclusion in the Americas*, edited by Luis Roniger, James Naylor Green, and Pablo Yankelevich, 127–54. Brighton: Sussex Academic Press.

Mayr, Ernst. 1988. *Toward a New Philosophy of Biology: Observations of an Evolutionist.* Cambridge, MA: Belknap.

McAdam, Doug. 1983. "Tactical Innovation and the Pace of Insurgency." *American Sociological Review* 48: 735–54.

McAdam, Doug, and Dieter Rucht. 1993. "The Cross-National Diffusion of Movement Ideas." *The Annals of the American Academy of Political and Social Science* 528: 56–74.

McAdam, Doug, and Yang Su. 2002. "The War at Home: Antiwar Protests and Congressional Voting, 1965 to 1973." *American Sociological Review* 67 (5): 696. https://doi.org/10.2307/3088914.

McCammon, Holly J., Christine Mowery, Ellen M. Granberg, and Karen E. Campbell. 2001. "How Movements Win: Gendered Opportunity Structures and U.S. Women's Suffrage Movements, 1866 to 1919." *American Sociological Review* 66 (1): 49–70.

McDermott, Terry. 2002. "The Plot: How Terrorists Hatched a Simple Plan to Use Planes as Bombs." *Los Angeles Times*, September 1, 2002. https://www.latimes.com/archives/la-xpm-2002-sep-01-na-plot-1-story.html.

McWhinney, Edward. 1975. *The Illegal Diversion of Aircraft and International Law.* Leiden: Sijthoff.

Merari, Ariel. 1999. "Attacks on Civil Aviation: Trends and Lessons." In: *Aviation Terrorism and Security*, edited by Paul Wilkinson and Brian Michael Jenkins, 2–6. Cass Series on Political Violence 6. Portland, OR: Frank Cass.

Metcalfe, J. S. 1998. *Evolutionary Economics and Creative Destruction.* The Graz Schumpeter Lectures 1. London: Routledge.

Meyer, David S., and Sidney G. Tarrow, eds. 1998. *The Social Movement Society: Contentious Politics for a New Century. People, Passions, and Power.* Lanham, MD: Rowman & Littlefield Publishers.

Miami News. 1961. "Castro to Release EAL Airliner." August 13, 1961.

Mickolus, Edward F. 1980. *Transnational Terrorism: A Chronology of Events, 1968–1979.* Westport, CT: Greenwood Press.

Mirowsky, John, and Catherine E. Ross. 1981. "Protest Group Success: The Impact of Group Characteristics, Social Control, and Context." *Sociological Focus* 14 (3): 177–92. https://doi.org/10.1080/00380237.1981.10570394.

Mizuta, Jonathan Juichi. 2013. "An Evaluation of the Conceptual Similarities and Differences between the Strategic Logic of the Religiously Motivated Suicide Attacks of Tokkotai Kamikaze and Al-Qaeda Shahid." PhD diss., Baylor University, Waco, Tex. https://baylor-ir.tdl.org/handle/2104/8734.

Moher, Andrew A. 2003. "The Lesser of Two Evils - An Argument for Judicially Sanctioned Torture in a Post-9/11 World Notes and Comments." *Thomas Jefferson Law Review* 26: 469–90.

Mokyr, Joel. 1998. "Induced Technical Change and Medical History: An Evolutionary Approach." *Journal of Evolutionary Economics* 8: 119–37.

———. 2000. "Knowledge, Technology, and Economic Growth during the Industrial Revolution." In: *Productivity, Technology, and Economic Growth*, edited by Bart van Ark, S. K. Kuipers, and G. H. Kuper, 253–92. Boston, MA: Kluwer Academic Publishers.

———. 2001. "Useful Knowledge as an Evolving System: The View from Economic History."

———. 2002. *The Gifts of Athena: Historical Origin of Knowledge Economy.* Princeton, NJ: Princeton University Press.

———. 2005. *The Gifts of Athena: Historical Origins of the Knowledge Economy.* Princeton, NJ: Princeton University Press.

———. 2006. "Useful Knowledge as an Evolving System: The View from Economic History." In: *The Economy as an Evolving Complex System III*, edited by Lawrence Blume and Steven N. Durlauf. Santa Fe Institute Studies in the Sciences of Complexity. New York: Oxford University Press.

Montgomery, Jacob Michael. 2011. "An Evolutionary Theory of Democracy: Dynamic Evolutionary Models of American Party Competition with an Empirical Application to the Case of Abortion Policy from 1972-2010." PhD diss., Duke University, Durham, NC.

Morris, Aldon. 1981. "Black Southern Student Sit-In Movement: An Analysis of Internal Organization." *American Sociological Review* 46 (6): 744–67. https://doi.org/10.2307/2095077.

———. 1993. "Birmingham Confrontation Reconsidered: An Analysis of the Dynamics and Tactics of Mobilization." *American Sociological Review* 58 (5): 621–36. https://doi.org/10.2307/2096278.

Morris, Benny. 2011. *Righteous Victims: A History of the Zionist-Arab Conflict, 1881–1999.* New York: Harper and Row.

Mowbray, Joel. 2002. "How They Did It - An 'Evil One' Confesses, And Boasts." *National Review* 54 (24): 36–38.

Mueller, Carol. 1999. "Escape from the GDR, 1961–1989: Hybrid Exit Repertoires in a Disintegrating Leninist Regime." *American Journal of Sociology* 105 (3): 697–735. https://doi.org/10.1086/210358.

Murphy, John F. 2005. "The IRA and the FARC in Colombia." *International Journal of Intelligence and CounterIntelligence* 18 (1): 76–88. https://doi.org/10.1080/08850600590905753.

Myers, Daniel J. 2000. "The Diffusion of Collective Violence: Infectiousness, Susceptibility, and Mass Media Networks." *American Journal of Sociology* 106 (1): 173–208. https://doi.org/10.1086/303110.

NACLA Newsletter. 1971. "Pan Am the Wings of Imperialism." *NACLA Newsletter* 5 (2): 13–18.

Naftali, Timothy J. 2005. *Blind Spot: The Secret History of American Counterterrorism.* New York: Basic Books.

Nagin, Daniel S. 1998. "Criminal Deterrence Research at the Outset of the Twenty-First Century." *Crime and Justice* 23: 1–42.

National Commission on Terrorist Attacks upon the United States, ed. 2004. *The 9/11 Commission Report: Final Report of the National Commission on Terrorist Attacks upon the United States.* 1st ed. New York: Norton.

Nelson, R. 2003. "Physical and Social Technologies and Their Evolution." *Laboratory of Economics and Management* no. 61: 13–31.

Neria, Yuval, David Roe, Benjamin Beit-Hallahmi, Hassan Mneimneh, Alana Balaban, and Randall Marshall. 2005. "The Al Qaeda 9/11 Instructions: A Study in the Construction of Religious Martyrdom." *Religion* 35 (1): 1–11. https://doi.org/10.1016/j.religion.2005.02.001.

Nettle, Daniel. 1999. *Linguistic Diversity.* New York: Oxford University Press.

New York Times. 1930. "Violence Hits Peru; New Dictator Rules: Governor of Tacna Is Slain." August 28, 1930.

———. 1931a. "Peru Quells Revolt: 61 Killed in to Callao; Try Free Ex-President." February 21, 1931.

———. 1931b. "Revolt in Peru Gains as Garrisons Rise' Navy on Rebel Side: Battle at Arequipa Near." February 22, 1931.

———. 1931c. "Troops March on Rebels: Loyal Forces Sent Against Revolting Arequipa Garrison." February 22, 1931.

———. 1931d. "Americans Won't Join Rebels." August 30, 1931.

———. 1931e. "Court-Martial for H.B. Grow Is Ordered by Peruvian Junta." August 30, 1931.

———. 1931f. "Grow Denies Plan to Bomb Arequipa: American Says Only Shell W. as to Attract Peruvian Rebels; Attention to Leaflets." September 10, 1931.

———. 1964. "Pistol Is Traced in Crash On Coast." May 10, 1964.

———. 1967. "Cuba Asks Landing Fee for a Hijacked Airliner." August 21, 1967.

———. 1969. "Hijacking Victims Term Treatment by Cuban Hosts Royal but Tiresome." February 4, 1969.

———. 1970. "4 Jets Hijacked; One, a 747, Is Blown Up." September 7, 1970.

———. 1972a. "Hijacker Gets $500,000, Bails Out of Jet Over Utah." April 7, 1972.

———. 1972b. "$155,000 Recovered in Reno Jet Hijacking." June 6, 1972.

———. 1975. "Cuba Surrenders 3 in Plane Hijackings." June 3, 1975.

Newson, Lesley, Peter J. Richerson, and Robert Boyd. 2010. "Cultural Evolution and the Shaping of Cultural Diversity." In: *Handbook of Cultural Psychology*, edited by Dov Cohen and Shinobu Kitayama, 2nd ed. New York: Guilford Press.

Newton, Michael. 2002. *The Encyclopedia of Kidnappings.* New York: Facts on File, Inc.

Newton, Wesley Phillips. 1978. *The Perilous Sky: U.S. Aviation Diplomacy and Latin America, 1919–1931.* Coral Gables, Fla: University of Miami Press.

North, Douglass C. 1990. *Institutions, Institutional Change, and Economic Performance. The Political Economy of Institutions and Decisions.* Cambridge: Cambridge University Press.

———. 1994. "Economic Performance Through Time." *The American Economic Review* 84 (3): 359–68.

Nyampong, Yaw Otu Mankata. 2013. *Insuring the Air Transport Industry against Aviation War and Terrorism Risks and Allied Perils: Issues and Options in a Post-September 11, 2001 Environment.* Berlin: Springer. http://site.ebrary.com/id/10641777.

Oberschall, Anthony. 1973. *Social Conflict and Social Movements.* Prentice-Hall Series in Sociology. Englewood Cliffs, NJ: Prentice-Hall.

———. 1989. "The 1960 Sit-Ins: Protest Diffusion and Movement Take-Off." *Research in Social Movements, Conflict, and Change* 11: 31–53.

O'Neill, Bard E. 1978. *Armed Struggle in Palestine: A Political-Military Analysis.* Westview Special Studies on the Middle East. Boulder, CO: Westview Press.

O'Reilly, Bill, and Martin Dugard. 2015. *Killing Reagan: The Violent Assault That Changed a Presidency.* New York: Henry Holt and Company.

Organista, Kurt C. 2007. *Solving Latino Psychosocial and Health Problems: Theory, Practice, and Populations.* Hoboken, NJ: John Wiley & Sons.

Orr, H. Allen. 2009. "Testing Natural Selection." *Scientific American* 300 (1): 44–51.

Pape, Robert A. 2003. "The Strategic Logic of Suicide Terrorism." *American Political Science Review* 97 (03). https://doi.org/10.1017/S000305540300073X.

———. 2005. *Dying to Win: The Strategic Logic of Suicide Terrorism.* 1st ed. New York: Random House.

Patrick, Stewart. 2001. "The Evolution of International Norms: Choice, Learning, Power and Identity." In: *Evolutionary Interpretations of World Politics*, edited by William R. Thompson, 113–74. New York and London: Routledge.

Pearlman, Wendy. 2011. *Violence, Nonviolence, and the Palestinian National Movement.* Cambridge: Cambridge University Press.

Pedahzur, Ami. 2007. *Suicide Terrorism.* Reprint. Cambridge: Polity.

Pedahzur, Ami, and Arie Perliger. 2006. "The Changing Nature of Suicide Attacks: A Social Network Perspective." *Social Forces* 84 (4): 1987–2008.

Pedraza, Silvia. 2001. "Cuba's Refugees: Manifold Migrations." In: *Cuban Communism*, edited by Irving Louis Horowitz and Jaime Suchlicki, 10th ed, 411–36. New Brunswick, NJ: Transaction Publishers.

Petras, James, and Maurice Zeitlin. 1967. "Miners and Agrarian Radicalism." *American Sociological Review* 32 (4): 578–86. https://doi.org/10.2307/2091025.

Petrov, Vladimir. 1950. *My Retreat from Russia.* New Haven, CT: Yale University Press.

Phillips, David. 1973. *Skyjack: The Story of Air Piracy.* London: Harrap.

Pinker, Steven. 1999. How the Mind Works. New York: Norton.

Pirogov, Peter. 1950. *Why I Escaped.* New York: Duell, Sloan, and Pearce.

Piven, Frances Fox, and Richard A. Cloward. 1979. *Poor People's Movements: Why They Succeed, How They Fail.* 2nd ed. New York: Vintage Books.

Polanyi, Michael. 1962. *Personal Knowledge: Towards a Post-Critical Philosophy.* Chicago: University of Chicago Press.

Popper, Karl R. 1972. *Objective Knowledge: An Evolutionary Approach.* Rev. ed. Oxford: Oxford University Press.

"PPS 22: Utilization of Refugees from the Soviet Union in U.S. National Interest." 1949. Policy Planning Staff. RG 59, Microfiche 1171, card 62. National Archives and Records Administration.

"PPS 54: Policy Relating to Defection and Defectors from Soviet Power." 1949. Policy Planning Staff. RG 59, Microfiche 1171, card 62. National Archives and Records Administration.

Preston, Edmund. 1998. *FAA Historical Chronology: Civil Aviation & the Federal Government, 1926–1996.* Washington DC: US Government Printing Office.

"PSB Draft Program for Soviet Orbit Escapees." 1951. Psychological Strategy Board. EP, File 1. National Archives and Records Administration.

Quinlivan, James T. 1986. "The Taran: Ramming in the Soviet Air Force." Product Page. Rand Corporation. https://www.rand.org/pubs/papers/P7192.html.

Raguraman, K. 1997. "Airlines as Instruments for Nation Building and National Identity: Case Study of Malaysia and Singapore." *Journal of Transport Geography* 5 (4): 239–56. https://doi.org/10.1016/S0966-6923(97)00021-5.

Ranstorp, Magnus, ed. 2006. *Mapping Terrorism Research: State of the Art, Gaps and Future Direction.* Cass Series: Political Violence. London: Routledge, Taylor & Francis Group.

Rapkin, David P. 2001. "The United States, Japan, and the Power to Block: The APEC and AMF Cases." *The Pacific Review* 14 (3): 373–410. https://doi.org/10.1080/09512740110064820.

Reitan, Ruth. 1999. *The Rise and Decline of an Alliance: Cuba and African American Leaders in the 1960s.* East Lansing: Michigan State University Press.

"Relatives Claim Passenger in 1958 Plane Crash off Cuba Was a Hijacker." 2008. November 19, 2008. https://www.theguardian.com/world/2008/nov/19/usa-cuba.

Reuters. 1994. "Philippine Airline Explosion Kills One." December 10, 1994.

Rhodes, Bernie, and Russell P. Calame. 1991. *D. B. Cooper, the Real McCoy.* Salt Lake City: University of Utah Press.

Richards, Anthony. 2014. "Conceptualizing Terrorism." *Studies in Conflict & Terrorism* 37 (3): 213–36. https://doi.org/10.1080/1057610X.2014.872023.

———. 2015. *Conceptualizing Terrorism.* First edition. Oxford: Oxford University Press.

Ricolfi, Luca. 2005. "Palestinians, 1981–2003." In: *Making Sense of Suicide Missions*, edited by Diego Gambetta. Oxford: Oxford University Press. https://doi.org/10.1093/acprof:oso/9780199276998.001.0001.

Riding, Alan. 1994a. "Hijacked Airliner Forced to France." *The New York Times*, December 26, 1994, sec. World. https://www.nytimes.com/1994/12/26/world/hijacked-airliner-forced-to-france.html.

———. 1994b. "Police Say Hijackers Planned to Blow Up Jet Over Paris." *The New York Times*, December 28, 1994, sec. World. https://www.nytimes.com/1994/12/28/world/police-say-hijackers-planned-to-blow-up-jet-over-paris.html.

Rogers, Everett M. 1983. *Diffusion of Innovations.* 5th ed. Hoboken, NJ: Wiley.

———. 2005. *Diffusion of Innovations.* New York: Free Press.

Rousseau, Charles. 1967. "Deroutement et Destruction Par Palestiniens de Quatre Avions Commerciaux - Deux Americans, Un Swisse et Un Britannique." *Revenue Generale de Droit International Public.*

Rousseau, Claude. 1970. "Deroutement et Destruction Par Palestiniens de Quatre Avions Commerciaux - Deux Americans, Un Swisse et Un Britannique." *Revenue Generale de Droit International Public* 4: 1018–66.

Rudé, George. 1964. *The Crowd in History: A Study of Popular Disturbances in France and England, 1730–1848.* New York: John Wiley and Sons.

Rupp, Leila J., and Verta A. Taylor. 1987. *Survival in the Doldrums: The American Women's Rights Movement, 1945 to the 1960s.* New York: Oxford University Press.

Sancton, Thomas. 1995. "Anatomy of a Hijack." *Time* Magazine, January 9, 1995. http://content.time.com/time/magazine/article/0,9171,163487,00.html.

Sandler, Todd, John T. Tschirhart, and Jon Cauley. 1983. "A Theoretical Analysis of Transnational Terrorism." *The American Political Science Review* 77 (1): 36–54. https://doi.org/10.2307/1956010.

Sayigh, Yezid. 1999. *Armed Struggle and the Search for State: The Palestinian National Movement 1949–1993.* Oxford: Oxford University Press.

Schlembach, Raphael. 2009. "Some Notes on the 'Baader-Meinhof Complex'!" *Ephemera: Theory and Politics in Organization*, 9.

Schotter, Andrew. 1981. *The Economic Theory of Social Institutions.* Cambridge: Cambridge University Press. https://doi.org/10.1017/CBO9780511983863.

Schweitzer, Yoram. 2011. "Innovation in Terrorist Organizations? The Case of the PFLP and Its Offshoots." *Strategic Insights* 10 (2): 17–29.

Seale, Patrick. 1993. *Abu Nidal: A Gun for Hire.* London: Arrow.

Shapiro, James A. 1999. "Genome System Architecture and Natural Genetic Engineering in Evolution." *Annals of the New York Academy of Sciences* 870 (1 MOLECULAR STR): 23–35. https://doi.org/10.1111/j.1749-6632.1999.tb08862.x.

———. 2005. "A 21st Century View of Evolution: Genome System Architecture, Repetitive DNA, and Natural Genetic Engineering." *Gene* 345 (1): 91–100. https://doi.org/10.1016/j.gene.2004.11.020.

Silke, Andrew, ed. 2004. *Research on Terrorism: Trends, Achievements & Failures. Cass Series on Political Violence.* London: Frank Cass.

Simmel, Georg. 1950. "The Fundamental Problems of Sociology." In: *The Sociology of Georg Simmel*, by Kurt H. Wolff, 289–320. Glencoe, IL: Free Press.

Simpson, George Gaylord. 1984. *Tempo and Mode in Evolution. A Columbia Classic in Evolution.* New York: Columbia University Press.

Singer, Benjamin D. 1970. "Mass Media and Communication Processes in the Detroit Riot of 1967." *The Public Opinion Quarterly* 34 (2): 236–45.

Smith, Terence. 1976. "Hijackers' Orders Challenge Israel." *New York Times*, June 30, 1976.

Smith, Wayne S. 1987. *The Closest of Enemies: A Personal and Diplomatic Account of U.S.-Cuban Relations since 1957.* 1st ed. New York: W. W. Norton.

Snow, David A, and Robert D. Benford. 1988. "Ideology, Frame Resonance, and Participant Mobilization." *International Social Movement Research* 1 (1): 197–217.

Snow, David A., E. Burke Rochford, Steven K. Worden, and Robert D. Benford. 1986. "Frame Alignment Processes, Micromobilization, and Movement Participation." *American Sociological Review* 51 (4): 464. https://doi.org/10.2307/2095581.

Sober, Elliott. 1984. *The Nature of Selection: Evolutionary Theory in Philosophical Focus.* Chicago: University of Chicago Press.

Somit, Albert, and Steven A. Peterson, eds. 1992. *The Dynamics of Evolution: The Punctuated Equilibrium Debate in the Natural and Social Sciences.* Ithaca, NY: Cornell University Press.

Soule, Sarah A. 1997. "The Student Divestment Movement in the United States and Tactical Diffusion: The Shantytown Protest." *Social Forces* 75 (3): 855–82. https://doi.org/10.2307/2580522.

———. 1999. "The Diffusion of an Unsuccessful Innovation: The Case of the Shantytown Protest Tactic." *Annals of the American Academy of Political and Social Science* 566 (1): 120–31.

———. 2004. "Diffusion Processes within and across Movements." In: *The Blackwell Companion to Social Movements*, edited by David A. Snow, Sarah A. Soule, and Hanspeter Kriesi, Nachdr. Blackwell Companions to Sociology. Malden, MA: Blackwell.

———. 2011. "Diffusion Processes within and across Movements." In: *The Blackwell Companion to Social Movements*, edited by David A. Snow, Sarah A. Soule, and Hanspeter Kriesi, Nachdr. Blackwell Companions to Sociology. Malden, MA: Blackwell.

Spilerman, Seymour. 1976. "Structural Characteristics of Cities and the Severity of Radical Disorders." *American Sociological Review* 41: 771–93.

Spruyt, Hendrik. 2001. "Diversity of Uniformity in the Modern World: Answers from Evolutionary Theory, Learning, and Social Adaptation." In: *Evolutionary Interpretations of World Politics*, edited by William R. Thompson, 110–32. New York: Routledge.

St John, Peter. 1991. *Air Piracy, Airport Security, and International Terrorism: Winning the War Against Hijackers.* New York: Quorum Books.

Staggenborg, Suzanne. 1991. *The Pro-Choice Movement: Organization and Activism in the Abortion Conflict.* New York: Oxford University Press.

Steedly, Homer R., and John W. Foley. 1979. "The Success of Protest Groups: Multivariate Analyses." *Social Science Research* 8: 1–15.

Steinberg, Marc W. 1999. "The Talk and Back Talk of Collective Action: A Dialogic Analysis of Repertoires of Discourse among Nineteenth-Century English Cotton Spinners." *American Journal of Sociology* 105 (3): 736–80. https://doi.org/10.1086/210359.

Steinhoff, Patricia G. 1989. "Hijackers, Bombers, and Bank Robbers: Managerial Style in the Japanese Red Army." *The Journal of Asian Studies* 48 (4): 724. https://doi.org/10.2307/2058111.

———. 2016. "Transnational Ties of the Japanese Armed Left: Shared Revolutionary Ideas and Direct Personal Contacts." In: *Revolutionary Violence and the New Left: Transnational Perspectives*, edited by Alberto Martin Alvarez and Eduardo Rey Tristán. New York: Routledge.

Sterling, Claire. 1981. *The Terror Network: The Secret War of International Terrorism.* 1st ed. New York: Holt, Rinehart, and Winston.

Sterling-Folker, Jennifer. 2001. "Evolutionary Tendencies in Realist and Liberal IR Theory." In: *Evolutionary Interpretations of World Politics*, edited by William R. Thompson, 61–109. New York: Routledge.

Stern, Robert Cecil. 2010. *Fire from the Sky: Surviving the Kamikaze Threat.* Annapolis, MD: Naval Institute Press.

Sternberg, Richard V. 2006. "On the Roles of Repetitive DNA Elements in the Context of a Unified Genomic-Epigenetic System." *Annals of the New York Academy of Sciences* 981 (1): 154–88. https://doi.org/10.1111/j.1749-6632.2002.tb04917.x.

Stokes, Susan Carol. 1995. *Cultures in Conflict: Social Movements and the State in Peru.* Berkeley: University of California Press.

Strang, David, and Sarah A. Soule. 1998. "Diffusion in Organizations and Social Movements: From Hybrid Corn to Poison Pills." *Annual Review of Sociology* 24 (1): 265–90. https://doi.org/10.1146/annurev.soc.24.1.265.

Strang, David, and John W. Meyer. 1993. "Institutional Conditions for Diffusion." *Theory and Society* 22 (4): 487–511.

"Summary Statement of Facts: The September 12, 1994 Plane Crash." 1995. US Department of the Treasury. Public Report of the White House Security Review. US Department of the Treasury. http://prop1.org/park/pave/rev6.htm.

Sweet, Kathleen M. 2002. *Aviation and Airport Security: Terrorism and Safety Concerns.* Lewiston, NY: Edin Mellen Press.

Taillon, J. Paul de B. 2002. *Hijacking and Hostages: Government Responses to Terrorism. Praeger Studies in Diplomacy and Strategic Thought.* Westport, CT: Praeger.

Tarrow, Sidney. 1993. "Modular Collective Action and the Rise of the Social Movement: Why the French Revolution Was Not Enough." *Politics & Society* 21 (1): 69–90. https://doi.org/10.1177/0032329293021001004.

Tarrow, Sidney G. 1998. *Power in Movement: Social Movements and Contentious Politics.* 2nd ed. Cambridge Studies in Comparative Politics. Cambridge: Cambridge University Press.

———. 2013. *The Language of Contention: Revolutions in Words, 1688–2012.* Cambridge Studies in Contentious Politics. Cambridge: Cambridge University Press.

Taylor, Verta, and Nella Van Dyke. 2007. "'Get Up, Stand Up': Tactical Repertoires of Social Movements." In: *The Blackwell Companion to Social Movements*, edited by David A. Snow, Sarah A. Soule, and Hanspeter Kriesi, 262–93. Oxford, UK: Blackwell Publishing Ltd. https://doi.org/10.1002/9780470999103.ch12.

"Terrorist Group Profiles." 1989. Washington, DC: Vice President's Task Force on Combatting Terrorism.

Tester, Hank. 2012. "Ponce de Leon Admitted Role in Cubana Hijacking: FBI - NBC 6 South Florida." *NBC Miami*, November 2, 2012. https://www.nbcmiami.com/news/local/Ponce-de-Leon-Admitted-Role-in-Cubana-Hijacking-FBI-176892791.html.

Thayer, Bradley A. 2004. *Darwin and International Relations: On the Evolutionary Origins of War and Ethnic Conflict.* Lexington: University Press of Kentucky.

The Economist. 1978. "Look Both Ways." April 15, 1978.

The Naples Daily News. 1976. "Kamikaze' Hits Home." March 23, 1976.

"The Sandinistas and Middle Eastern Radicals." 1985. Declassified Intelligence Report. Department of State.

The Senate Intelligence Committee Report on Torture: Committee Study of the Central Intelligence Agency's Detention and Interrogation Program. 2014. Brooklyn, NY: Melville House Publishing.

Thompson, William R., ed. 2001a. *Evolutionary Interpretations of World Politics.* New York: Routledge.

Tilly, Charles. 1978. *From Mobilization to Revolution.* Reading, MA: Addison-Wesley Pub. Co.

———. 1986. *The Contentious French.* Cambridge, MA: Belknap Press.

———. 1992. *Coercion, Capital, and European States, AD 990–1992.* Studies in Social Discontinuity. Cambridge, MA: Blackwell.

———. 1993. "Contentious Repertoires in Britain, 1758–1824." *Social Science History*, no. 17.

———. 1995. Popular Contention in Great Britain, 1758–1834. Cambridge, MA: Harvard University Press.

———. 2004. "Terror, Terrorism, Terrorists." *Sociological Theory* 22 (1): 5–13. https://doi.org/10.1111/j.1467-9558.2004.00200.x.

———. 2005. *Regimes and Repertoires.* Chicago: Chicago University Press.

———. 2006. *Regimes and Repertoires.* Chicago: University of Chicago Press.

———. 2008. Contentious Performances. Cambridge: Cambridge University Press. http://dx.doi.org/10.1017/CBO9780511804366.

Tilly, Charles, Louise A. Tilly, and Richard H. Tilly. 1975. The Rebellious Century: 1830–1930. Cambridge, MA: Harvard University Press.

Tilly, Louise, and Charles Tilly, eds. 1981. *Class Conflict and Collective Action. New Approaches to Social Science History*, v. 1. Beverly Hills: Published in cooperation with the Social Science History Association [by] Sage Publications.

Times. 1959. "Flight 482 Is Missing." November 17, 1959.

———. 1968a. "Grenade and Gun Attack on Israel Jet at Airport." November 28, 1968.

———. 1968b. "Israelis Hail Punitive Action." December 30, 1968.

———. 1968c. "Lloyd's Meets Today for Talks on Aircraft War Hazards." December 30, 1968.

———. 1969. "Arab 'Tiger Cubs' Attack Embassies." September 5, 1969.

———. 1970a. "Security Blackout as Leila Khaled Flies off to Cairo." October 4, 1970.

———. 1970b. "Israel Condemns Hijack Hostages Deal." October 5, 1970.

———. 1971. "Dynamite Pulled out in Fight on Hijacked Jet." 1971.

———. 1972a. "Parachuting US Hijacker Caught by FBI." January 22, 1972.

———. 1972b. "Algeria May Return £192,000 Ransom." June 5, 1972.

———. 1972c. "Hijacker Sentenced to Life in Jail." September 30, 1972.

———. 1972d. "Hijackers Threatened Dive into Nuclear Station." November 13, 1972.

———. 1972e. "US Hijack Victims Attack FBI Shooting." November 14, 1972.

———. 1973. "Arabs Fail in Twin Attacks on Israel Envoy and Airliner in Nicosia." 1973.

——— 1974. "Charges against White House Helicopter Man." February 19, 1974.

Tosaw, Richard Thomas. 1984. *D. B. Cooper, Dead or Alive?* Ceres, CA: Tosaw Pub. Co.

Townshend, Charles. 2011. *Terrorism: A Very Short Introduction.* Very Short Introductions 78. Oxford: Oxford University Press.

Traugott, Mark. 2010. *The Insurgent Barricade.* Berkeley: University of California Press.

Tyson, Timothy B. 2009. *Radio Free Dixie: Robert F. Williams and the Roots of Black Power.* Chapel Hill: University of North Carolina Press.

United States v. Ramzi Yousef, Eyad Ismoil, also known as Eyad Ismail, and Abdul Murad. 2003. 2nd Cir.

United States v. Raymond Johnson. 1968. 5th Cir.

United States v. Richard Floyd McCoy. 1973. 10th Cir.

Unites States v. Martin J. McNally. 1973. 8th Cir.

Varon, Jeremy. 2004. *Bringing the War Home: The Weather Underground, the Red Army Faction, and Revolutionary Violence in the Sixties and Seventies.* Berkeley: University of California Press.

Von Eschen, Penny M. 1997. *Race against Empire: Black Americans and Anticolonialism, 1937–1957.* Ithaca, NY: Cornell University Press.

Von Hippel, Eric. 1988. *The Sources of Innovation.* New York: Oxford University Press.

Wada, Takeshi. 2012. "Modularity and Transferability of Repertoires of Contention." *Social Problems* 59 (4): 544–71. https://doi.org/10.1525/sp.2012.59.4.544.

Wald, Matthew L. 2002a. "EgyptAir Pilot Sought Revenge by Crashing, Co-Worker Said." *The New York Times*, March 16, 2002, sec. U.S. https://www.nytimes.com/2002/03/16/us/egyptair-pilot-sought-revenge-by-crashing-co-worker-said.html.

———. 2002b. "Report Finds Co-Pilot at Fault In Fatal Crash of EgyptAir 990." *The New York Times*, March 22, 2002, sec. U.S. https://www.nytimes.com/2002/03/22/us/report-finds-co-pilot-at-fault-in-fatal-crash-of-egyptair-990.html.

Warrick, Jo, and Joe Stephens. 2001. "Before Attack, U.S. Expected Different Hit." *Washington Post*, October 2, 2001. https://www.washingtonpost.com/archive/politics/2001/10/02/before-attack-us-expected-different-hit/3e9666e6-51ab-4e0a-b9c6-274fd5088f00/.

Washington Post. 1975. "Cuba Delivers Hijackers." June 3, 1975.

Weber, Max. 1988. *Gesammelte Aufsätze zur Wissenschaftslehre.* Mohr: Tübingen.

Weinberg, Leonard, Ami Pedahzur, and Sivan Hirsch-Hoefler. 2004. "The Challenges of Conceptualizing Terrorism." *Terrorism and Political Violence* 16 (4): 777–94. https://doi.org/10.1080/095465590899768.

Wilber, Del Quentin. 2012. *Rawhide Down: The Near Assassination of Ronald Reagan.* New York: Picador.

Williamson, Oliver E. 1985. *The Economic Institutions of Capitalism: Firms, Markets, Relational Contracting.* New York: Free Press.

Witt, Ulrich. 2006. *The Evolving Economy: Essays on the Evolutionary Approach to Economics.* New ed. Cheltenham: Elgar.

Wood, Elisabeth Jean. 2003. *Insurgent Collective Action and Civil War in El Salvador.* Cambridge Studies in Comparative Politics. New York: Cambridge University Press.

Wood, Lesley. 2007. "Breaking the Wave: Repression, Identity, and Seattle Tactics." *Mobilization: An International Quarterly* 12 (4): 377–88.

Yallop, David A. 1993. *To the Ends of the Earth: The Hunt for the Jackal.* London: Corgi Books.

Zolberg, Aristide R. 1972. "Moments of Madness." *Politics & Society* 2 (2): 183–207. https://doi.org/10.1177/003232927200200203.

Zulaika, Joseba, and William A. Douglass. 1996. *Terror and Taboo: The Follies, Fables, and Faces of Terrorism.* New York: Routledge.

Index

About the Author

Yannick Veilleux-Lepage is an Assistant Professor in the Institute of Security and Global Affairs at Leiden University, Netherlands. He previously worked as a Senior Researcher in the Transcultural Conflict and Violence Initiative at Georgia State University, where he worked on a Department of Defense–funded project analysing media products and online discourse produced by extremist groups.